Good Things Come

LINDA SHANTZ

Good Things Come

Copyright © 2020 Linda Shantz

Cover Artwork: Linda Shantz Fine Art

Book Design: Natalie Keller Reinert

PAPERBACK EDITION

ISBN: 978-1-7773003-0-2

For my parents.
I'm sorry I didn't become a vet, but at least I outgrew my dream
of being a jockey!
Raising a horse girl isn't easy!

CHAPTER ONE

January

There was a weight to the stillness, the tangerine band streaking across the inky horizon holding something contrary to the promise of a new day. Liv's nostrils stuck together as she drew in a breath. *So cold.* Maybe not as cold as the winters she remembered as a child *à Montréal,* but the record-breaking polar vortex sweeping Southern Ontario made her forget some of her hardy *Québécois* pride. She tugged her hood down and pushed gloved hands deeper into the pockets of her down-filled jacket, the squeak of her boots on the laneway's hard-packed snow like Styrofoam to her ears.

She'd take these frigid mornings over what was to come. Inventing creative ways to keep her fingers from freezing as she legged up feisty two-year-olds in the indoor arena was still preferable to hours spent imprisoned in the University of Guelph's stuffy lecture halls and labs. Just three more days of winter break, and that's what she'd be back to—pursuing a degree she wasn't convinced she wanted.

Back to reality. Back to expectations.

Light spilled from the barn's overhead apartment, and she

almost expected to feel warmth as she sliced through the bright pool of light in her path. She slid through the side door, frost condensing on her eyelashes, her face starting to thaw, and a chorus of whinnies greeting her even before she switched on the lights.

"'Morning girls," she called, inspiring another singsong as she ducked into the feed room and scooped the breakfast ration of grain into a pail. When she turned the corner to the well-lit aisle, the faces of two mares jutted out of boxes on either side. The third, though...

"Hey, 'Tisse, what's up?"

Sotisse stood in the corner of the deeply bedded straw, oblivious. The mare took a deliberate turn, huge belly swollen with the life she carried; her tail slightly raised, patches of sweat on her flank and neck darkening her bright chestnut coat to liver. Liv's heart rate took off, and she scrambled to feed the other two horses.

Nerves and muscles were at odds with her brain, but she summoned enough self-control to keep from racing back to the feed room, the grain bucket clattering to the ground. Vapour from the hot water flushed her face as she filled a stainless steel pail. In her other hand she scooped up the foaling kit she'd prepared—just in case—and power-walked back to the stall.

Hold it together, Liv. Her hands were trembling so badly she fumbled with the elastic bandage as she wrapped Sotisse's long golden tail, something she should be able to do in her sleep.

Three weeks. Sotisse was three weeks early. Not technically premature, but still.

She glanced at the time on her phone, then up at the ceiling. Both she and the exercise rider who lived upstairs were due at the training barn for seven, but she definitely wasn't going to make it now. Calling on an extra set of hands was the sensible thing to do, even though complications were rare. This was Sotisse, Papa's favourite racemare, having her first foal, by none other than Just Lucky. And she could be as practical as she wanted about the breeding business, but there was no denying she'd been waiting for this foal. This foal was special.

Foaling was messy, and fast. But there was something intimate about it too, ushering a newborn into this world, and part of her didn't want to share it with a stranger. Because even though Nate Miller had been working on the farm since September, he was really still a stranger to her.

She'd just get him to hold Sotisse while she checked the foal's position and washed under her tail and udder. Once she knew all was well, he could go. Taking two steps at a time, she flew up the stairwell.

Meaning to knock softly, she rapped a staccato beat on the apartment door. There was no hiding the welling combination of panic and excitement in her eyes. The whole being professional and under control thing was definitely not coming off at the moment. She was ready to knock again when the door swung open.

"Everything okay?" Nate stepped back to let her inside, eyebrow tweaked, but she stayed where she was, and dodged his eyes when they landed on hers.

Damn the way her stomach tumbled. Normal, physiological response, right? Sure he was good-looking, but she had enough trouble being taken seriously because she looked fourteen without acting it. She'd leave the gushing to her younger sister Emilie, and the girls who worked on the farm— all of whom had applauded her for hiring him to break yearlings last summer. She'd given him the job because of his experience and references, not because a hot guy would be a welcome addition to the female-dominated staff.

"Sotisse is in labour. I need someone to hold her while I check the foal's position. I won't keep you long." Words ran together, the heat wafting from the apartment threatening to turn her into a puddle of sweat. *Winter? What winter?*

"She's pretty early, isn't she?"

Liv nodded, already dashing back down the stairs.

Sotisse was sinking to her knees in the straw, glancing uncomfortably at her side before rocking back to roll as she tried to adjust the uncomfortable pressure inside her. The mare righted herself, resting, her well-sprung rib cage heaving with laboured breaths before she pitched into another roll, hooves clattering against the wall's wooden boards. She lurched back to her feet, circling with head low, steam rising.

Liv discarded her coat and adjusted her dark ponytail before sliding on a sterile sleeve, aware of Nate's appearance beside her. She waited, balanced on the balls of her feet, shaking her arms loose at her sides like a runner ready to step into the starting block.

"No…"

The word caught in her throat, the sac appearing under the mare's bandaged tail gleaming red instead of pearly white. Nate was already dragging open the door, like he must know what this meant. *Red bag delivery, placenta previa, premature detachment of the placenta…*more importantly, the foal wasn't getting oxygen.

Liv grabbed the sharp scissors from the foaling kit, Nate already at Sotisse's head. She sliced through the thick membrane, a pungent soup of blood, faeces and amniotic fluid sluicing out, soaking her through jeans and long johns and coursing down the mare's hocks. Reaching inside the birth canal to find the foal, her chest seized—one tiny foot was missing from the expected triad of two hooves and a nose.

"You need to get this going," Nate said, his eyes locking onto hers.

"I know that," she snapped, stepping back and ripping off the sleeve. "There's a leg caught."

She peeled off layers until she was stripped to a tank top, beyond any memory of cold, and drew on a fresh sleeve. Sotisse's contractions were powerful, closing in on her arm as she eased it inside the mare, following the foal's neck past the pelvic rim to the shoulder wedged against it. How could such a tiny baby get it so wrong? Not that it wasn't a good thing the foal was small, because it might be what made the difference between getting it out alive instead of dead. Braced against the mare's hindquarters, she pushed the shoulder back and found

4

the uncooperative limb, stretching farther to cup the soft hoof in her hand, struggling to flip it up to join its mate. *Got it.*

Liv withdrew her arm and stepped back, still humming with adrenaline. Now they needed to get it out. Fast. "Turn her loose."

Sotisse lumbered around the stall, sweat and straw matting her thick coat, then buckled into the bedding and flattened herself with a grunt. Liv dropped to her knees, Nate right with her, the foal's tiny feet inching out with every contraction. They each grasped a leg, and Liv looked at him sideways. Nate nodded, and when the next contraction came, they pulled.

"C'mon, 'Tisse." Liv tried not to give in to the desperation creeping into her voice.

"You got this, momma," Nate murmured. "Just one more push to get those shoulders clear and we'll do the rest, promise."

He sounded a lot calmer than Liv felt. They strained with the mare, Liv clenching her jaw and putting her bodyweight behind one last heroic heave, and the foal's shoulders popped through. Another grunt from all three of them, and Nate and Liv drew the foal out onto the straw with a slippery mess of blood and membrane and fluid. Liv fretfully looked for signs of life.

Nate reached for the towels, passing her one, and started to vigorously rub the small, still, body. Liv lifted the foal's head, propping its shoulder against her own hip as she cupped the tiny muzzle to clear the nostrils.

"Filly," Nate said with a quick peek under the wispy tail.

"She's not breathing," Liv responded flatly, overwhelming dread paralyzing her as she cradled the foal's head in her lap.

"Get out of the way."

She was too dumbfounded to protest as he double-checked the foal's airway, stretched out the neck, then closed off the far nostril to start resuscitation. The foal's delicate rib cage rose and fell with the timing of his breaths, and as much as it irked Liv that she wasn't the one doing it, it made no sense to interrupt him. She crept closer to check the filly's pulse, and noticed Nate had stopped, his lips moving soundlessly, eyes fixed on the filly's side. They both saw the faint flutter.

"You got her." Liv pressed her eyes shut, opening them again to assure herself it hadn't been her imagination.

"Welcome to the planet, baby girl," Nate said softly.

Neither of them moved, watching as each breath came more strongly than the last. Sotisse stirred with a low rumble, rocking up onto her sternum and curling her neck towards the foal. Liv turned to Nate, at a loss as to how to express the emotions flooding her, so she pushed herself to her feet instead.

She grabbed the door frame as her legs cramped, then reached down for a dry towel and tossed it to him. "Stay with her?"

Her legs slowly regained function as she shuffled to the office, heartbeat tempering. The newborn foal's heritage surrounded her on the walls of the small room—framed images of their stallion, Just Lucky, winning the Queen's Plate, and Sotisse's victory in the Canadian Oaks. A large oil painting of the pair posing on either side of farm manager Geai Doucet dominated the room from behind a huge old desk. Liv paused —she could never just ignore that painting—then picked up the landline, not trusting the reception of her cell phone, and put in a call to Geai, leaving a message.

By the time Liv returned, the foal was alert, her long forelegs stretched in front of her. Nate still rubbed the baby with the towel, a huge grin on his face as the filly shook her head and struck out with a hoof, trying to get her hind end underneath her. Sotisse was on her feet, supervising anxiously over his shoulder. While it got old, the way Emilie and the girls went on about Nate—the charm, the sandy blond hair, the azure eyes—he looked pretty good at the moment.

A rush of incoming air from the door interrupted the sentiment, Liv glancing up the aisle. A fresh smile took over her face as Geai appeared around the corner. "You must not have been far away."

The old man ambled towards her and threw a well-bundled arm around her shoulders, pulling her into him as he squeezed. "Put some clothes on! It's freezing!"

"I'd forgotten," Liv said wryly, bending down to scoop up the discarded pile. She eased her shirt on, everything aching.

Geai peered through the stall door. "A filly?"

Nate nodded, and draped the towel over his shoulder as he climbed stiffly to his feet, hand outstretched. Geai grasped it firmly.

"All good?" The farm manager turned back to Liv.

"I could have done without the drama, and some oxygen would have been nice… but yeah, now, so far." The list of things that could still go wrong lurked in her brain.

Geai crossed his arms, the corners of his eyes crinkling as they went from Liv to Nate. "Great work, you two. But who's getting on the horses this morning while our two exercise riders are here playing midwife?"

Nate glanced at Liv with a smirk. "I'll get going. Don't expect I'll see you over there anytime soon."

"I think you're on your own this morning, sorry." Her sweater hid the upward curve of her lips as she pulled it over her head, the adrenaline wearing off and leaving her with a chill. "Thank you," she said, which was totally inadequate, but she wasn't good at putting feelings into words.

He flashed an easy grin, zipping his jacket and extracting a toque from the pocket. "Pleasure was all mine."

Maybe it was a good thing she was going back to school, because that, there, was a distraction, and there was no room for distraction in any of her plans.

"At least her early arrival means you'll get a few days to dote on her before your classes start, eh?" Geai's voice pulled her back to the filly in the stall.

She wasn't going to think about classes right now. She fished a tiny cup out of the foaling kit and filled it with chlorhexidine, then went back in, interrupting Sotisse's devoted cleaning of her new daughter to douse the foal's umbilical stump. Sotisse rumbled worriedly, bumping Liv with her nose.

"Don't worry, momma, I'll just be a second."

The filly kicked and struggled, amazing Liv with her rally. There were no markings on the jumble of legs, and only a few white hairs on her small wedge of a head, bobbing as her mother resumed her doting. A defiant whinny escaped from the filly's throat.

"Those lungs seem to be working fine now." Liv grinned at Geai.

"*On dirait une p'tite chique,*" Geai said, lapsing back into French now that Nate was gone.

Chique—that name was going to stick. The comparison was amusing, but fitting—the filly kind of looked like a little quid of tobacco someone had chewed up and spit out on the straw. Liv went in once more to give the foal an enema, and started removing the soiled bedding, replacing it with a deep, dry, bed, banked up the walls.

Geai's steady gaze landed on her when she rejoined him. "You will make a great vet. But I'm not sure you can practice veterinary medicine and be ready to ride this one in the Plate in three and a half years."

"They're all Plate horses at this stage," Liv scoffed, deflecting the way he pinpointed her real dream with logic. Because that was the dream—to ride races, the Plate the ultimate goal, this filly worthy of a place in her fantasy. She'd made it this far, overcoming her first hurdle and moving on to the next, all legginess and hope.

Geai chuckled, and pushed up the sleeve of his heavy coat to check his watch. "I'll leave you to it. Keep me posted." He gave Liv a pat on the back and ambled off.

She tossed Sotisse a flake of hay and shrugged into her coat, hugging it around herself as she headed to the feed room to make the mare a hot mash. Then she left mare and foal to bond, and in the warmth of the office collapsed into the chair behind the desk to write up the foaling report, the painting of Lucky and Sotisse overseeing.

The Queen's Plate—Canada's most prestigious race,

restricted to three-year old Thoroughbreds foaled north of the forty-ninth parallel. Twelve hundred foals might be born across this country that spring; a hundred might be nominated for the classic; as many as twenty might go postward. Only one would get their picture taken in the winner's circle under the royal purple and gold blanket of flowers. One winning team would be on the podium accepting the fifty gold sovereigns from the Queen's representative. *Many are called, few are chosen...* and only one comes home first.

Liv wrote it down like a prophecy: *SOTISSE: January 2, 7:05AM, dk.b./br.filly by Just Lucky...*

Breed the best to the best, they said. And hope for the best.

Her own future was as mapped out as Chique's. She'd gone along with the assumption she'd become a vet for so long; now here she was, with a year and a half left of the DVM program and a surgical internship hers for the taking after she graduated, questioning the whole thing. Sure, it would be an asset to have a vet in the family, between the farm, and the string of racehorses at the track, currently wintering in Florida. Liv's heart was with those horses, her passion pitch perfect on their backs, not at the end of a scalpel or reading radiographs. There was no doing both, because both were all-or-nothing paths.

She finished up the foaling report, and went back to the stall. The little filly struggled with determination to get to her feet.

"Let's see if I can help you out."

Positioning herself behind the foal's rump, she wrapped her fingers around the base of Chique's tail, and when the filly's next scrambling effort came, Liv scooped an arm under the narrow ribcage for added support. The filly bobbled, but with Liv steadying her, parked a leg at each corner. Chique gave a definitive snort and minced forward, instinctively looking for her first meal.

"You're a fighter, *ti-Chique.*"

Being a vet was a responsible choice. A safe choice. Giving up what she'd spent years in school for? Was crazy. Period. But

Liv had done sensible her whole life. Maybe this filly was her chance to break free.

CHAPTER TWO

May

The clock on the tack room wall read ten to six, and outside Woodbine's Barn Five, it was beginning to get light. A radio that was probably older than he was hung in the doorway, playing painful top-40 shit to which Nate found himself humming along, in spite of himself. He sat on top of the cupboards with *The Daily Racing Form* in his lap, worn brown boots beneath his faded jeans, waiting for his first mount of the morning. The light jacket and sweatshirt over his safety vest and t-shirt would be gone by the time they were finished with the last set of horses.

"'Morning."

Trainer Roger Cloutier's lengthy shadow appeared in front of the door beneath one of the covered light bulbs illuminating the shed, his back to Nate as he reviewed the whiteboard training schedule.

"Hey, Rog."

"Claire ready to go?"

The question wasn't directed at Nate—he glanced up to see Liv at Roger's side.

Claire was a bay two-year-old—officially, *L'Éclaircie*—the only one Nate hadn't started last fall when he was breaking the yearlings. Liv's father, Claude Lachance, had purchased Claire at the Keeneland Breeding Stock Sale as a scruffy little weanling with no pedigree, apparently because he'd felt sorry for her, getting her for cheap. Liv had taken Claire on as her own project, somehow working around her insane school schedule to break the filly with the help of the farm manager, Geai. Claire had gone to Florida—without her—and came back last month with the rest of the Triple Stripe string, transformed over the winter into an athletic Amazon of a filly.

Since Liv had finished her exams, she was here each morning to get on her share of the twelve horses Roger trained for her father, but she arrived way before Nate to muck Claire's stall, take off her bandages, and clean her feed tub and water bucket—just like the grooms did for each of their charges. After she was done for the morning, she went on rounds with Roger's vet, or helped out at the nearby equine hospital. She was definitely a novelty when it came to owners' daughters.

"'Morning Liv," Nate said when she walked into the room.

She smiled at him briefly, finding her Kroops in the corner and kicking off her shoes to slip into the tall black boots. He'd gotten used to that reserved, almost aloof smile. Small talk was definitely not her thing.

"All set?" She twisted in his direction as she tied a kerchief over her dark hair and covered it with her helmet.

Nate nodded, leaving *The Form* on the counter. He pushed his own helmet on with one hand, and picked up his whip.

"Michel's on the shed with your filly, Nate." Jo St-Laurent, Roger's assistant trainer, emerged from the stall next to the office with Claire towering beside her, bay coat shimmering.

Claire was flashy, the kind of filly that stopped people in their tracks. Legs for days with high white on three of them; a big star connecting to a wide stripe that covered her face before falling off her nose into one nostril; a little bit of a wall eye that made you wonder if you could trust her. Wall eyes weren't often attractive, but Claire pulled it off.

Michel came around the corner leading a smaller, stockier, bay filly, and the groom greeted Liv with a lazy grin as he went by. He stopped in front of Nate.

"How's Gemma today, Mike?" Nate checked the tack, the last over-played pop song loitering, unwelcome, in his head.

"Good to go, Miller." He legged Nate up and walked Gemma off, turning them loose.

Gemma bounced as Nate took her a short turn, cutting through the middle of the barn. *Small but mighty.* Maybe she didn't have Claire's height, but Gemma was a full sister to Just Lucky, Claude's horse-of-a-lifetime, with the associated high hopes. Heir apparent, while Claire was auditioning as Cinderella.

He picked up the slack in his lines when they caught up to Claire back on the Triple Stripe side, Gemma's quarters swinging out as they stopped. Claire curled her head around and bumped Jo in the shoulder, knocking her off balance, while Roger threw Liv up.

"Meet you outside," Roger called over his shoulder, walking down to the stable pony's stall as Claire marched off, Jo leaning into her while Liv got tied on—knotting her reins, tightening the girth, adjusting her stirrup irons.

The gradually rising sun cast a golden glow over the landscape, picking up brilliant highlights in the gleaming coats of both fillies as Roger steered Paz, the pony, between them. Liv reached forward and scratched Claire under her flip of black mane, Claire stretching her neck down and snorting happily.

Gemma jigged a few strides, flinging her head and crowding Paz before Nate reeled her in. "See how nice Claire is being?" he chided. "Why can't you be more like that?"

They joined a growing stream of horses on the tree-lined path to Woodbine's main oval. Toronto's racetrack was the largest in Canada, one of the top racing venues in North America. Nate's hometown Calgary didn't have anything close.

He'd told people that was why he'd left—it sounded reasonable. If he never went back, it would be too soon. He'd lucked out, getting this job. Claude had nice horses, and he'd even let Nate keep the apartment on the farm, though he'd been full time at the track since the Florida horses had returned.

"L'Eclaircie and Just Gemma, a half." Roger called the pair of fillies in to the clocker as they reached the tunnel to the main, just as it opened.

The cadence of aluminum-shod hooves on the rubberized paving stones echoed off the concrete walls as they passed under the turf course. Claire was alert, head up and ears zeroed forward, and when they came out the other end, Liv let her jog up the slope to the on-gap. Gemma matched her enthusiasm, and even Paz sprang to life.

"Meet you at the pole," Roger said before turning off to the right and nudging Paz into a canter down the backstretch.

Nate glanced over his shoulder and laughed as he and Liv jogged off the other way. Paz gave Roger a hard time, bouncing like a spring horse, ready to take up the chase when he saw horses already on the track ahead of him. Every. Single. Day. The old sprinter loved his job.

Claire and Gemma jogged the wrong way along the outside rail—backing up—until they reached the wire, stopping with the towering grandstand behind them as they faced the infield. The sun coming across the track was blinding, bathing the surface. Horses galloped by while they stood: Claire a statue, Gemma bowing her neck and pawing impatiently.

"Are you ready to get your ass kicked?" Liv smiled nonchalantly with a rare outward display of confidence in her filly.

Nate held back a laugh. Liv was so bloody serious most of the time. The only time she loosened up was when she was with Claire. "Oh yeah?"

"You have the privilege of being among the first to view the sight that will frustrate many a jock this year." She slapped Claire's well-rounded rump.

"We'll see who's watching what."

"Dream on, Miller. Let's go."

They turned, both fillies leaping into a gallop—Claire on the inside, Gemma close beside her. Nate relaxed, standing in the irons and keeping Gemma next to Claire in the middle of the track, rounding the clubhouse turn and entering the straight. Liv glanced ahead at Roger's silhouette astride Paz, standing on the outside rail a furlong away from the red and white half-mile marker that would be their starting point. Nate pulled down his goggles, and when Liv dropped Claire to the rail, Gemma locked onto her like a missile onto a target.

The fillies matched strides, figuratively—Gemma was taking two for every one of Claire's. Claire dragged Liv around the turn, when Nate didn't have anywhere near that much filly beneath him. As they came down the stretch, Claire's ears flickered forward and she accelerated, each thrust of her hindquarters dismissing the smaller filly, Liv still poised motionless in the tack. Nate sent Gemma after them with a chirp and a crack of his stick, Gemma inching up on Liv's boot bravely, but with the wire looming, Claire cleanly changed leads, regaining a length advantage on her stablemate by the time the watches stopped.

Gemma caught up as they galloped out. Nate ran his eyes over Claire, the easy bunching and extending of her muscles, then Liv. The smile she gave him lacked her usual restraint.

"Nice ass," he called, and ducked the look she shot back. *Real original, Miller.*

They pulled up and turned in on either side of Roger and Paz. The trainer looked his two charges up and down.

"That looked pretty easy," Roger said to Liv.

She shrugged, but the slight curve of her lips and the way her grey eyes shone belied her indifference.

Roger glanced at his stopwatch. "She's something else. If she turns out to be as good as I think she is, she'll look like quite the bargain."

Liv withdrew back into herself as the endorphin rush subsided on the walk back to the barn. That's the way it went

—Nate had learned not to take it personally. She intrigued him, sure. Under different circumstances, he'd be into figuring that out. *I mean, why not?* She wasn't hard to look at, and had that whole dark and mysterious thing going on. But there was a whole list of reasons why it stopped there, not the least of which was, owner's daughter? Definitely off limits.

Michel and Jo met them in front of the barn, exchanging halters for bridles and taking the fillies a turn while Nate and Liv set the tack for the next two horses. Back outside, Nate took the lead shank from Michel as Liv started to douse Claire's neck with suds while Jo held, leaving the tall bay glimmering beneath a slick film.

"So when do we head to New York, Rog?" Michel dipped a sponge in his own pail of steaming water, squeezing it over Gemma's crest when the trainer rejoined them after putting Paz away.

Roger crossed his arms. "A couple of weeks. Your father wants to send Claire now, too, Liv."

Nate arched an involuntary eyebrow, and noticed the sharp turn of Liv's head in Roger's direction. News to her too, apparently. Claire shook her head and lashed her tail, Jo cursing while Liv wiped her face on her sleeve before carrying on like she hadn't just been christened with bathwater…or had that boulder of information dropped in front of her.

"Why the hell do you get to go, Mike?" Nate grumbled once he'd passed Gemma over to a hotwalker. Of course it made sense to send a groom—Roger was planning to ship three horses to Don Philips, Claude's trainer at Belmont. *I wouldn't mind rubbing horses for a bit if it meant going to Belmont Park.*

"Think it's called seniority, Miller." Michel flicked the sponge at him before dropping it in the empty bucket.

Nate dragged the back of his hand over his face. "Obviously not maturity."

"Boys," Jo reprimanded. "Don't worry, Nate, he'll only be gone for a couple of weeks."

Liv actually smiled, though her eyes were on Claire as another hotwalker relieved Jo and started walking the

Amazon.

"I've never been to Belmont." Nate stopped himself. No whining. One thing at a time. Woodbine was already a move up.

"I'll send you a postcard." Michel slapped him on the arm as Nate followed him into the barn.

Jo pulled out his next mount, a dark bay three-year old. "Throw Nate up, will you, Michel?"

Nate gathered the lines, and Michel thrust him aboard carelessly.

"Miss you already, Mike." Nate grinned as the colt walked off.

Liv waited outside, circling her colt to keep him moving. The colt tried to bite Nate's gelding playfully, and she smacked him on the neck with her stick and pulled him away, chasing him forward. Roger jogged Paz up and inserted the pony in between the two three-year olds.

Liv glanced at Roger, a slight furrow to her brow. "So I guess I'm going to New York."

Napoleon's whole hind end wagged in welcome as Liv pushed through the door of Geai's bungalow. Rubbing the black Lab's head helped still the nerves her sprint here hadn't.

Geai appeared from the kitchen, ushering her into the living room. "So? How'd the filly work?"

Liv tucked a leg under herself as she perched on the sofa, pulling a cushion to her midriff. "She was brilliant. Forty-five flat, just breezing. Put Just Gemma away without even trying."

Geai frowned. "Gemma? Roger worked them together?"

"She's the only one in the barn who can go with Claire."

"Who was on her? She must have an excuse." Geai was ever loyal to their homebreds.

"Nate Miller."

"Ah, you should have had a rider on her, then you'd be telling me something different."

"He can ride all right."

"I'll get you some water. You must be light-headed from

your run."

Liv grinned as she and Napoleon followed him to the kitchen, fellow devotees.

Geai poured a glass from a jug in the fridge. "He's really as good on a horse as I hear he is?"

"I think he probably is."

"You obviously like him, then."

With Geai Liv had no fear her words of praise for Nate would be misinterpreted—Geai would realize her admiration was limited merely to his way with horses. The same conversation with her sister Emilie or her best friend Faye would quickly get twisted.

"Did you know about New York?" Napoleon rested his chin on her knee when she sat at the kitchen table, and she stroked his well-padded side to try and settle herself again. Back-up therapist, when her stress was related to her usual one—Claire.

Geai nodded, silently, setting the glass in front of her.

"A little warning would have been nice." Liv abandoned the disappointed Labrador to take a gulp, like the water offered fortitude. "I'm going with her."

Geai's eyebrows peaked. "Have you discussed that with your parents?"

"No, but I'm twenty-three, what can they say?"

"Well, your father owns the filly, I think he could say a lot."

"You and I both know it's not my father who'll be the problem."

Geai chuckled, and parked himself opposite her. "Have you actually thought this through?"

Liv pressed her lips into a line, hands encircling the glass. "Still processing."

"You want to get your apprentice license down there."

"Is that crazy? It's crazy, isn't it?" She went back to stroking Napoleon. Science, right? Petting an animal was supposed to lower blood pressure. At this rate, poor Napoleon would be bald by the time she left.

"Completely." *You weren't supposed to agree with me, Geai.*

"But I doubt that will stop you." *True.* "You'll need a good agent." Like he'd already thought about it, and had it figured out. "I hear Kenny O'Connell is looking for a new bug rider. He handles Ricky Acosta's book."

"Ricky Acosta?" Liv squeaked. Only the leading rider at Belmont, not to mention movie star good-looking, fangirl-worthy. *Poor, poor Napoleon.* "He's like an idol, Geai."

"I'll give Don a call and have him mention you. Acosta rides for him a lot."

Her stomach spasmed. This was making it all the more real and terrifying.

"You should eat something, you're looking pale." Geai pushed himself up, grinning.

Liv choked on a laugh. "I'm not feeling so hungry at the moment, thanks. Besides, I guess I need to watch that now."

He glanced over his shoulder as he opened a cupboard. "You don't eat nothing as it is. You be careful."

"It's just a couple of pounds." She waved off his concern. "Any more advice?"

Geai opened a bag of potato chips, and started nibbling. She shook her head when he offered it to her. She ate better than he did, that was for sure.

"You see those French riders when they come over for the International? They come, they go in suits. You be like that. It shows class. It shows respect for your profession. The sport of kings, eh?"

"Kings?" The corner of her mouth curved up.

"Would you prefer Princess? See how you like that, because that's what you're going to get. They'll say the only reason you have the mount on Claire is because your father owns her."

"Which is true, but too bad for them, right?" Claire made all the other stuff fade away. Claire was her secret weapon. Napoleon scrambled, dancing beside her on the hardwood as she rose. "Sorry, I can't sit still, I'd better go. Please tell me I'm not crazy?"

Geai followed her to the door, and he patted her on the shoulder as he smiled. "Only a little bit."

"Is my mother going to kill me?"

"Probably. Find some nice young man in New York to sweep you off your feet, and maybe she'll forgive you."

"Like that's going to happen."

"You must be such a disappointment to her."

She laughed, putting her arms around him and squeezing. She just needed Geai and Napoleon to come with her, and everything would be fine. She skipped down the steps and broke into a run to chase away a fresh flutter of nerves, following the path through the woods that separated the stallion barn from the mares' paddock.

Mares and foals milled by the gate, waiting to be brought in. It wasn't hard to locate Sottise's little filly, dodging the girl who sought to catch her while Sotisse waited patiently at the end of a rope shank. Chique didn't seem to care that the rest of her companions were on the way to the barn—she tore off, showing admirable athleticism as she threw bucks and leaps into her performance.

"Cheeky little bitch, eh?"

Liv started, her head snapping to the side. Nate Miller, slowing from a jog in shorts and a good pair of shoes, his blond hair damp.

He pulled the back of one wrist across his brow. "Sorry."

No he wasn't. Not one bit. It was as if he liked to make her squirm, with his nice arms and easy grin. She glanced at him sideways when he joined her at the fence.

Chique was losing interest in her game, her circles getting slower and smaller. She finally lapsed into a jaunty walk, shaking her head and snorting happily, short tail flapping. When she sidled up to her mother, doing a perfect turn on the forehand to line herself up alongside the mare to nurse, the girl crept up and snapped the rope to her halter.

Nate fell in beside Liv as she began walking towards the barn. It would probably be rude to tell him to go away. Besides, she couldn't just run and hide every time someone made her uncomfortable. She had to get better at this. *Think of it as training.*

"So, New York." His eyes caught hers, pulling them away

from the filly's progress. "Why New York?"

Yes, Why? She'd been working on that since Roger had announced it this morning. "My father likes to have a couple horses with Don. He spends a lot of time in New York with work. I galloped there a few summers ago, actually." Some kids went to Europe after graduating high school; she'd gone to Belmont Park. "Claire is New York-bred, and they have a good incentive program. She really only came here from Florida because...well...because I asked." She glanced at him quickly, tucking a flyaway strand of hair behind her ear. "I should know better than to get attached in this business."

"Some of them get to you no matter how much you tell yourself that, don't they?"

She tilted her head. It wasn't the reaction she'd expected from the guy who always had a quick comment.

"It takes guts, what you're doing," he went on. "Quitting school."

"You did." She stopped by the empty paddock gate and crossed her arms.

The way he shifted his weight and his eyes was uncharacteristically self-conscious. "I'm surprised you remember that."

"Not many people come to an interview for a farm job with a resumé, not to mention a university education."

"Like you said, I dropped out."

"Still."

"Not vet school."

She rolled her eyes. "It's so cliché. Smart horse girl has to go to vet school, right? Don't get me wrong, I'm a total science geek. I love it. I just love this more."

"So with what, a year left, I'm betting you'll be pissing off a lot of people by bailing?" He threw her that grin.

"Right?" Those connections who'd supported her, the faculty, the relatives who'd told her for as long as she could remember she was going to be a vet, so much so she'd finally believed it herself. At least Geai was on her side. And, it would appear, Nate. Only because of his similar aspirations, she was sure. "Do you think it would make my mother feel better if I told her one of my classmates is dropping out to pursue his drug addiction?"

He choked on a laugh. "Seriously? Not sure, though. Riding racehorses is its own addiction."

She sighed, and started walking towards the barn again. "Yeah. Exactly."

It was weird, this. Almost comfortable. She didn't do comfortable. Especially not with guys anywhere near her own age. It wasn't as if there were men lining up to ask her out in vet school, where her class was 80 percent female. Which was fine, because keeping her focus on her studies, and now her career, was her shield; an easy excuse to put off things that, she had to admit, scared her. Not that she thought Nate was coming on to her. Maybe that was what made him bearable.

They found the dark filly nose-deep in the corner feed tub next to her long-suffering mother. She still wasn't very big, and was losing her foal coat in patches, leaving her with a decidedly moth-eaten look.

Liv would miss Geai and Napoleon, that was a given. But she'd also miss seeing Chique change and grow. "You'll keep an eye on this filly for me?"

Nate arched an eyebrow—it was an odd request, considering there was farm staff responsible for such things, but he'd been there from day one—a big part of the reason the little filly was here to torment them all.

"For sure."

Back outside in the daylight she faced him, folding her arms across her body. "Can you do me one other favour? Can you check on Geai from time to time?"

There was a glint of curiosity in his eyes. "Sure. Can I ask why? Is he all right?"

"I just worry about him getting lonely—not that he'd admit to it. And you're easy to talk to." When she actually got over herself enough to have a conversation. They'd worked together every day since the middle of April, but this was the longest they'd talked since last August's interview.

Nate reflected her posture, one corner of his mouth twisting up. "No problem. I'm guessing he's got a story or two to share."

"Geai's forgotten more about horses than you or I will ever know." She made no attempt to hide her affection. "And by the way, he calls Sotisse's filly Chique, so you two are on the same page already."

"You know I'm still going to call her Cheeky, right?"

She backed away a few steps before leaving him with an amused look, breaking into a run towards the woods. Nate Miller was definitely safer left behind.

Liv slipped in the front door, her courage bolstered, and kicked off her shoes. She skipped down into the sunken living room, grabbing the new copy of *The Blood-Horse* resting on the coffee table with the day's mail. The clinking of dishes in the kitchen brought her tension right back. She flipped through pages of coloured ads and reports from tracks across the world...stalling.

Just get it over with.

Taking the magazine with her, she sat on the bench at the kitchen table, pressing it open at the article about this year's Preakness Stakes. "Hi Maman."

Anne Lachance reached up with the clean glass she'd just taken from the dishwasher, placing it in the cupboard before bending down for the next. Her dark hair, peppered with grey, brushed her jaw where it fell, and she tucked it behind her ear. She always looked as if she belonged in the pages of a women's magazine; that mother who had it all together—raising kids, keeping an immaculate house, looking good doing it.

"Have a good run?"

Liv nodded, fingering the edge of the page.

"Ready for New York?"

Liv's eyes shot from the magazine, meeting Anne's. "Am I the only one who didn't know about this?"

"When your father told me he was sending L'Éclaircie, I

assumed you'd want to go and gallop for Don until your internship starts. I'm sure you can find a vet to work for at Belmont while you're there."

At least her mother wasn't totally clueless. Liv turned the page, and tried to sound casual. "I'm going to get my apprentice license down there."

Anne closed the cupboard and turned slowly. "I'm sorry, what did you say?"

"I'm not going to let someone else ride Claire when I'm perfectly capable."

The silence was so loud it pierced her eardrums; the weight of her mother's realization terrifying.

"You're dropping out." Her mother's words were like an accusation. "You can't be serious."

"I am. Completely. I've always wanted to do this. I didn't plan for it to be now. That's just the way it worked out."

"But—vet school, Olivia. You only have a year left! And the internship! I thought that's what you wanted."

It's what you *wanted*...but she bit back the retort. "Roger thinks this filly is good. You know there's nothing like being on these horses. You can't tell me, if you'd had this kind of a chance thirty years ago, you honestly could have turned it down?"

She couldn't tell if there was more than displeasure in her mother's dark brown eyes. It was because of horses her parents had met—but marrying Claude Lachance had ironically been the end of Anne's aspirations as a rider, as instead she chose to raise a family. That wouldn't be Liv's story. A man wasn't going to derail her dreams.

"There's so much more to life than horses, Olivia," Anne said—reading her mind, if not her heart.

Was there, though?

CHAPTER THREE

June

Sometimes when he ran, it all came back. At work it was easy to believe he'd reinvented himself, but here the solitude and calm of the farm exposed his raw and busted parts, and it was as if he was running away all over again, trying to put distance between past and present, but getting nowhere.

He stopped and forced himself to look around. To look up at the huge maples towering on either side of the lane, the perfectly clear blue sky peeking through cloaked branches, down to where leaves cast dappled shadows beneath his feet. He breathed in their oxygen, and sent some CO_2 back. He had this job. He had a plan, of a fashion, even if today he felt like he was standing still. Or worse, left behind.

The maples gave way to a clearing, tall double fence lines forming the stallion paddocks in front of him. Even though the busiest part of the breeding season was done, Geai still had both stallions in this time of day.

Wasn't doing something for someone else the best way to get your sorry-ass thoughts off yourself? Even if that someone was the one who'd inadvertently induced this current frame of mind. The interior of the barn was cool and dark after the brightness outside. He walked down the aisle as his eyes adjusted, following up on a promise.

"Ah, Mr. Miller. To what do I owe the honour?"

Geai was in the stall with a small bay horse, currying dried mud off into clouds of dust. The sign on the door told Nate what he knew already—this was Just Lucky, the farm's pride and joy. The stallion wasn't very big, but the look he gave you when you entered his presence warned you not to be fooled by that. As a sire, he was still unproven, Chique the first foal of his first crop.

"Figured maybe now things were slowing down around here, I'd pop in and say hi to my fellow Chique guardian." He'd barely seen Geai since he'd started at Woodbine. Most days he just ran by the stallion barn, because there was inevitably a trailer pulled up outside, bringing a visiting mare to be bred.

Lucky grabbed the chain—doubled up so he was tied short, no doubt to keep him from using those teeth on his handler. The stallion stepped abruptly into Geai, who hopped spryly out of the way before reprimanding him with a deft poke behind the shoulder and a short verbal rebuke in French.

"Everything go smoothly this morning?"

Nate nodded, even though Geai's back was to him. "The van left around nine, with Liv right behind it."

Geai laughed and slipped around Lucky's hindquarters to the other side. Geai wasn't all that tall, but he could still look over the stallion's back. Just Lucky was what, maybe fifteen-two? Chique had come by at least some of her lack of size naturally.

"Of course she would. She'd ride in with the horses if they'd let her."

The old man's accent was heavy, but you didn't grow up watching *Hockey Night in Canada* without learning how to understand a French-Canadian. Geai ducked under Lucky's neck and picked up a set of brushes, then started knocking off the layer of fine dust that left both him and Lucky sneezing.

After turning the stallion loose, Geai slid the stall door shut behind him and left the halter on the door. "You want a drink? Water? Pop? Beer?"

Nate followed him to the tack room at the end of the barn, stopping in the doorway. It was a big room, one corner of it breeding lab, another mini office. No-nonsense, like the man who spent the most time there. The fridge looked like a typical farm fridge—all three of the beverages on offer, half a sandwich and some snack-size yogurts, plus an assortment of injectable medications. He didn't want to know what else.

When Nate didn't give him an answer, Geai held out a beer. "Don't tell me you're all healthy like Livvy."

Nate grabbed the bottle. "Thanks." So much for the rest of his run.

Geai led the way to a picnic table on the lawn outside the barn, and unscrewed the cap on his bottle. "Has Roger hired another exercise rider?"

"Not yet." Nate settled across from him. "It'll be okay for a couple of days, with those three horses leaving. Emilie will help on the weekend. I'm sure Rog will fill those stalls with some two-year olds pretty quick though." He shrugged. "I can get on twelve if I have to. I don't mind."

"How long before you run off and start riding races too?"

The old man propped his bottle in front of him with both hands, and Nate could practically hear the whizzing in his brain as questions queued up.

"I agreed to babysit a foal, I'm not going anywhere." He threw out a grin.

"Probably below your paygrade, though."

Nate picked at the label, the sodden paper peeling easily in his fingers. "I admire her, going off to New York like that. Admire her conviction." *Envy it.* "I'm not in a hurry myself. Still sizing things up around here."

"Patience is a virtue?"

"Something like that."

The old man was still sizing him up, like he saw right through the casual excuses to the doubt beneath.

"Livvy says you're good. She's stingy with compliments."

"She's stingy with words," Nate quipped dryly. What did she know? But she *was* good. And she had connections. He should probably just be content staying on the sidelines. Career exercise rider, that was him.

"She asked you to watch Chique. Don't take that lightly. She doesn't like to let people help her."

"Should I be honoured, or scared? I'm pretty sure your crew here on the farm is perfectly capable of looking after that filly." This visit had been inspired by the fact she'd asked him to keep tabs on Geai, too, but Nate didn't mention that. He didn't know if he wanted the responsibility of Liv's trust. It didn't fit with his goal of underachiever.

"It's just her way of showing respect. You stepped up when she foaled Chique. She won't ever forget that."

"I think I pissed her off as much as anything. I'm sure she knows how to resuscitate a foal."

Geai chuckled. "Kind of hard to stay mad when you saved the filly's life. She froze, and she knows it."

"There's a reason they don't let doctors treat kin, right?"

Geai tipped the bottle to his lips. "You were in the right place at the right time. If you have ambitions to be a rider, it won't hurt to have Livvy as a friend. She may be young, but she does have a fair bit of influence around here."

He'd let her believe that's what he wanted, at the interview. Once, at least, it had been true, before he'd tried to rewrite his life into what he thought would please someone else. Which had backfired, big-time. Deep down, that was what he envied most about Liv. That she'd gone after what she wanted, everyone else's expectations be damned.

"She's one of those really smart kids who has trouble dealing with humans, isn't she? Does she even have friends?"

Geai's eyes narrowed slightly, and it was a moment before he responded. "So like I said...don't take her loyalty lightly."

Nate stewed when he left, crossing the lawn in front of Geai's cottage to the trailhead through the woods. The beer left him with a mild buzz...*lightweight*...but he broke into a run anyway. Running away again, the confusion that conversation left him with piled on top of the same old broken record in his head. He always thought if he went fast enough, he could outrun it all, but it always caught up.

He didn't stop today, merely identifying Chique as he ran past the mares and foals, back to his apartment. Maybe a glass of cold water would dilute what remained of the alcohol in his bloodstream and clear his head.

The piano under the big picture window in the main room had been there when he'd moved in. He'd never asked what the hell it was doing in a barn apartment, let alone how they'd got it up here, but it was what made him think this job had been meant to be. That piano was his best friend. He slid onto the bench and placed the glass on a coaster next to a picture frame, resting his fingers on the keys and playing a few bars from a song that had kept him company in his beat-up old Mustang last summer as he drove east.

The photo always won, though. He stared at it—he and his two brothers, and a blonde girl who still gave his heart a jolt. He didn't know why he tortured himself, keeping that photo out. It would be better off at the bottom of a box somewhere. Except when it didn't pitch him into misery, it fueled a fire.

Ambition. It wasn't that he didn't have it. His was just a slow burn, eating away at him. One day, he'd show them all—when he figured out what exactly that meant.

"Give her back, Liv."

The voice broke through her self-absorption, coming from behind her as she walked Claire down Don Philips' shedrow at Belmont. Liv glanced over her shoulder and slowed, Don's assistant, Jeanne, standing there with hands on hips.

"You're going to have to start acting more like a rider if you want to be taken seriously around here."

Liv relinquished the shank to the hotwalker, and with it, a portion of her sense of security. "The track's not even open yet."

"So don't show up so early tomorrow." Jeanne's face

softened, and Liv followed her to the training board. "Kenny said he'd be here at six. Sit down and have a coffee or something."

She didn't do caffeine; besides, she was jittery enough. She forced herself to study the win pictures decorating the walls around Don's messy desk, then, perched on the spare chair, flipped distractedly through status updates on her phone.

Footsteps jolted her back to reality. Kenny O'Connell didn't acknowledge her as he walked over to the coffee maker and filled a Styrofoam cup. Liv rose slowly, waiting while he took his time adding generous portions of cream and sugar, then slurped carefully. He gave a satisfied nod, and finally turned to her.

The way he looked her up and down made her leery, but she squared her shoulders and offered her hand. When he grasped it, he didn't let go.

"Harder," he said, with the faint lilt of an Irish accent.

"I'm sorry?" She pulled back, but he hung on.

"You're going to have to work on that handshake, darlin', if you want trainers to believe you're stronger than you look."

She flinched, pressing her lips together as he finally released her. "Thanks for agreeing to take me on." Though she wasn't completely convinced of it, at the moment.

"Thank Don. He's the one who talked me into it. I could use a good bug, so guess we'll see if we can make you into one." Kenny took another sip of his coffee. "Girl jocks do well at Woodbine, why didn't you stay there?"

There it was again. Why New York? She couldn't answer without discrediting herself by bringing up Claire, so she returned his challenging gaze, channeling assertiveness she didn't feel. "What matters is I'm here now, so why don't we just go with that?"

"Fair enough. How 'bout we go meet some people, darlin', and we'll talk."

"How about you stop calling me darling?"

Kenny cracked a wide smile and put an arm around her shoulders. "You might be all right. Put your helmet on, so you look the part."

She wriggled out from under his arm, suppressing a shudder, and followed him to a shiny black Lexus, feeling conspicuously like a child being lured with the promise of candy. *Come with me, darlin', and I'll make your dreams come true.*

He set the coffee cup in the console and poked the start button. "How's your weight?"

Right to it—good thing she hated small talk. "Almost there."

"Well get on that, 'cause almost ain't good enough." He reached across and grabbed her bicep beneath the sleeve of her polo shirt, and she winced, resisting the urge to slap his hand away. "Start by laying off the weights. You're never actually going to be as strong as the guys, and muscle weighs too much. You need finesse, not power. I'll get Ricky to help you with the rest."

She nodded, even though it was counterintuitive to sacrifice strength—not to mention health. That was the whole warped truth of this profession. It's what she'd signed up for.

He pulled up to a barn, and she walked behind him, her eyes on the horses reaching heads out of the stalls with radar ears. *Yeah, I'm not sure what I'm doing here either.* She tried to smile pleasantly and think about her grip as Kenny introduced Rod Milotski. *That's Mister to you.*

Milotski's eyes skimmed over her, finally resting on her face. "She's better looking than your last bug, at least, huh Kenny? I hope this one can ride."

Talking like she wasn't even there. Was a little respect too much to ask? The Woodbine backstretch wasn't Disneyland—but compared to this? No one at home acted like this to her face. But her father was somebody at Woodbine. Here, once she left Don's barn, if they even knew who Claude Lachance was, they didn't care. It was starting to hit her just how sheltered—and privileged—she'd been.

"Why don't you see for yourself, Rod? What about that little filly of yours? She might like a lighter touch. When you gonna breeze her again?"

"How 'bout you gallop her this morning?" Rod finally spoke directly to Liv.

And she had to defer to Kenny. He nodded.

In a few minutes the groom brought a pale chestnut filly around, and after legging Liv up, Rod took over the shank.

"What's her name?" Liv stroked the filly's neck, her washed-out colour tending towards pink instead of orange or red.

"Blush. She's a bit of a nervous thing. Back her up as best you can, then go once around."

As soon as she was on the filly, Liv's edginess dissolved, sitting quietly as they jigged their way to the track. When Rod turned them loose at the gap, Blush jumped ahead, then settled into Liv's cross when she realized no one was going to fight with her. They eased to a walk just past the wire, but only for a second, Blush rocking back on her hocks and doing a half-pirouette. Liv decided not to push the whole standing thing, and let the filly go.

Blush leapt forward, feeling like she wanted to run off, giving Liv visions of barreling around the clubhouse turn in front of the trainer. Not a good first impression. Liv concentrated on keeping still, and the filly started to trust. She tried to trust back, praying Blush didn't duck out the on-gap.

The trainer was waiting at the off-gap when they were done, Kenny beside him still nursing his coffee. Rod snapped the shank to the bit and Blush tossed her head and started to jig again.

"She looked good," Rod said, not hiding his surprise.

"She was great once she started to relax. She'd be a lot happier if you took that ring bit off her and put something kinder in her mouth."

"You gonna come gallop her every day, then?" Rod glowered up at her.

Liv looked beyond him to Kenny, whose face was telling her to shut up. She leaned forward and rubbed Blush under her flouncing mane, lower lip between her teeth. "She's a nice filly."

Back at the barn, her tension returned as soon as her boots hit the ground, like it was crawling up from the mats under the straw in Blush's stall. She slid off the tack, thanking the groom. Now to see if she'd blown it.

Kenny and Rod stopped talking as she approached. Rod still didn't look happy.

"She breezes Wednesday. Six AM work?"

Liv caught herself—it was easy enough to transform her disbelief into a smile—and endured the handshake ritual again. "Thank you."

"I'll be sure to put a rubber D on her," Rod crowed as he walked away.

Liv allowed herself a skip step once she and Kenny were out of sight. "He asked me back to work her."

"Don't get excited until your name's in the entries, or you'll find yourself a glorified gallop girl," Kenny countered. "And maybe wait till people get to know you a bit before you start saying stuff about the equipment."

"It was the truth, though. I'd think they'd want feedback."

"You come off a little like a snob, darlin'." He raised his hands in surrender as she grimaced at the endearment. "They have to like you a little, at least until you prove you can ride. Try and show some personality."

Her teeth hurt, she clenched them so hard. "Is there a book I can buy? Or maybe I could hire a life coach." An online course, maybe.

He howled. "Maybe some less sarcastic personality."

She left Kenny to chat up trainers with his stereotypical Irish gift of the gab—selling the ten-pound weight advantage she'd receive as a shiny new apprentice; gambling on his reputation until she built her own. It was up to her to ignore the affront of every sneer and derogatory comment. Smile anyway, practice a killer handshake, laugh at their jokes, say nice things about their horses, and keep the other stuff to herself. *Get yourself some mounts so you make them forget you're a* girl. She lost track of time and barns visited.

"One more stop." Kenny pulled up outside of Don's shed,

and it felt like coming home.

Don sat behind piles on his desk in the office. Under normal circumstances, between his impressive build and brusque demeanor, she found him totally intimidating, but after being plugged to strangers all morning, Liv could have hugged him.

"How'd it go?" Don sat back in his chair.

"It's a start," Kenny said. "What have you got for our girl?"

"I'll enter that gelding Roger sent from Woodbine for Friday and give you the call, assuming you get the all-clear from the stewards and starter. Get your feet wet."

Kenny put an arm around her shoulders, and the muscles in her neck ratcheted tighter, but she kept her feet planted. "Don't worry, before you know it, I'll have you swimming in the deep end."

"Speaking of..." Don pushed an open booklet towards her.

The current condition book, listing the races written for the next two weeks. There was Claire's name, scribbled at the top of a maiden special weight for two-year-old fillies. Her chest tightened at the sight.

"All right, darl—" Kenny stopped himself with an unapologetic grin. "See you in the morning. Call me if you need me."

Liv had always been lucky, naturally lightweight, but this was a whole new dimension. She stepped off the scales—scales that would rule her life, at least as long as she had the ten-pound bug. It was a significant allowance for a racehorse—*one pound equals one length,* the saying went—but to ask that kind of a reduction from an already slim human was...inhumane.

She looked up, finding Ricky Acosta watching her. Another step closer to real now, starstruck in the Belmont jock's room. He wouldn't remember the times they'd breezed horses together for Don—with helmet, kerchief and goggles on, she was just another no-name gallop girl to him—but each time was emblazoned on her memory.

He sauntered over, his face as hard and hollow as his body, an unlit cigarette hanging out of the corner of his mouth. He didn't look nearly as attractive as he did on TV. The camera added ten pounds, right? *Ten pounds*...that number haunted her.

"Kenny asked me to give you some tips."

Somehow it felt like he was looking down his nose at her, even though she had two inches on him. He slung an arm around her shoulders, paralyzing everything but her eyes, which shifted sideways to his leer.

"Here's one. Lasix isn't just for horses. It'll suck the water out of you. Works a treat." He tilted his head into hers, lips close to her ear. "But you look all pure, and I can think of a perfect drug-free way to work up a sweat. It'd be an honour to help you break your maiden."

The words crawled up her spine, working into her brainstem and igniting a signal that finally got through to her legs. She spun away, face burning, her still-frozen tongue thwarting a snappy comeback.

"Think she might be a bit of a slow starter, boys." Fed by their laughter, he called after her. "This ain't high school, princess. And this sure as shit ain't a team sport."

Whatever he said as she bolted was in Spanish, garnering more laughter, and it certainly wasn't anything she'd picked up in the intro course she'd taken as an elective during her undergrad. She crumpled onto the bench in the safety of the women's change room, her heart still pummeling against her chest wall.

Princess. Geai had called that one. It was clear: Acosta would never let her forget she was a woman. Not on the track, and not in ways in which she had even less experience. His physicality had made her shamefully aware of *that*.

She closed her eyes, controlling her breathing—crush officially crushed. *As it turns out, your idol is an asshole.*

The density of the safety vest under the nylon colours Liv wore gave her body an illusion of substance she didn't feel, arms folded to keep them steady. Just five wins, and the allowance would drop from ten pounds to five. It sounded straightforward enough, until you went two weeks riding nothing but also-rans. She was starting to understand why guys like Acosta were such bastards. Hangry. All the time.

"Riders up!"

She glanced at the trainer, and he threw her up on the walk.

"Stay out of trouble," was all he said.

She didn't know if her heart palpitations were from nerves or dehydration, grateful for the pony's steady influence escorting her mount through the post parade and warm up. They filed into the gate, the doors slamming shut behind them.

Her horse broke sideways, brushing the runner next to her —of course it was Acosta, Liv catching his dirty look as they were drawn along in the charge of bodies vying for position. In a blink she was trailing the pack.

The race was only six furlongs, and everything was happening so fast. They were already heading into the turn. Her horse moved up steadily, and the field swept into Belmont's broad stretch.

Going to the outside was the safest plan—making her own room wouldn't be following the trainer's instructions. But was staying out of trouble the best she could do? She wanted to win this race. *Needed* to, tired of finishing at the back of the pack all the time. Tired in general.

The leader was running out of gas, and Liv pulled her horse out a lane so they didn't get stuck behind the stopping pacesetter. One on the outside started to drift out, leaving room—but the hole left on the rail was the shortest path. Her horse was game, and Liv was determined to show these guys she had grit.

Her exhale came like a maniacal cackle as her horse bullied his way through. They scraped the rail, and her mount veered sideways, clobbering the horse next to her, the curses reaching Liv's ears unmistakably Acosta's—*again*. Liv drove on, throwing everything she had into the drive to the wire.

Acosta's horse caught up as Liv eased hers, galloping out.

"You're coming down, princess."

"Did we win?" she asked.

"Don't know. Don't matter." He pulled his horse up as Liv let hers go on.

She was the last to return to the front of the grandstand. Her heart soared seeing the tote board, her number on top, then plummeted at the bold red letters of the inquiry sign.

The groom peered up at her as he snapped a paddock shank to the horse's bit. "Acosta claimed foul."

"Of course he did."

Liv tossed her whip to her valet, hanging her head as they circled, and waited for the stewards' verdict. She didn't like her chances of it being in her favour.

* * *

Faye: *Are you coming home for the Plate? Dean's running Playing Catchup!*

Liv: *Wouldn't miss it for the world.*

Faye: *What? Seriously? How?*

Liv: *Suspension.*

Faye: *That's the best news! I mean, sorry. See you Saturday!*

* * *

Woodbine felt like a heartening embrace after the harshness of Belmont, even on a day like today when it was dressed up almost beyond recognition. Liv felt that way herself, but the Plate was special. It was history and pageantry and pride, distinctly Canadian, and worth a little social discomfort.

She and Emilie threaded their way through the masses, pressing on to find Faye, who was, naturally, right in the middle of it. Faye didn't spend a lot of time around the track, even though her older brother was a trainer, but Queen's Plate was an event, so Faye was in her element.

Faye hugged her gingerly, as if she were afraid Liv would crumble. "You look fabulous—in an anorexic, runway model sort of way."

"Um, thanks?"

"I do have to applaud you for picking out that cute dress without my help, so something about this crazy New York thing has been worthwhile."

They were jostled, and Faye grabbed Liv's arm to steady herself, then steered them out of the crowd to a free bench.

"So who gets a suspension when they haven't even been riding three weeks?"

Liv smirked. The win had been taken away from her, but her actions had served a purpose. She'd shown Acosta she'd come to play. "I guess I got carried away trying to prove something."

"Brilliant." Faye didn't buy into the whole horse thing, but she was in full support of beating men at their own game, whatever game that happened to be. Her eyes dropped back to Liv's spare frame with a sweep of her hand. "This, not so much. There's nothing to you under normal circumstances. You're not doing anything stupid, are you?"

Liv dropped her eyes, crossing her legs and tugging at her skirt. "There's always some sort of compromise. Where's Nate, Em?" She needed to distract Faye from probing further into how she met the low weight assignments. "I thought he'd be here."

Faye's perfect eyebrows peaked. "He's real then, is he? I've been convinced he's a figment of Emilie's imagination."

Emilie tilted her head and stuck out her tongue. "He stayed at the farm to watch the race with Geai. Geai had a mare booked for a rebreed to Lucky this afternoon."

Faye's face fell to a frown, her lower lip jutting out. "So disappointing. I need to meet him."

Liv buried her own sense of letdown. Not that she'd been hoping to see him or anything. "Maybe Em wants to keep the exercise rider for herself."

"Chasing an older man," Faye teased.

"As tempting as that is, because he is completely gorgeous, and also super nice, I'm really just protecting him from you, Faye." Emilie gave Faye a pointed look. "Older man. Four years. Besides, you only date jocks."

Faye's mouth curled upward. "True. For future reference, though."

Liv's phone chimed, and she glanced at the screen. "Speak of the devil."

She opened the message, making out a selfie of little Chique nuzzling Nate's hair, Sotisse grazing passively behind them. *She's gonna come watch the Plate with me and Geai* he'd typed below it, as if the power of suggestion could fashion the filly's destiny. The word *adorable* came to mind—because of Chique, of course. She handed the phone to Faye.

Faye lifted the device, studying it approvingly. "How do I get on that list? You do have good taste, Emilie."

Faye gave the phone back and Liv glanced at the photo again, letting Emilie's crush be the decoy. She didn't know what to think of Nate, with his regular updates on Chique, and his faithfulness to Geai. Sure, she'd asked him to keep an eye out, but she didn't want to mistake his devotion for something it wasn't. As in, anything to do with her.

She felt Faye zero back in on her, and quickly turned the phone over.

"So, your agent's creepy, your idol's an asshole...you're still determined to do this riding thing?"

Liv shrugged. "Kenny's kind of grown on me."

"Like a fungus?" Emilie chirped.

Liv had to laugh. *Kind of.* "I haven't officially withdrawn from school yet."

Faye's eyebrows shot up. "Are you seriously thinking about going back?"

"I can't win a race to save my life, can I? Maybe this was a big mistake. I've still got time to decide."

Faye looped an arm through Liv's and pulled her to her feet. "Let's go up to the Turf Club and see Dean and have something to eat. Free lunch."

"I can't. If I got started on that buffet I might not be able to stop. I'll see Dean when he comes down for the Plate."

Emilie led the way as the horses left the paddock for the current race, taking the shortcut to the trackside apron at the west end of the grandstand.

"Hey Liv, how's it going in New York?" A voice behind them caught her attention as they climbed the stairs.

She couldn't remember the guy's name, or place him out of context—someone who worked on the backstretch—but she gave him a polite smile. "It's going."

"How's your filly?"

"Great. She runs next week. Don almost entered her a week ago, but decided to wait for a longer race."

"Acosta going to ride her? First time starter and all."

Liv curled her fingers into fists at the mention of Acosta's name, but sweetened her smile. "Nope, that one's mine."

"Well good luck. Nice to see you."

Faye made a face, muttering under her breath, "Everyone's your friend when you're a big-time New York rider."

"Right." Liv rolled her eyes, but it reinforced her feeling of warmth for the home crowd, after weeks of being an outsider at Belmont.

The guy walked away with his buddy when they reached the apron, voices drifting.

"I thought they were pretty high on that filly when she was up here," the buddy said.

The first guy answered, "Yeah, me too. Can't be much if they're going to put Liv on her when Acosta rides the rest of the barn."

"Don't listen to them." Faye pulled Liv to the spot Emilie had secured on the rail.

Liv gazed across the track to the infield, flags billowing gently in front of the shrubs and lakes. "They're so wrong. Claire is the real deal."

Later, waiting at the gate to board the plane back to New York, she scrolled distractedly through the first photos and reports from the Plate—Dean's horse had run a gutsy third.

The Plate magic lingered, reminding her of the whole point behind her decision to get her license at Belmont; her dream to be here with Chique in three years. She opened up Word, and started drafting a letter to her academic advisor about her intention to withdraw from the DVM program.

She couldn't expect to be successful at this riding thing if she wasn't all in. It had only been three weeks; Claire hadn't even started yet.

Claire would change her luck.

CHAPTER FOUR

July

When Liv had stood in this walking ring in the past month, she'd often questioned herself. But Claire was here this time, shimmering black and gold and white; the reason she'd come to New York. She flexed and extended her toes against the thin leather of her lightweight boots, little more than slippers. Suspension over. Recommitted. *All in.*

Her father stood on the other side of Don, but their conversation didn't register amid the hum in her brain. Had she expected her mother to be here? Not really. That might have been misconstrued as acceptance of this mad life choice. Just as well. Her mother wouldn't have ignored her drawn face, or the fact that a gust of wind could have blown her over. Don legged her up like she was a feather, and the groom led them into the tunnel, passing them off to the pony.

She shook off her guilt that Claire didn't have the benefit of a more seasoned rider for her first outing. It was Liv's job to make sure the filly had a good experience today, because this race could shape Claire's opinion on the whole game. Fillies weren't forgiving. She couldn't screw this up.

Behind the gate an assistant starter took over, Claire swinging her head and bumping him before Liv could stop her. He shoved back, and led them in. Liv reached down and touched the sheen of sweat on Claire's neck. Claire was feeling her tension. She needed to pull it together.

They missed the break, Claire popping out a beat behind the others when Liv had schooled her ad nauseam. Dirt flew back, pelting their faces as Liv parked the filly on the rail. Claire would either deal with it, or she wouldn't. She settled into her big stride, undeterred...*good girl*.

Even though they were at the back of the pack, they weren't all that far behind. The front-runners were flying—that would work in Claire's favour in the lane. One thing about Belmont's long homestretch, it would give them lots of time to get there. On the turn Claire passed a couple of fillies on her own, Liv still holding her. *Not yet.* The speed freaks on the lead would come back to her. She needed to be content to build momentum, wait for the right second to throw Claire into gear.

Turning for home, there was Acosta, ahead of her—elbows flying, cross thrown, the sound of his voice carrying back to her. Claire's ears flicked forward when Acosta's filly accelerated.

Yes. Now.

Claire launched, Liv's body mirroring the thrust of her neck as they drove for the wire. Claire's nose reached the other filly's saddle towel, then shoulder. But Acosta intentionally let his filly drift, nudging Claire wide. Liv gritted her teeth. *You don't get to mess with Claire.* She unsheathed her stick and struck Claire in the haunches—once, twice—and Claire dug in, pushed back, pulled even, and stuck her glorious pink nose in front.

Liv barely remembered the picture—or dismounting, or unsaddling, or weighing in—jogging back to the jock's room in a blissful daze. When the ice water drenched her, she welcomed it, letting herself think, just for that moment, she was one of them.

* * *

43

Chique's yell pierced Nate's eardrums—for such a tiny thing, she had a voice on her. She contorted her body as only an indignant foal could while he attempted to stand her in the aisle of the broodmare barn for the blacksmith.

"She's right there, Cheeky."

Sotisse poked her head over the stall door with a mouthful of hay to check in, but went back to the pile with an unconcerned snort. The little filly braced all four legs solid as fence posts as the blacksmith sidled up to her shoulder, scratching under her spiky mane, trying to convince her they were friends. Chique rolled an eye, unconvinced

"Whatever you're selling, she's not buying," Nate quipped.

"Each time I come it's like she's never seen me before." The blacksmith ran a hand down Chique's leg. She sighed and lifted it.

"She just has to make her point."

"Remember that when you're breaking her." Geai observed, amused, sitting on a bale of straw.

"I'm pretty sure Liv is going to be the one breaking her," Nate responded, stroking the filly's neck, her coat shiny and sleek now that the baby fuzz was gone.

"Ah, not if she's setting the world on fire in New York!"

"That filly of hers run huge the other day, eh?" The blacksmith rasped Chique's tiny hoof, then gently placed it down. Chique lifted it back up and stomped it to the ground for emphasis.

"It was a solid performance." Geai nodded. "Livvy kept her cool with that little bit of race-riding Acosta threw at her." The grin that overtook his face was all pride.

Geai opened the stall door for Nate when the blacksmith was finished. Chique shook her head once she was free, going immediately to Sotisse's side to nurse, like she'd just suffered an unthinkable injustice and her mother's milk would erase the memory.

"She says Don wants to run Claire in a stake at Saratoga next time out," Geai mused, pulling the door shut when Nate slipped out.

"We should go, Geai."

The old man looked at him like he was insane.

"Breeding season is over. The farm will survive without you for a couple of days."

Geai turned and walked away from him.

"I've got vacation days coming, and I'm guessing you've probably collected a few months' worth over the years." When the old man still ignored him, Nate played his trump card. "Think of how happy Liv would be. I bet she'd appreciate the moral support. It'd be nice to see Claire run, wouldn't it?"

"Shouldn't you be going home to see your folks or something?" Geai protested.

Hell no. He felt the recurrent pang of guilt knowing how much his mother wanted him to come back to visit, but she'd know it was impossible, that first anniversary looming, flaring like a gunshot wound in his chest.

"Not sure I'm welcome. My dad kicked me out when I quit school." That really wasn't enough to keep him away, but Geai didn't need to know he'd dropped out for less inspiring reasons than Liv had.

"Bah, parents get over stuff like that. You should go home. Why do you want to go to Saratoga?"

Nate handed the lead rope to the girl waiting to hold the next foal. "Everyone wants to go to Saratoga. It's like Mecca for racetrackers."

"You want to spend your holiday with an old man? Don't you have any friends?"

He put an arm around Geai's shoulders, grinning. "You're it."

Geai studied the next foal when the girl brought him out, assessing the sturdy chestnut colt's conformation. "I'll talk to Claude. No promises."

CHAPTER FIVE

August

A year ago he'd climbed into his ancient Mustang, packed with as little as he could get away with, and started heading east. He'd had no business driving a car that night. Not a recollection he was proud of. Saratoga was as good a distraction as any.

They'd left before dawn, because Geai insisted they get there to see Liv ride in the first race. The playlist was carefully chosen to exclude anything that would stir the wrong memories, the timing of Eve 6's *Open Road Song* perfect, hitting the speakers as Nate accelerated onto the New York State Thruway. He started belting out the lyrics. Geai was a good sport about the music, though he'd spare the old man the Cursive and Three Days Grace that had featured prominently in his escape last summer.

"Is this song personal, Mr. Miller?" Geai yelled over the volume.

Nate threw Geai a grin, but only said, "It's the perfect road trip song," when it was almost as if it had been written for him. He could have looped it for the whole drive.

In just under four hours, they left the Thruway at Amsterdam. Forty-five minutes later, there it was: *Saratoga Springs.*

Geai complained about the sweltering heat as he and Nate walked toward the legendary racetrack—the closest lots were full, so they'd had to park on one of the sidestreets. Nate didn't mind, sauntering past stately old homes under towering trees before he recognized the sales grounds and pavilion, Saratoga's famous "Oklahoma" training track across the road, and the rustic barns beyond it. Geai left him behind. The old man couldn't disguise the excited glint in his eyes, the energetic swing in his step. Nate jogged to catch up before they crossed Union Avenue.

"I'm going to grab a program," he said once they were through the gates.

"They're just leaving the paddock." Geai didn't wait for him, swallowed up by the crowd.

Nate dodged bodies to catch up again. They passed tents of vendors—photographers and artists and fancy hats—before Geai led him through the grandstand, the smell of fresh pizza wafting from a concession stand. When they emerged at the trackside apron, Nate stopped and turned, bombarded by the history here.

"Why are you standing there?" Geai huffed, mopping sweat from his brow with a kerchief.

The old man pushed up to the chain link that kept the spectators from the outer rail, staring down towards where the green-coated outrider led the procession of horses onto the track. Before Nate could pick out Liv from her colours and program number, Geai had spotted her, dark hair braided down her straight back, focus absolute.

The horses warmed up off the other way, headed to the gate over in the chute. When the field came down the stretch minutes later, riders yelling and whips popping, Liv's horse was one of those struggling at the back of the pack. She probably rode a lot like that, though she'd won a couple of races at this meet, her tally resting at four. One more win and she'd be done with the ten-pound allowance. It put a whole new spin on the meaning of hungry.

Geai elbowed him and set off again. "We'll catch her coming back."

"Maybe I can get her autograph."

"Don't make fun."

"How do you know I'm not serious?"

Geai might've been stocky, but he nimbly darted around people with the single-mindedness of a forward intent on scoring a game-winning goal. They easily beat the jockeys back to the room.

Liv approached amid the bobbing helmets, aloof and businesslike—head down, stick under her arm, the goggles around her neck encrusted with dirt. When she finally glanced up, her eyes popped. She sprinted, launching herself at Geai, and clung to him like a homesick kid seeing her dad after a week at camp.

Liv grinned at Nate over Geai's shoulder, her cheeks flushed. "Hey, Miller!"

That smile wasn't meant for him, not at all, but it knocked him sideways. He pulled his eyes away and pushed his chin out, indicating behind her. "I think you've got another fan waiting."

Liv seemed almost as shy as the young girl as she accepted the pen and scribbled an autograph on the kid's program. The girl lit up as she took it back, holding both edges of the program and gazing at it, her father mouthing *thank you* as he ushered her away.

"Ah, my celebrity." Geai beamed.

"Hardly," Liv said, still looking unsettled by the girl's adoration. "I can't believe you made it for the first race. What time did you leave?"

"Dark o'clock." Nate elbowed Geai. "No traffic at the border, anyway."

"I can't believe you're actually here." She squeezed the old man again. "Gotta go."

Who was that? Definitely not a version of Liv Lachance he'd ever met; almost like a normal girl. She disappeared, and Nate smirked at Geai.

"You almost look happy I dragged you here, kicking and screaming." He ducked as Geai flicked him in the head with the back of his fingers.

Liv had one more mount between now and the Adirondack Stakes, in which she and Claire would make their stake debut. Her other mount looked like it had no chance.

"Must get pretty disheartening, riding all those longshots," Nate commented when they watched the horses load, the gate set up in front of them.

"It's horse racing. As long as you remember anything can happen, there's hope."

Especially in a maiden claimer. Liv's mount blasted out and assumed the lead. She was still on top when they came down the stretch, Geai rattling the chain link with both hands, screaming so loud Nate dissolved into laughter as Liv brought the 30-1 shot home first by five lengths.

"You're not allowed to leave!" Liv skipped up to them after she'd posed for the win photo and weighed in, pressing a finger to Geai's chest. She threw her arms around him and gave him a quick kiss on the cheek, then bounced to Nate and hugged him too before she realized what she was doing.

He caught her, hands on her impressively solid biceps, the body protector under her silks hard against him. *Put down the boss's daughter, Miller.* She pushed herself back looking mortified.

"Can I get you a slice of pizza?" He gave her a twisted grin.

"*Ohmygosh,* I could have pizza." Liv laughed. "Claire first."

Liv checked herself; checked Claire, reeling in the filly's enthusiastic gallop. Don had said it was okay to warm her up away from the pony, but getting run off with would be bad. She was still riding the high from the win—had she really hugged Nate? Thank goodness it had only been Geai there. The look on Nate's face, though.

There was no weight allowance for an apprentice in stake

races, so she rode on equal terms with the journeymen. She probably could have eaten a whole pizza and still made weight.

They loaded into the gate, six and a half furlongs from the wire. Liv laced her fingers through Claire's mane, every muscle poised on the brink—Claire's too—every nerve under control, her focus unwavering between Claire's rigid ears.

Claire bounded out perfectly, but Liv sat back, convincing her to let the speed go. Claire's ears flickered, listening, and she settled into a big loping stride that carried her easily along the backstretch. The front-running grey started opening up on the turn, and Liv had a flash of indecision. Claire was on the bridle, pulling, asking. *No, just wait…*

They closed the gap as the field thundered into the stretch, Liv sighting the clear path before them. Claire took aim, wearing down the grey's lead until she drew even. But the grey eyeballed her, digging in, and fought back. Liv stopped herself from screaming as they blazed under the wire, beaten a head. Damn it! *Damn, damn, damn.*

She gritted her teeth. She should have moved sooner. She tried to talk herself down as they galloped out.

Placing in a stake earned Claire coveted black type designation, and in a Grade Two contest no less. This is where she belonged—she'd shown that today, and the way she'd come flying at the end, they'd just have to look forward to the longer fall championship races back at Belmont. And maybe… just maybe…did she dare think it? The Breeders' Cup.

When she got back to the barn, Geai was talking to Don, dwarfed by the trainer's commanding physique. Geai broke away, throwing his arms wide when he saw her. Nate stood off to the side with his hands jammed in the pockets of his chinos, watching.

"Ah, see? That was . . . *fantastique.*" Geai pulled her close.

"I really wanted to win."

"So win next time."

"Black type for the big filly." Nate offered his hand, then recoiled as she gripped it. "Holy shit! Careful, I can't get hurt on vacation."

Kenny would be proud, Liv thought with satisfaction as he rubbed his fingers.

"You look nice, by the way," Nate said. "But that dress doesn't go with the handshake."

It was the same outfit she'd worn to the Plate, and definitely not out of place at Saratoga, but she had to stop herself from pulling at the hem of the skirt, having him notice her appearance. Instead she swept the hair from her face with a sly smile. "That's the whole idea. The element of surprise."

When Claire returned from the test barn, the hotwalker walked her a few more turns before taking her out to graze, the sound of her teeth tearing the grass easing away the remnants of Liv's disappointment. At the end of the day, all that mattered was that the filly came back healthy and happy.

Nate appeared at her elbow. "Geai's right, she ran a big race."

"You're a miracle-worker, Miller. I owe you."

His forehead wrinkled in confusion. "What are you talking about?"

"Geai hasn't ventured very far from the farm since his wife died five years ago. I don't know how you talked him into this."

He shrugged, looking back to Claire. "He misses you. That's a pretty strong motivator."

"Thank you." She fought a sentimental urge to hug him again, and might have, if she hadn't thrown herself at him like a freak earlier.

He pushed his hands deeper into his pockets, still not looking at her. "It was nothing."

Nothing? It was everything.

CHAPTER SIX

September

Blush was like a kid with no friends. Once upon another September, Liv had been that kid, climbing on the school bus for her first day in a new high school after moving to Ontario. Faye had adopted her introvert self, much like Liv had now adopted Blush.

Liv didn't normally buy into the chestnut filly stereotype, but Blush made a good case for it. Sore shins had set the filly back and delayed her debut, but if she got her gate card today, there was a race for her next week. Liv had earned that call—not that anyone else wanted it. Blush was a quick little thing though, and her trainer Rod was practical, running his horses where they belonged. They might get lucky with her first time out.

The filly quivered beneath Liv from the tip of her fiery forelock to the tail skirting her hocks. Not that Liv didn't understand—being locked in that huge metal contraption went against the most valued of equine instincts. She scratched the filly's rock-hard trapezius, hoping to relax the drum-tight muscle. Liv had lost track of how many times they'd gate schooled. Almost every day since she'd returned to Belmont after the Saratoga meet.

"All right, baby girl. Let's do this." The assistant starter at Blush's head led her forward.

Blush walked into the stall next to her workmate like a pro, save for the trembling. The starter's assistant climbed onto the frame beside them, turning Blush's head slightly and rubbing her forehead. The filly's heart pounded through her ribcage.

"We got one more," called another gate crew guy behind them.

Blush's ears flicked back as her head tilted, and the assistant gently straightened her.

"Can we just get these two on their way, please?" Liv begged. Blush was being so good, she hated to push their luck. Sure enough, the filly started sinking. "Don't you dare," she hissed, shifting her weight and tapping lightly with her stick.

Mistake. Blush rocked forward and pitched her head, dragging the assistant down and leaving him hanging precariously from the frame before he hauled her back up. As soon as the filly scrambled to her feet, she threw herself left, unbalancing the assistant before exploding vertically with a panic-driven twist. Liv crouched, ready to bail. She dropped the lines and grabbed at the frame, but Blush was tipping over, and the momentum sent Liv out the back of the gate without a chance to push herself away.

She heard the snap as her arm struck the ground first, and cursed herself for not better controlling her fall. Someone grabbed her as she crumbled to the dirt, dragging her away from the filly's thrashing hooves.

"You okay?"

Searing pain siphoned the breath from her lungs as she cradled the limb against her body, but she forced a nod, her smile coming off more like a grimace. Somehow Blush was free of the gate, clambering to her feet, the crew on top of the filly before she realized she was loose.

"Is she all right?" Liv asked through clenched teeth, staggering to her feet and trying to shake off the hand on her elbow, even though her head was swimming. "Athletic little bitch, isn't she?"

"You don't look so good. You better sit down."

The voice seemed suddenly remote, Liv's ears ringing, and her legs abruptly gave way. The elbow-holder softened her landing as she collapsed.

Unbelievable. Taken out by a chestnut filly.

Silence, and more silence. Liv wasn't about to break it. All she had in her head were self-defeating thoughts. Only six more hours of this, and they'd be home, the trees and water of the Adirondacks in upstate New York flashing past like a movie on fast forward.

"I know this is hard for you," her mother finally said from behind the wheel, because of course driving a stick shift with one arm in a cast was impossible. So much for independence.

Which part did Anne mean? The six-week sentence this injury had served Liv? The part where she'd left Claire on a path leading towards the Breeders' Cup, and champion two-year old filly? Or just being faced with relying on her mother for basic things like driving her car and pulling back her hair?

"But please tell me you're done now, with this riding madness. Tell me you'll finish your degree. It's only mid-September, surely—"

Liv's bitter laugh cut her off. "Do you really think I'd let a fluky gate accident scare me away?"

Her mother sighed. "It's just such a waste, Olivia."

"How embarrassing for you, to have a *pinhead* for a daughter." She spat out the slur, immediately ashamed Anne could so quickly reduce her to a petulant teenager.

"When I was your age…"

Here we go. Liv braced herself for the life lessons speech.

"…there was a boy, before I met your father. A rider."

Liv's eyes shot from the window. Her mother's remained fixed on the highway, fingers tightening and releasing on the wheel.

Anne glanced at her. "He lost his life in a spill. My not

wanting you to ride...it's not just about quitting vet school."

Liv's gaze dropped to her lap. "I'm sorry, Maman. Why didn't you tell me?"

"It seemed better to make an argument out of logic than fear —though I think any rational parent would be terrified. I had a hard enough time watching you do cross-country on a pony, let alone seeing you out there on the track on a racehorse."

The smile Liv suppressed seemed wrong given the gravity of the conversation, but the memory of her pony—who'd actually been a small firecracker of an off-track Thoroughbred —inspired nostalgia.

"And I know this..." Anne looked down at Liv's cast quickly. "It's not going to stop you. But it doesn't help. So if I don't watch you ride, now you know why."

"You don't need to dry it. It's just going back up in a ponytail." Liv glanced at the stylist, itching to let Faye have her turn so she could watch the replay of the Frizette Stakes again.

"Yes you do, because no it's not," Faye interjected. "We're going for dinner, because at least you can eat now, right? Then to a club to pick up guys. Kidding, of course," she added before Liv even reacted.

"What happened to Hot Bug Boy?"

Faye waved her hand airily. "I got bored."

Hacking a few inches off her hair made it more manageable with her cast, but she probably should have just chopped it off. Her mother was still going to have to braid it or pull it back. Her wrist ached constantly, and her fingers didn't want to move like they should.

She escaped from the chair as soon as the stylist removed the cape, trading places with Faye, then tuned their conversation out while she hit play on the video.

Claire running like she should, eating up the mile at Belmont, winning her first stakes race by two. Without her. Worse yet, with Ricky Acosta. Okay, Acosta rode a lot of horses for Don, and he was Kenny's other rider, and still leading the standings at Belmont, so yes, not a hard call to make, but really? It just stung all the more.

But she had to be happy for Claire. The filly deserved it. Deserved better than her, obviously.

"You're still thinking about that race, aren't you?" Faye said when they were settled at the restaurant.

Liv asked for water to Faye's wine. Maybe she should take up drinking, only she didn't really like the stuff.

"The universe has it out for me. You know my dad is seriously talking Breeders' Cup now? Claire paid her way with that win. I should have just stayed in school and let Acosta ride her from the start like my mom said. Then I wouldn't know what an ass he is and be that much more pissed about it all." She stabbed a chip into the bowl of salsa.

Faye smirked, and pushed the glass of wine towards her. "Want some?"

Liv took a sip, then shook her head as the alcohol burned at the back of her throat. Nope. Not happening.

"Guess we don't have to worry about you turning to the bottle to drown your woes," Faye quipped. She set the glass to the side as the server came with their food.

"What am I even going to do for six weeks? Roger won't let me go into the track to help until the ortho is sure I won't need surgery."

"Maybe we could actually hang out." Faye smirked. "Between the horses and your crazy school schedule, I feel like I've barely seen you since undergrad. Some best friend you are. Remember that first day you got on the bus?"

"And you adopted the poor French girl?" Liv grinned, then sighed. "Sorry."

"That's okay. When you're famous you can hire me as your image consultant."

Famous. Liv wasn't sure she wanted to be famous; she just wanted to be respected. This need of hers to be successful was at odds with the attention that went along with it. She wouldn't have to worry about that for a while, at least.

"We're having cake, right?" Faye tilted her head, perfect eyebrows quirked.

"Hell yes." That much she was sure of.

CHAPTER SEVEN

October

Few people called Liv—anyone who knew her learned to use text, or email, because she hated answering the phone—but she picked up on the first ring when she saw Don's name on the screen. *Three weeks until Breeders' Cup.*

"Claire's caught that virus that's going around," the trainer said without preamble. "She's pretty sick."

The tone of his voice scared her, his pause loaded.

"I've already talked to your father, and we're sending her to the clinic for treatment. You know the drill. Fluids. Anti-inflammatories."

"I'll come down." She couldn't leave Claire to fight on her own while a deadly infection attacked her immature immune system.

"She'll be in isolation, so you won't be able to see her. It'll be easier for both of you if you stay put. Trust me. All you can do is hope for the best."

And plan for the worst, Liv finished in her head.

CHAPTER EIGHT

November

Claire pushed out her nose, twisting her neck first one way, then the other, upper lip contorted in a full-fledged peppermint appeal. Her two stablemates looked on with interest, but Claire was stealing the show—which Liv videoed with her phone. She reached into her pocket for Claire's inspiration, and the filly quickly lipped the candy up, the affection in Liv's eyes reserved for the leggy bay.

Claire gave him away with a low rumble, and Nate started down the aisle so he didn't feel so conspicuous for watching.

"Nice to see you embracing my suggestion. Give me the phone, I'll get one of both of you."

Liv frowned, and shoved the phone into her pocket. "I'm not as photogenic as Claire."

"I doubt that. Your fans want to see you too."

She looked away, but handed over the device, self-consciously tucking her dark hair behind an ear.

Claire was happy to provide an encore. Liv loosened up when the filly started her performance again, her smile so sweet and natural Nate forgot himself for a moment.

"Maybe it's that block to having your picture taken that's getting in the way of you winning races."

"That's pretty woo, Miller." She smirked as she took the phone back and posted the new—in his mind, improved—video.

At first she'd scoffed at his idea to use social media to keep herself out there while she was off, but if her posts were any indication, she was actually enjoying it. She really did need more pics of herself in there, though. Cute bug girl needed to work that.

"I'm starting to think you might be the life coach I so obviously need." Her lips went a little less smirk and a little more smile, and he would have enjoyed that so much more if her comment hadn't inadvertently stirred something else.

"I'm hardly qualified for that." The slight furrow of her brow indicated she hadn't missed his flat tone. He pushed aside morose thoughts. "How'd it go this morning?"

She pulled back the sleeve of her coat to reveal her atrophied left arm, freshly cast-free, and rubbed it, opening and closing her fingers. "Rehab next."

"Maybe you'll be ready to ride the last couple weeks of the Woodbine meet."

"Because that would be so much fun. Spoken like someone who's leaving for Florida soon."

"Not my fault you're not bringing Claire down till January."

Liv touched the filly's pink nose, then let Claire lick her palm. "That was one scary virus. We could have lost her. She's going to need the time to gain back some weight before she trains again."

He'd felt Liv struggle, being away from Claire while she was so sick. There had been a couple of days when the reports from the clinic in New York had been grave, before the filly had turned a corner.

Nate checked the time. "Still coming to Geai's to watch the Breeders' Cup?"

"Yeah." She looked wistfully back to the big bay filly. "A few months ago I thought there was a chance we'd be there."

"It was hard enough having her win the Frizette without you, right? Can you imagine what it would have been like if you had to watch someone else ride her at Santa Anita?"

"If you're trying to cheer me up, it's not working."

"Next year. Everything happens for a reason."

"Any thoughts on what that might be?"

"Building a social media following?" He flashed a crooked grin. "Good things come to those who wait."

"Who knew you were such a philosopher, Miller."

He zipped up his coat, motioning in the direction of the door. "Shall we?"

Liv looked up at him quickly, then back to Claire, like she was searching for assurance from the filly, but Claire just stretched her neck back out looking for more treats. Nate almost laughed at her indecision—it wasn't like he was asking her out on a date.

"I was just going to walk," she said, and he had to stop himself from saying, *you're cute when you're all self-conscious.*

"I can walk."

A little smile tugged at the corners of her mouth. "Fine."

It was fun to push her, make her uncomfortable, try and get a reaction. He jumped ahead to open the door, standing back with a sweep of his arm. She rolled her eyes as she went through, pulling up her hood.

The farm's tall maples had lost most of their foliage, looking like skeletons against the grey sky, the paddocks reduced to mossy green scrub, and a cold wind stirred dead leaves around their feet making him wish he'd grabbed a toque. He glanced at Liv, her face hidden behind her hood as she held it tight to her cheeks.

She was a fast walker, but he wasn't going to complain—it would get them there sooner. He really should have just taken the car, left her to her exercise obsession. But this was kind of nice. That's what he liked about Liv. She wasn't afraid of silence. And he could throw out comments that poked at his past and she just let them go, never probed. Probably thinking *I'll stay out of your head, Miller, if you stay out of mine.*

The weanlings lived outside—colts in one big paddock, fillies in another. And cold as it was, when Liv stopped at the fence of the fillies' field, he didn't complain about that, either. Chique, never one to shun visitors, led the inquisitive group of youngsters over.

"Watch this." He dug into his jacket pocket.

Chique dropped her whiskery nose to his palm, and picked up the mini English mint with careful lips. She seemed to suck on it for a moment before working it back to her molars, grinding, then lifted her muzzle to blow a hot minty breath in his face. He planted a kiss between her nostrils.

"Impressive," she said. "I don't think I've ever known a weanling to figure that out. Let's hope peppermint-eating precocity is an indicator of racing prowess."

Talk nerdy to me, baby. But he stopped himself from saying that, too.

Chique leaned into his fingers as he scrubbed under her wild mane, then torqued her neck to try and grab his sleeve. He'd caught Liv smiling out of the corner of his eye when he'd kissed the filly. *C'mon, you like me, just a little, admit it.*

Napoleon gave them the royal welcome when they arrived at Geai's. There had been many afternoons here since Liv had come back, watching the racing channel; many days where she'd played restless spectator with her broken limb as he and Geai worked with the yearlings.

He couldn't help the flirting, or the things that popped into his head, but he didn't have any illusions. The only reason Liv even tolerated him was because of Chique and Geai. And he wasn't looking for anything more. There was still the owner's daughter thing —and the scar tissue holding together his heart.

CHAPTER NINE

December

Liv was getting claustrophobic. Her mother was running true to form, preparing the traditional Christmas Eve *réveillon*. Geai, Faye, and Faye's brother Dean were over to join the celebration. Too many people, even if they were good friends and family. Time to escape.

Everything lay dormant around the farm, from huge maples to expectant mares. Solitary. Peaceful. Soft flakes drifted from the sky, melting on her face when she peered up into the blackness. The apartment over the office barn was dark, Nate in Florida with the rest of the Woodbine crew. Liv and Claire would join them in just over a week. The van was booked for New Year's Eve. That would put an end to her calm. She slipped through the barn door, flicking on the lights.

Three faces surfaced hopefully from the stalls when she looked down the aisle, but first she unlocked the office. She smiled at the painting as she went to the desk, picking up a small pile of mail and flipping through it. Business envelopes that were probably flyers advertising Ontario stallions; Christmas cards from some of the other stud farms. One card was addressed to Nate—glancing at the return address, she saw it was from Calgary, last name Miller. Odd they didn't have his Florida address, but she could take it with her when she went next week. She placed the envelopes back on the desk, glanced at the painting again, and locked the door behind her.

The water buckets were half-empty, so she topped them up, and threw all three horses more hay. Claire ignored hers, her toe tap-tap-tapping the mat until Liv unwrapped one of the starlight mints she'd stuffed in her pocket at the house. Claire inhaled it.

"See you later, Amazon filly." The Nate-assigned moniker had slipped into her own vocabulary. One last glance at the white-lined eye, the wide blaze—a face that never failed to give her heart a surge —and Liv turned off the lights, returning to the crisp darkness.

The weanlings came in at night now so they didn't become completely feral. Liv could pick Chique's voice from the chorus of whinnies that greeted her, the throaty declaration contradicting the dark filly's diminutive stature. Chique's head shot over the stall door at the crinkling wrapper, and Liv placed the red and white mint on her palm. The filly swept it up confidently, thanks to Nate's training, but spat the disc onto the ground, looking offended as she worked her lips and tongue.

"Fair. You're not used to the fancy ones."

Chique snuffled in her ear, then nibbled on her toque. Liv stepped out of reach and snapped a picture, sending it to Nate. *Cheeky Little Bitch says Merry Christmas.*

She pushed the filly back gently to peek at her bucket, and started topping up waters with the hose. The click of the door latch made her jump, and she froze, until she recognized Geai's familiar bulk, hands deep in the pockets of his parka, stomping snow from his heavy boots.

"It's too early for night check," he reprimanded.

She dragged the hose to the next stall. "Well, whoever is supposed to do it will just have an easier time."

"That would be me."

Just like Geai to volunteer for the task so everyone else could enjoy Christmas Eve uninterrupted. Only a skeleton crew was on tomorrow—no one had to work Christmas Day if they didn't want to. The colt in the stall grabbed hold of the hose, and Liv poked him below a nostril to keep the stream going into the bucket instead of soaking the bedding.

"Your mother's getting twitchy."

"You're saying I have to go back?"

He chuckled. "I think you'd better. Your friend Faye is kind of miffed too. They're joining forces."

"Might as well finish what I started."

Geai started doling out flakes.

She rolled up the hose once the buckets were full, then wandered back to Chique, stalling. Chique was quick to leave her hay, and Liv ran a finger over the velvet between the filly's nostrils.

"It kind of feels like the calm before the storm." She felt Geai beside her, but kept her eyes on Chique, making sure the filly's investigation of her gloves didn't turn into a nip. "I'm ready to get back to it, but…it feels like I'm starting over."

"You don't have to go through the ten-pound bug again."

She laughed. "Thank goodness for that. But more expectations this year, right? For me and Claire." She'd been so restless while she was off—too much time to feed her doubts, relegated to social media posts that left her feeling like a fake. "It was hard to take, getting hurt when it seemed everything was finally going well."

"If this is what you want to do, it's not going to be the last time."

Chique latched onto the fabric at her elbow, tugging. "At least I got to know this monster better. You have developed some seriously bad habits, cheeky one." She pushed her finger into the corner of Chique's mouth and the filly let go.

"You kids spoil her." But there was fondness in Geai's eyes. Chique got to him as much as any of them.

"And I got to spend more time with you. Thanks for putting

up with my whining." She gave him a sheepish grin.

Geai pulled a small box from his pocket, and held it out. "Might as well give this to you now."

Liv looked up at him, accepting it, and held it for a moment before removing the red bow and wrapping. She lifted a delicate medallion on a fine chain from its bed of tissue paper, and laid it in her gloved palm to study it.

The face of the medallion was decorated with a miniature painting of a bay horse with markings just like Claire, a woman in a nun's habit pressing her forehead devotedly to the animal's. Her eyes crinkled as the corners of her mouth turned up.

"I hope that's not supposed to be me," she joked, feeling a tiny bit bad that was her first response to something so exquisite.

"Ste-Anne. Patroness of horseback riders, protector from storms."

Liv bit her lip. So perfectly appropriate. "You and your Catholic superstitions." She blinked back a tear, closing it in her hand, and hugged him tight.

"Also the patron saint of unmarried women."

He chuckled as she pushed him back and smacked him in the arm, a lump constricting her throat.

CHAPTER TEN

January

It was just past ten PM when Liv pulled into the sandy driveway of Payson Park—in the Middle of Nowhere, Florida. The grounds were still, enveloped in the dark closeness—all except Barn Six. Jo waited, standing by with a lead shank in hand while the transport driver finished setting up the ramp.

Liv climbed out of the car, yawned and stretched, and accepted the shank when Jo offered it. No lectures from Jo about having to act like a rider to be taken seriously. Claire looked as bleary-eyed as she felt herself. Liv kissed her pink nose, and the filly shook her head half-heartedly.

"Grumpy girl." She smiled, winding the chain around the halter's sheepskin-covered noseband.

Claire stepped down the jute-lined ramp with exaggerated caution, and Jo held her while Liv dropped to her knees in the deep straw of the stall to remove the protective bandages and bell boots. The big filly took a languid drink from the pail of fresh water hanging by the door, then dribbled over Jo's arm before rubbing her face on the assistant trainer's elbow.

"Lovely, Claire." Jo wiped her arm dry with the hem of her

t-shirt. "Just leave the bandages on the rail, Liv. I'll take care of them. Sleep in tomorrow. We'll bath and walk her for you."

"Thanks." She was exhausted enough not to turn down that offer. Liv gave one last touch to Claire's fuzzy bay shoulder before ducking out of the stall.

Shadowy orange groves and scrubby fields whizzed by her Nissan's open window on the way into the town of Stuart, and Liv checked into the first reasonable hotel she found. She'd be staying with Roger and his wife Hélène, but didn't want to disturb them this late. First she threw herself under the shower, washing away two days of sweat and hay and dirt, then she collapsed into bed.

She couldn't remember the last time she'd slept late enough to see daylight, rolling out of bed at eight AM. After the heavy winter clothing she'd needed at home, it was liberating to put on shorts and a tank top. The gloriously stifling air hit her as she stepped outside, sun shining through the haze, asphalt in the parking lot steaming from an earlier rainfall.

The final horse to train was cooling out when she got to the Triple Stripe barn. She passed Jo the box of doughnuts and tray of coffees she'd picked up for the crew, the card that had been delivered to the farm for Nate tucked under her arm. Claire looked happy and relaxed as she pulled at her haynet, bathed and walked as promised.

"How's my girl?"

"Temp's normal, no problems." Jo glanced at Liv's bare legs, her mouth twisting as she started for the tack room. "You're a brave one, walking on the shed your first day in Florida wearing shorts. I think you're going to wish you hadn't."

What a ridiculous thought. Liv touched the bay filly's nose lightly in parting, and Claire tossed her head, spraying her with alfalfa leaves.

She heard Nate's voice before she saw him, unmistakable as he sang along to the radio. Bridles and martingales moved on their hook in the doorway, Jo brushing by with a mouthful of doughnut, coffee raised in appreciation as she headed back to her stalls.

Liv stopped short. "Have you been doing any work down here, Miller, or do you spend all your time at the beach?"

Even in the dimness of the tack room the brown of his muscled arms against his light turquoise golf shirt added a beat to her pulse. The blue eyes, the sun-bleached hair, the tanned beach body—she caught herself. A normal girl might fall for that. But this wasn't spring break. She was here to get her career back on course, and falling of any sort wasn't part of the plan.

"Hey, Liv! How was the drive?"

"Fine, thanks. Just don't stand too close to me till I have a chance to catch up, all right?" She held out the card. "This came before I left."

He scanned the return address, then tossed it to the side and went back to work. *Well that wiped the cheery expression from his face.*

"Where's Rog?"

Nate glanced at the clock to his left—he wasn't wearing a watch. Heaven forbid he should have a tan line. "He's around here somewhere."

As if on cue, Roger walked up behind Liv and gave her a gentle squeeze. "Welcome to Payson. Weather warm enough for you?"

"Clearly you've been having plenty of it." She tilted her head towards Nate.

"Your filly made it in good order."

"She'll feel much better when I get her clipped out. Maybe once Mr. Florida here is done his tack he'll give me a hand."

Nate fished a second sponge from his bucket and tossed it directly at Liv. She deftly caught it to avoid getting soaked, scowling as she squeezed the excess water out onto the sandy shed.

"Just thought if you helped me finish, we'd get to the big filly sooner."

Liv conceded, taking the bar of glycerin from him. "Now I know where you get the time to lie on the beach. You pawn off your work on everyone else." She started on the saddles resting on the rail.

"It's called delegating." He flashed his ever-ready grin.

Nate was hanging the last of the bridles when she pushed past with the final saddle, pads piled on top, and hoisted it onto the rack. He adjusted the bridle just so on the nail, the browband straight and the lines hanging evenly. Sometimes the simple things seemed to make Liv happiest, and the line of clean bridles, glowing rich Australian nut brown, was one of them. She took down the tack hook as Nate dumped the water pail, and found the clippers and an extension cord. Nate followed her to Claire's stall with a shank over his shoulder.

"Might actually be too hot out here," he said when he led Claire to the grassy expanse beside the barn.

Liv ran the extension from the closest outlet. "How could it possibly be too hot?"

The blades hummed to life, the thick fuzz of Claire's winter coat soon dropping in clumps around the filly's white feet. Fine hair tickled Liv's face and arms, but she wasn't about to give Nate the satisfaction of hearing her complain. She drew an arm across her brow and sneezed.

"Having fun yet?" he asked.

"I love clipping."

"Sure you do." He scratched Claire's white forehead. "So how come you didn't have my girl Cheeky stowed away somewhere?"

She took a moment to clean the blades, his fondness for the little yearling making her smile. "Next year."

"She'll be so mad I missed her birthday."

Liv laughed, stepping away as Claire shuddered, shaking loose the latest rows. "Where did you learn how to do respiration on a foal, anyway?"

He hesitated, eyes dropping to where he tickled the sensitive skin between Claire's nostrils with the end of the shank. Claire's lips flapped, trying to grab it.

"The trainer I worked for in Calgary had a few mares, and I did some nightwatching for him. One of them had a red bag delivery. Foal needed a bit of help when it came out, so Al taught me. Al was kind of my Geai."

"I'm surprised you didn't mention that, seeing you went to the trouble of putting together a resumé."

"Wasn't really relevant for breaking yearlings, was it?" He passed the loop of leather into his left hand, and brushed Claire's forelock to the side with his fingers. "Couldn't talk Geai into another road trip, eh?"

The abrupt change of both the subject and his manner was suspect, but she let it go. She didn't like it when people probed her either. "That's your superpower, Miller. Maybe you could work on it. He has another month or so before breeding season starts."

She finished Claire's body, and exchanged large clippers for small, moving up beside Nate to do the filly's head. Sweat soaked through her tank top, clinging as she reached for one of Claire's ears to trim the protruding wisps.

"You know you're going to end up with a sunburn from this, right?"

Liv blew the hair out from the blades, not quite in his face, before continuing. He seemed aggravatingly acclimatized to the heat, considering he'd galloped the barn, while she was a disgusting, sweaty, mess. "I'm accepting the consequences of my choice, Miller. Unless you want to finish the job for me."

"I'd just wreck it, and Claire would be all embarrassed. We can't have that, can we?" He tickled the filly's nose again. Claire snorted. "You're almost done anyway."

Claire shook from head to haunches when Liv stood back to assess her work. "You're a pale girl now, Amazon filly."

"Don't you worry, Claire, in a couple of weeks no one will know you haven't been here since November like the rest of us." Nate slid Liv a sly smile.

She gave him a tired look, then fished her phone from her back pocket, composing a shot. "Thanks, Miller, you can put her away."

She glanced at the photo before writing the caption. Unlike her, the camera loved both of them. *Hey, pretty...*Mr. Florida would definitely help the post's engagement.

Liv followed him into the tack room as he hung the shank with the others. That card still rested where he'd tossed it.

"Not going to open that?" she couldn't help asking.

He glanced over his shoulder. "It's just a card."

Liv shrugged, and leaned back against the doorframe. "Kenny's on me to get back riding again."

"That's good, right?"

"Well…yeah. Because I'll still have my apprentice allowance for most of the year, he thinks I have a shot at an Eclipse award. I think he might be dreaming. But either way…Claire."

Spending the better part of twenty-eight hours in the car had given her time to think, to accept reality—she couldn't be two places at once.

"I'm sure someone would have a stall at Gulfstream for her."

"I know…but she's better off here. I was jogging her back home, so she's ready to start galloping, but after being so sick last fall, we should really take our time bringing her back." She hesitated, hating that Gulfstream Park, where she'd be riding, was an hour and a half away. "You're going to have to get on her for me."

His eyebrow quirked, not hiding his surprise, and it reinforced her guilt, that she was abandoning Claire for her own career. Sure, like he said, they could get a stall for her at Gulfstream, but at Payson Claire could be turned out. She could go for hacks, she could gallop on the turf…there were so many alternatives to training on the track.

He recovered, the grin surfacing. "Is that supposed to be a hardship?"

"It's an extra horse."

"What's one more? I'll manage. Maybe not get to the beach as early. Too much sun isn't good for you anyway, right?" He sobered. "You know I'll take good care of her."

"It won't be right away. I'll gallop here for a couple of weeks to get back into shape." She found Nate's eyes. "I seem to be entrusting you with the things that matter most to me. Don't screw up, Miller."

He shifted uneasily, forcing a laugh. "No pressure."

It wasn't a big ask, not really. And maybe for the best, given how she wondered if Claire was actually better off without her. But it felt significant, somehow. Like she'd shared with him another part she'd always kept to herself.

CHAPTER ELEVEN

February

Her old friend Blush minced around Gulfstream's paddock, washed out and showing the whites of her eyes as Liv tried to find something nice to say about her. Rod was one of the Belmont trainers who wintered at Palm Meadows, about an hour north. He seemed unexpectedly excited to have Liv back in the picture, quick to agree to a reunion with the filly to give Liv her first Florida ride. Blush's past performance was uninspiring—a few short lines summarizing lacklustre maiden claiming attempts at Aqueduct last fall when Liv had been off.

"See what you can do." Rod threw her up, with no other instructions. The groom led them out of the paddock, Blush's neck a dark sheen of sweat.

"Hey, little girl, sure you can handle that horse?"

"I never bet girl jocks. Girls don't belong on the racetrack."

She was used to blocking out hecklers, but Liv recognized the voices, and looked, breaking her other rule by responding. "Well, if it isn't Triple Stripe's dynamic duo."

"Your horse have a shot in here, Lachance?" Nate said behind sunglasses, sun-bleached hair falling over his forehead, grin reliably in place.

"Sure, she's got a shot. A 50-1 shot!" Michel elbowed him and started laughing as they followed along behind the spectators lining the rail.

"Good luck," Nate called after her.

She was afraid there would be nothing left of Blush by the time they made it to the gate. The starter's assistant loaded her, and Liv pushed aside the flashback of that moment at Belmont last fall, channeling confidence to counter the filly's nerves. The doors crashed open, and Blush fired away like she was being chased by zombies.

Blush started to relax once they were away from the scary metal barrier, letting Liv park her behind the leaders and on the outside where the claustrophobic filly wouldn't stress. She pulled around the turn, passing one of the fading pacesetters, and Liv started to think they might get a piece.

Okay...let's see what you've got. She picked Blush up and chirped, keeping her stick quiet because she remembered all too well what the filly thought of the whip. Ears flickering forward as she changed leads in the lane, Blush romped past the field, and galloped home in front by two lengths—much to Liv's own shock, not to mention that of most of the grandstand, she was sure.

The groom was all smiles when he met them, chattering excitedly in Spanish. Liv heard Nate's whoop, and found the guys in the crowd just as Michel let the torn pieces of a losing ticket fall from his hand.

"Those your friends?" Rod waved them into the winner's circle before Liv could answer.

She dismounted after the photo was taken, Rod patting her on the back as she scrubbed Blush on the neck. Her valet took her tack, and she overheard Rod talking to the guys.

"Maybe you'd better come next time she runs. You're good luck."

"Naw, you just had a good rider," Nate said. "Here, take our picture." He passed the phone to Rod, and pulled Liv over.

"Oh come on, Miller," she protested.

"Just be a sport and smile." He wedged her between himself and Michel. "I'll send it to you so you can share it with your followers."

"I'll get right on that."

"You've been a little slack since you started trying to be three places at the same time. Sign this for me?" He just laughed when she made a face. "I don't want your autograph, it's a model release."

That earned him a smirk and a shove. "Why are you guys bothering me? You should be trying to pick up paddock girls."

"She has a point, Miller," Michel said.

"We're paddock guys," Nate said. "It's new."

She shook her head and headed for the scales.

"Are you done for the day?" Nate asked after she'd weighed in. "We should grab a bite before heading back."

Liv stopped, frowning as she looked from Nate to Michel. They had come all the way from Payson for her return to the races. "Maybe something quick."

She suggested somewhere off the track complex, quiet and casual, where they could be in and out in a reasonable time. The guys beat her there, securing a booth, and she looked from Nate to Michel, deciding sitting next to Nate was the better option.

Michel scanned the menu. "Nate's buying. He cashed a ticket on that."

"Did you really?" She wished there was just a little more room, feeling a swell of awareness faced with sitting so close. "I'm not sure I would have bet her."

"Fifty to one? That was worth a couple of bucks." Nate glanced up as the server placed glasses of water on the table. "Thanks."

The server's expression transformed from boredom to attentiveness as she looked from Nate to Michel. *Yes, they're both good-looking, you're right. Careful, you're drooling.*

"Are you ready to order?" Her fresh smile bypassed Liv.

Nate lifted his arm from the table and dropped it on Liv's shoulders like it was the most natural thing in the world, leaning in. "Know what you want, hon?"

She sat straighter and shot him a look—if she thought he'd been close before, well, this was a definite invasion of personal space. The server's eyebrows all but knitted together as she sized Liv up. It was worth going along with it just for that, except that the bump in her pulse was sending blood rushing to places she didn't care to acknowledge, and every last one of her nerve endings was on fire.

"I'll have the garden salad, thanks. Dressing on the side?" She handed over her menu with her sweetest fake smile, and got an eye roll so hard back she thought the girl's head would fall off her shoulders. It didn't, her perkiness rebooted as she turned to Michel.

When she sashayed away, Nate started laughing, his arm falling back to his side where it belonged. "Don't think she's one of your fans."

"*Hon?*" Liv glared.

"Too much? I was just helping Mike out. Removing myself from her options."

"And here all I ordered was a salad," she said dryly.

"You think I need your help, Miller?" Michel glowered at him, putting down his phone. Michel would probably be trying to get the server's number before they were done.

Nate grabbed for the cheque as soon as it came, Liv poking him. "You don't really have to pay."

He kept it out of her reach. "I don't mind. I probably made more than you did for riding her."

"How much did you bet?"

Nate smirked, throwing some bills on the table and crowding her so she'd get up. "Let's go."

She waved as they parted ways in the parking lot, then checked her messages before starting the car, the screen of her phone littered with congratulatory texts for the win. The last one was from Faye.

Nice win. Cute date.

Liv: *??*

Faye: *Check IG.*

Liv opened the app—Michel had tagged her in a post. Three photos: coming into the winner's circle on Blush, the one Rod had taken of the three of them, and another Michel had snapped in the restaurant, of course at that exact moment Nate had put his arm around her.

It was like looking at someone else, a little bit of fiction; the looks on their faces easily misconstrued, if someone didn't know better. Because he was cute, and she'd had fun, and if she'd thought any of it had been real, that never would have happened. As fictional dates went though...she could do worse.

You know you're jealous, she typed back, wondering what it would be like to be that girl.

CHAPTER TWELVE

March

"Nate! You're breezing Claire this morning."

He stopped in his tracks, looking up the shed to where Roger appeared from the murky darkness outside the barn.

"What happened to Liv?"

"There's one Kenny says she has to work at Gulfstream this morning. She was gone before I got up."

*Kenny says jump...*but that was the life of a bug rider. She knew she'd be on Claire no matter what when the filly made it back to the races, so it was a no-brainer to skip out and leave Nate to get on her...even if it would kill her control-freak self. She'd never missed a breeze on the filly down here, always taking that one day a week to be at Payson.

"We'll get a couple of sets out first, let it get light. She'll go at seven. Maybe the bloody fog will have lifted by then," Roger said. Not that the horses really went out in sets when Liv wasn't here. Nate got on all ten of them, one by one.

It wasn't like getting on Claire made him feel exceptionally skilled. Claire was easy. Claire could go alone, or in company. She could hack out by herself without drama. Hell, he was pretty sure he could do mounted archery on her and shoot some of those wild boar out in Payson's back forty, if that legend was true. It was Geai's words getting in his head that complicated it all. *Don't take her loyalty lightly.*

Jo had Claire ready to go when he got back on the second horse. She took the filly a turn, and legged him up.

Even at the walk Claire had a smooth, fluid swing to her step. Saying she was the best horse he'd ever been on wasn't a stretch—while Roger had some nice ones, none of them were Grade One stake winners. He pulled his phone from his pocket, shooting a few seconds of the steady pulse of her head, the relaxed flop of her ears. He was more of a lurker when it came to social media, but this was noteworthy.

Up where the air is rarefied. #moving up #bigfilly #leclaircie #oakscontender

"Head out next turn," Roger called.

Horses appeared eerily from the mist like wraiths as they walked to the track, the usual sounds of the comings and goings dampened and distorted. It almost had a sedative effect —or maybe it was the rhythm of Claire's walk lulling him.

"I don't even know why I'm coming out," Roger muttered. "I'm not going to be able to see a damn thing."

"Because you'd drive them crazy back at the barn?" Nate suggested as they reached the on-gap.

"Don't get lost out there."

He backed up, Claire jogging smoothly until he turned her in on the backstretch, pausing to pull down his goggles before setting off counter-clockwise. She galloped like a pony, all the way around, but when he dropped her to the rail the switch flipped.

He crouched over the lick of her black mane, content to be a passenger as she made the turn perfectly and switched leads automatically at the head of the lane. Cutting through the mist just made it more exhilarating, adding an element of danger because of the near-zero visibility—whizzing past the gallopers in the middle of the track, not knowing if there was a worker on the flight path in front of them. They swept under the wire, and he let her roll around the clubhouse turn galloping out, finally easing her on the backside.

Roger waited near the off-gap. "How'd she go? No surprise, I didn't see a damn thing."

"Wow."

"I'll take that as good."

"When does she run?"

"Florida Derby Day. First Saturday in April. She'll ship to Gulfstream for the next couple of works so she can go over the track."

Liv wouldn't have to worry about anything getting in the way of her being aboard for those final trials.

"Then it's back to Don at Belmont." Roger looked a little rueful.

"So unfair," Nate said, sharing the sentiment.

Once he finished cleaning and putting away the tack at the end of the morning, he stood in the doorway looking out as he dialed Liv. The fog had finally burned away, leaving behind steamy humidity.

She picked up immediately. "Is everything all right?"

He always texted, so he could see how a call might spook her. "Sorry, just thought you'd want to know how she went."

"Of course." The breath she released was audible. "I hear it was so foggy they didn't get a time."

"Well the clock in my head," he paused for effect, "caught her in fifty-nine and two."

She laughed quietly. "She's something, isn't she?"

"She's perfection."

"Thanks, Miller."

"Again, it was no hardship."

He disconnected, and jammed the phone in his back pocket. The burn of his ambition amped up a few degrees. What was he doing, playing understudy when he could be out there riding races too? He'd told himself he was just buying time while he silenced the doubt in his head, but now it felt like he was just wasting it.

That envelope from his brother and sister-in-law was still

jammed on the shelf where he'd left it two months ago, addressed in his brother's handwriting, no less. Like a stupid Christmas card could make everything right, when nothing could erase what Phil had done. He grabbed it, ripped it in half, and stuffed the pieces in the garbage. Moving up? *Moving on.*

CHAPTER THIRTEEN

April

Paz gawked at the horrendous Pegasus statue as they jogged around the turn at Gulfstream Park. It wasn't anywhere close to them, but its sheer size made its presence inescapable, even though Liv had learned to block it out. Paz seemed convinced it was a Trojan horse, housing an army of goblins about to be set loose on the field of unsuspecting Thoroughbreds. Said Thoroughbreds, with the exception of Paz, remained unsuspecting.

"Stop being an embarrassment and do your job, old man." Nate dug his heel into the gelding to keep him from bumping into Claire. "I wonder who thought that was a good idea."

"I have no clue." Liv sat quietly, Claire snorting her disgust at the pony's performance—or maybe at the fact anyone deemed it necessary for her to have an escort postward in the first place. "Not that I've seen anyone but Paz react like that."

"He's just expressing what the rest of us wish we could."

Paz regained his composure once they were behind the gate, set in front of the grandstand for the Gulfstream Park Oaks. Liv pulled her goggles down as they milled with the other eight starters, waiting to be loaded.

"She's favourite," Nate noted.

Liv averted her eyes from the odds board. She didn't want to know; didn't want the pressure.

"Good luck. You got this." Nate waited for a fist bump before he relinquished them to the starter's assistant.

The bell ringing in her ears as the doors crashed open, the roar rising from the Florida Derby Day crowd—none of it rattled Claire. Liv asked her to relax, conserve, and Claire complied. Let the speed horses do their job, and set things up for the big filly's usual move in the stretch.

The leader was trying to run away with it as they turned for home, and Claire took aim, wearing the other filly down steadily with each stride. Liv unpacked her stick, putting it to work. One, two, smacks on her quarters, then back to the hands, pushing, imploring, but not getting the explosive kick she'd expected. Another burst with her stick—*just a little more, and we'll have her.*

Only just. *Would it kill you to win by more than a whisker?* But she slapped Claire's neck heartily, blowing out a big exhale of relief.

Nate should have been in the picture with them. He probably deserved more credit for this win than she did— galloping Claire day in, day out at Payson. There was that familiar guilt. She was just the rider, the one who worked the horse a time or two, then got all the glory on race day.

"See you back at the barn," Roger said after she'd weighed in, abandoning her to the little following of girls collected on the apron pushing programs and pens at her.

She scribbled her name, one program after another, the other riders back in the room by now. At least she was done for the day.

"Can we get a picture with you?" one girl asked, a woman —probably her mother—at the ready with phone poised.

Liv nodded, mustering a smile as they clustered around her —the up-and-coming, good-for-racing, girl jockey—even if that role grated on her, and she just wanted to get back to check on Claire.

"How is she?" Liv ducked into the barn and cut to the inside, looking all cooled out herself in a sleeveless sundress, her hair pulled neatly back, a chain with a small pendant drawing Nate's eyes to her neck.

"Great." He pulled Claire away from the haynet hanging from the rail and raised his free hand. "First stake win!"

She slapped it, though it seemed a little half-hearted. "For me, anyway. Couldn't have done it without you."

"I'll come to New York and gallop her for you if you want."

"Tempting."

She needed to not give him that kind of smile, saying something like that. It might make him forget they were just talking about Claire.

"Put her in, Nate," Jo said. "If we head back as soon as she's done up, we might beat the traffic out of here."

"I'll give you a hand." He snapped the stall guard in place and tied Claire in the doorway. She attacked the haynet as soon as he looped the rope through an eye hook, burrowing her muzzle into the nest and fiercely pulling out a mouthful before he even tied it off.

"No, I will," Liv intercepted.

He glanced at her dress and shoes. "I don't mind."

"Once I get back to Belmont, Jeanne won't let me touch her, so I'm going to do this while I can. I owe it to her after a landmark win like that, don't you think? Especially the way I've passed her off on you all winter."

"Here I thought I was helping you out, when really all this time you felt bad for Claire."

She smirked before ducking into the stall.

Roger pulled the truck and trailer up, and Nate helped him load Paz and the traps while Jo and Liv finished with Claire. At least Liv deferred to Jo when it came time to put Claire on the van.

Roger checked the doors were secure, and turned to Nate. "Jo and I can take them home if you want to stick around and watch the Florida Derby."

"You're assuming Liv will drive me back."

"You're not the worst company." She looked at him sideways with traces of that smile. She needed to stop.

He felt awkward for a moment after the rig eased out of the backstretch. "Guess we should get over there, then."

Liv hesitated, checking the time. "Do you really have your heart set on it? I think I'd rather beat the traffic out of here myself."

"So you were just trying to get me alone in your car, weren't you?"

She rolled her eyes and started walking to the little black Nissan. "My exact plan."

"I can drive if you're tired."

"I'm okay."

Of course she was. He let himself in when she unlocked the doors.

She started the engine, and Poe's *Control* blasted from the speakers before her hand snapped out to kill the volume.

He had to chuckle. "Your theme song?"

"Don't judge."

"I'm not. It's perfect. I sure as hell wouldn't mess with you."

She parried his grin with a smirk and a subtle shake of her head.

He kept watching her, while she navigated out of Gulfstream's backside. "You should be happy with today. Why aren't you happier?"

Her lips pressed into a line, and she gripped the steering wheel a little tighter as they headed for the interstate. "I am happy. It's just...she didn't do it easily, you know?"

"She's been off since October. Sure she's been training great, but maybe she needed the race. She still got there. They don't give you extra money if you win by open lengths."

"I sound ungrateful, don't I?"

"You're just worried about her, I get it."

Her eyes darted over, and she sighed. "I wish she had another race before the Oaks. I'd feel a lot better."

"You're not one of those people who can just enjoy the moment, are you? She needed the time; you gave her the time."

"And Don is good at training horses up to races."

"See?" He reached for the stereo and started advancing tracks, laughing when he heard the opening of Panic! At the Disco's *Victorious*. "There's the song you need."

Her eyes flickered from the road, to him, and back again, probably totally regretting agreeing to drive him home as he sang along, right to the end—but she didn't interrupt him.

"I admit I'm jealous." He turned down the volume as the next song started. "You're going to ride in the freaking Kentucky Oaks."

"No one's stopping you from getting your license."

He stared out the window, the ocean-side sky a deep indigo as the sun went down in the west, figuring out how to answer that.

"Me coming out here created a big stink. Like my dad and I? We don't talk anymore. That kind of stink. So I have to do this right. I have to do well. I can't go back. The thought of him saying I told you so...I'd rather live in a dorm room and walk hots for the rest of my life." If only it were that simple. Like why was it that the thought of actually succeeding held him back more than the prospect of failure?

"So you want to skip the part where it took me two months to lose my triple bug?"

"Do you regret it? Wish you were back at school stressing over exams instead of stressing over riding Claire in the Oaks?"

"Not a chance. Just do it, Miller. Though barring any broken bones or tragedies, I don't expect to be back this fall, so someone's going to have to start Chique."

"Oh sure, I'll put my career on hold to break her, then you can come back and win the Plate with her."

"I didn't mean—"

"That's okay, I'd do that for you." He cut her off, letting her feel bad for a moment. "You think I'd let anyone else do that job?"

"It is only fair." Liv looked relieved, grinning back. "She is what she is because of you, after all."

Emilie's head popped around the corner of the tack room at Woodbine and she beamed, scurrying over and swinging up on the counter beside him. Her Blundstones knocked the cupboard doors and she pushed a piece of her dark hair behind an ear, leaning into him as she glanced over his shoulder at *The Form* spread on his lap.

"Have I told you what a great tan you have?"

Nate lifted his head. "I'm pretty sure it's faded since the last time you did."

"And you really didn't find yourself a girlfriend down there?"

"You know I'm waiting for you, Em."

Emilie patted his leg. "Sure you are."

Em was just as bright as her sister, just more emotionally balanced. He couldn't remember exactly what she was taking. Environmental Toxicology; something relevant and virtuous like that.

Roger strode past the doorway. "Okay, Nate, let's go. Dave's here."

Dave Johnson was the perennial leading rider at Woodbine, and rode the majority of the Triple Stripe horses when they ran in Ontario. He could ride, no question, but the guy rubbed Nate the wrong way—too arrogant, too entitled. Maybe that wasn't a good enough reason not to like him, but it added fuel to Nate's building fire of determination. He'd knock Johnson off his pedestal. *One day.*

Nate grabbed Emilie's arm. "Toss me up?"

"Of course." She followed him out and legged him up on a maiden three-year-old named Sans Défaut.

The sun fought to get through a filter of clouds on the walk to the main track, and he shivered, willing it to break free. It was a morning-long cycle. Work up a sweat on the track, come back to the barn and get chilled waiting for his next horse. He blew on one of his black-gloved hands to test if he could still see his breath.

"It's a lot warmer now the sun's up," Roger said.

"What sun?" Nate grumbled. "Next year, we don't come back so early, all right?"

"It's the middle of April, Nate."

"What's the matter, Miller? Not as cozy here as it was at Payson?" Dave Johnson leaned forward, so Nate couldn't miss his sly grin from the other side of Roger.

"You heard I got to spend some quality time with the Oaks filly, did you?" Claire, who was on her way to Louisville soon, while he waited for spring to decide to show up in Southern Ontario.

"Pretty sure if Liv got hurt again, you wouldn't be the one getting the call."

Nate didn't allow himself as much as a foul look—he wasn't giving Johnson the satisfaction. Besides, he deserved the digs, him and his so-called patience, telling Liv he'd break Chique, like the brownie points it might earn him would ever mean anything. It helped, though, when his colt out-worked Johnson's—Claude's Plate hopeful, Excursion. He contained the rush he felt and kept his mouth shut as they galloped out.

"You're gonna have to learn not to take life so seriously, Miller," Johnson called over as they pulled the colts up.

"I was just having fun out there, Dave. What the hell were you doing?"

Back at the barn, Nate pulled off the tack, leaving Sans Défaut to Michel and the hotwalker with a pat. "He'll be all right, this colt, you watch."

He ducked into the tack room to grab one of the coffees Claude had brought—lukewarm now, but he sucked it back anyway. Emilie popped in behind him.

"Nice move, Nate. Kicked Johnson's ass, didn't you?"

"I keep telling everyone what a nice colt that is."

"Well, *cher Papa* was a little shook up his Plate horse got beat, but he was still impressed. That might convince him to keep Sans Défaut eligible. Maybe if you got your butt in gear you'd get to ride him."

"Next year, Em. Going to start doing some freelancing once you're here everyday to pick up the slack." Made sense, right?

"I see." Emilie peeked around the doorframe, looking down the shedrow. "Guess I have to go. Can't miss my first class now, can I?"

"One of you girls better stay in school." Nate grinned, and watched her go.

It wouldn't happen, even if he pulled himself together and got his license in time. If both colts ended up in the Plate this year, Johnson would be on one, and Liv would come back and ride the other. Liv would jump on the chance to ride in the big race if one came before Chique—while he found yet another excuse to stagnate.

CHAPTER FOURTEEN

May

Thurby, they called it, all part of the insanity that was Derby Week in Louisville. For Liv, it was the day before the biggest race of her not-yet-year-old career. Claire would school in the paddock with the Derby and Oaks contenders, and Liv would ride a couple of races at Churchill Downs to get a feel for the track. She didn't expect much from either of the mounts Kenny had found her, but maybe it would help settle her nerves. They weren't here for the Derby, but the twin spires still presided, passing judgement with the ghosts that haunted them.

It felt odd to have just one horse to get on in the morning—after galloping Claire under those spires as the sun came up, she had nowhere to be until she checked into the jock's room. So she got there early, changed into running gear, jammed in her ear buds, and found a treadmill.

And ran, maxing out the volume for some Poe to chase away the stress, going harder and faster until calm overtook her. When she finally slowed, saturated with sweat, she laughed at the looks she'd been blocking out...taking control. Nate was right. It was the perfect theme song.

Her first mount lived up to expectations, finishing nowhere, but the next one surprised her with some grit. Tucked behind the front-runners on the rail, a hole opened up. Liv went to the whip, but instead of the strike propelling the filly forward, she ducked in, bouncing off the rail and slamming into their neighbor, legs entangling. Liv grabbed mane as her filly scrambled, but the momentum was too much. She let go and tucked her arms in, tumbling, and the smack of her helmet sent her to blackness.

When she came to, the ambulance was just pulling up, and her horse was nowhere to be seen. She clutched the rail while her head cleared, and assessed body parts. All in working order.

The ambulance gave her a ride back, and she walked through the room with a silly smile. No one was blaming her for her mount's overreaction, and no one else had suffered as a result of it. The outrider had caught the loose filly, unscathed. Relief on all counts. The doctor checked her over but let her go. She didn't mention she'd hit her head and blacked out, not wanting to be on his radar for possible concussion. Her helmet was going in the trash, though.

First spill? *Check.* The medallion around her neck was cool as she fingered it. Protector of riders? Protector from storms? Maybe Ste-Anne was doing her job.

Even though she was only going to the backstretch, she put on the dress she'd brought, Geai in her head, insisting she keep this professional presentation when she left the room. It was crazy out on the front side. How could they pack any more people into this place? But they would, tomorrow for Oaks Day, and more yet for Saturday's Derby.

Claire dozed with her quarters to the door, one hind leg resting. Liv stole into the stall, apologetically offering empty hands to the seeking muzzle. She laced her fingers over the bridge of the filly's nose and pressed her cheek to Claire's. Her pulse slowed, her breathing synched.

The buzz of her phone jolted her. A text from Jeanne, Don's assistant, who had travelled to Louisville with Claire.

Where are you?

Um. *Claire's stall.*

Jeanne appeared at the door, her face looking like she wanted to tell Liv off, but she didn't. "You're okay?"

"I'm fine." Liv kissed Claire's muzzle, and slipped out.

Jeanne gave her a hard look, but seemed satisfied Liv was telling the truth. "I have tickets for one of the events around town, do you want to go?"

"Oh—no. I'm looking forward to going back to the hotel to start psyching myself out about tomorrow."

Jeanne laughed. "Come on, you're already dressed for it. You're in Louisville two days before the Derby. It's part of the experience. Besides, it's pretty tame. Just cocktails downtown, and the Derby artist signing posters. You'll be in bed by nine."

"I don't know, Jeanne."

"Let's go. We'll take a cab."

Maybe it wouldn't kill her.

The lobby of the downtown Louisville Galt House was already packed when they got there. These were partygoers, not track connections, so at least she should go unrecognized —not that anyone knew who she was anyway. She evaded curious looks from some of the men as Jeanne scooped two flutes from a passing tray, and handed her one.

"It seems wrong to be having champagne before the Oaks." Liv held up the glass and peered through the golden liquid.

"Afraid you'll jinx yourself? You did survive your first spill unscathed."

Liv nodded, and touched the rim of her glass to Jeanne's. "I can drink to that."

Geai placed a bowl on the coffee table, and handed Nate a beer before sitting in front of the television for the Kentucky Oaks. Napoleon planted himself squarely in front of Nate, soft brown eyes locked hopefully on his handful of chips.

It was strange, waiting to see Liv and Claire on television. An odd sensation came over him as he watched; a mix of unrest and anticipation. There was satisfaction for the part he'd played, however minor, but the envy stuck, gnawing inside him.

"Ah, there's my girl."

Geai's pride wouldn't have been greater had Liv been the old man's own daughter. She walked out with the other jockeys, adjusting the elastics around her wrists, whip tucked under her arm, eyes downcast in aloof concentration. The image she successfully put forward, anyway, though Nate thought he could detect a faint injection of nerves in her body. She released a tight smile as she greeted Don with a handshake, then chatted briefly with Jeanne—no doubt inquiring about the well-being of her beloved filly.

"Claire looks good, eh?" Geai commented once the fillies were on the track for the post parade. Claire was more on the muscle than usual, maybe picking up on that tense undercurrent from Liv. Eight minutes to post.

"Why are we not there, Geai? We should be there."

"Because we both have jobs?"

"Like you couldn't get a couple of days off to see your girl ride in the Kentucky Oaks. Now I know where Liv gets her hard-assery from when it comes to letting others do things for her. I'm pretty sure someone could have covered breedings for you. And Roger could have fended for himself. He owes me big-time for getting on everything for most of the winter."

"You wouldn't do that to him."

Nate sighed. "Yeah, you're right. Damn it."

"You like her, don't you?"

Nate looked over sharply. "Liv? She's all right, when she forgets to be so bloody guarded."

"You get along well."

"You really have to stop with the crazy matchmaking."

"I could see it."

"Of course you could, because you're a sentimental old man and we're your two favourite people. I hate to disappoint you, but I'm pretty sure Liv's thoughts on men are of the 'like a fish needs a bicycle' variety. And getting involved with the owner's daughter, if there were any chance of it even happening, is pretty high on my list of bad ideas."

"Ah, you're already like family. Chique's guardian, Claire's gallop boy."

Not to mention Geai's companion, while Liv was making a name for herself—though Geai had managed just fine without either of them for four months. None of it meant a thing. He was a glorified lackey. "It's my job. She's focused on her career, and I should follow her example." The texting back and forth around the pics he sent of Chique was fun, but it wasn't exactly the makings of a relationship.

"Never mind. It would just make me happy to know you were looking out for each other. I'm not going to be around forever, you know."

"Sure you are," Nate scolded. "Stop being so melodramatic. Can we watch the race now? They're coming up to the gate."

Claire balked uncharacteristically as the assistant starter led her forward—just a brief hesitation, really, but she'd never done anything but walk right in. *Breathe, Liv.* The camera view shifted to the front of the metal barrier, waiting for the break. *Breathe.* That one was for him.

Claire came out like a shot, getting first call, and Liv wrapped up on her right away. The big bay filly's head flew up, resisting as Liv tried to negotiate with her when Claire clearly wanted no part. That wasn't like Claire either. Nate glanced at Geai, concern mirrored in the old man's face.

"Easy, filly."

They murmured in unison at the television, like they had any influence.

Liv managed to get her tucked behind horses, saving ground around the clubhouse turn, but the filly still looked fired up, her head cranked to the inside against Liv's hold. *Breathe.* It wasn't a good feeling, to be in tight quarters with a horse running rank.

Along the backstretch, her stride evened out into a smoother rhythm, Liv balanced motionlessly on her back, both of them starting to look more composed. Around the turn Liv found enough room to let Claire move up steadily on the rail, still quiet in the irons. The field turned into the stretch.

In front of Claire, everything was breaking loose—the pacesetter was making a last-ditch effort to hold on, the stalking favourite giving chase and eating up ground. Liv pulled Claire off the rail in pursuit.

But Claire was struggling, looking like a horse Nate didn't recognize as the kickback pelted her in the face. Liv kept after her, a couple more hits with the stick, imploring with her hands, but there was no response. Liv eased her, and Claire galloped under the wire at the back of the pack.

Her face stung from the clods of dirt that had assaulted her on the track. At least her eyes had been protected by goggles—Claire's, rimmed red, had taken the full brunt. Jeanne had blown out the gritty residue, but they remained weepy and sore.

She'd watched the replay, beating herself up for getting into a battle, for not having enough faith to trust the filly—and her own instincts. It's not like Don had specifically told her to take the filly back, it's just what Claire did, came from off the pace. For some reason today, Claire hadn't been happy with that plan, and all Liv had done was frustrate her. Her own nerves had interfered despite her best intentions, and she'd made a mess of it, like some kind of amateur, for half the world to see.

Don stood outside with Jeanne as the hotwalker finished cooling Claire out. Letdown hung in the air, Liv contrite, waiting for Don to tear her apart. She deserved it, and maybe that would make her feel better, in some warped way—if she could explain away Claire's poor performance by assuming the blame. Claire had never *not* shown up.

Don looked down at her. "She bled."

Liv's mouth fell open and her brain rewound. "How bad?" Not that that let her off the hook. All that fighting could have compromised Claire's breathing, putting unnecessary strain on her lungs, inducing the hemorrhage.

"We'll take her back to Belmont, back off on her a bit, come up with a plan."

"She was so sharp today. That's just not like her."

"At least she has a good excuse, and we don't have to try and figure out what the hell we did wrong."

Liv caught the set of his jaw as he said the last part. She was still expecting some commentary on the way the race had played out, but it didn't come. Maybe he was content to let her beat herself up. She should have known better. She should have picked up on it. She knew Claire best, didn't she? But Claire seemed to make out much better without her. The Frizette last fall. All winter with Nate galloping her.

"Go back to the hotel, Liv. Get some sleep. And not a word about this to anyone."

She wanted to stay with Claire, but Don still scared her, more than a little.

The hotel was busy, revelry in the air—Oaks Day was Derby Eve—and it only added to her desperation to get to her room, away from all the happy flowing around her. She jabbed at the elevator button. Her gaze flew up in relief when the lift chimed promptly and the doors parted, then fell on Ricky Acosta as he stepped out.

He threw a black-clad arm around her waist and spun her away from the elevator before she could react. It chimed again as it closed, ascending without her.

"Thank you for that, princess. I should have the mount back on that filly soon."

Her flats slipped along the tile floor as she resisted, but he didn't let go, his lips so close to her ear as he continued that she could feel his breath.

"Such an ugly ride from such a pretty girl. I would run and hide, too, if I were you. Shame, though, when you look so nice. Come party with me. You'll look much better on my arm than you did out on the track this afternoon."

He wasn't any more appealing in a tux, his cologne making her gag as he pulled her against him. She pushed him away, trying to muster a smile to make it look like a joke instead of a struggle to assuage the turning heads in the lobby. "I think I'll pass. I'm not scraping the bottom of the barrel yet."

"Suit yourself, princess."

She dove for the stairwell; pounding her way up the steps because it forced her to breathe. Sometimes all that cardio came in handy. It didn't block out the truth though. Acosta probably would get the mount on Claire now. Probably should. It was only fair.

There was a bottle of wine on the table in her room with a note from room service—courtesy of Kenny, who apparently agreed she had sorrows to drown. Too bad she didn't like the stuff enough to do that.

She turned her phone over in her hand—how had she missed a call from Geai? But she didn't call him back. The letdown she felt...not even Geai could help.

CHAPTER FIFTEEN

June

Don picked an easy spot for Claire's first race back—one she could win going backwards over hurdles. He'd given Liv the mount. There was only one explanation for that—privilege. It was her chance to set things right again. Claire had been treated, and was training great. Had scoped clean every work since. But that only served to reinforce Liv's conviction that it had been her that screwed up the Oaks.

Liv stayed with the pony to keep Claire as calm as possible, fretting that the filly wasn't sweating enough in the scorching afternoon heat. Claire seemed to be back to her usual unflappable self, but Liv kept second-guessing—was she too quiet? *It's just the medication.* The race was only three-quarters, a glorified workout, really. Claire was picked across the board in *The Form. Much the best in here,* they said. Morning line favourite. Odds-on at post time. So much pressure.

Claire broke just right, and came back to her perfectly; running easily, coasting at the back of the pack. *Just believe.* They picked up a couple of horses on the turn, staying wide. *Don't ask too much too soon.* She waited for signs the filly was having trouble breathing; waited for her to fall apart at the quarter pole like she had in the Oaks. Claire hung as they straightened into the stretch and Liv froze, a sick feeling lurching inside her.

They were practically in the middle of the track, steering clear of any kickback that could impair the filly's respiration. But—there! A shift of gears as Claire realized she wasn't going to be stopped by an asphyxiating sensation in her lungs. Liv threw herself into supporting the drive, the filly zoning in on the leader, taking aim.

It was a big move, but a late move. Liv had spent so much time worrying if Claire was all right, she was going to pay for it. No amount of scrubbing and pleading was going to get them there on time.

A scattering of boos met her as they came back to the grandstand, and she deserved every one of them. She didn't make eye contact, didn't say a word to Jeanne as she pulled off the tack and went to weigh in.

There was really no point in putting on that post-race outfit today, was there? She wasn't a professional. She didn't even shower, sliding into her jeans, leaving on the t-shirt she'd worn under her silks. She dreaded going back to the barn. But she had to see Claire, just long enough to make sure the filly cooled out okay.

Don wasn't there, small mercies. Jeanne just shrugged.

"There's good news. She scoped clean. She ran a good race, Liv. She's not a sprinter. Six furlongs is just too short for her."

"She should have won. I got her beat."

She was losing it. Losing her timing, losing her confidence, losing her dream of Chique, and the Queen's Plate.

The maples were hitting their stride, in full plumage shading the farm's long lane. Nate stretched his arm out the window of the Mustang as it crept along, breathing in the warm breeze like a tonic. He was looking forward to a run, though the mosquitoes were going to be vicious through the woods. Maybe he'd stick to the access road that connected the barns.

He turned the corner by the main house towards his apartment, admiring the riot of colour spilling through the flowerbeds by the main house.

A form appearing from the driveway to the house startled him—Claude Lachance flagging him down, like he'd been watching for Nate's return. Nate braked abruptly, instantly conscious of his pulse. He was on good terms with Triple Stripe's owner, but their relationship was nonetheless formal; he saw Claude more often at the track than around the farm. The man's face looked much too serious.

"Could you come in for a moment, Nate?"

Nate swallowed and nodded, turning the Mustang into the driveway. He couldn't come up with an explanation for this. No one had tried to get hold of him on his phone. If something were wrong back in Calgary, someone would have called him. He waited until Claude caught up, following him up the steps.

Claude led him through the front foyer to a large main room decorated with neutral tones, racing-themed originals and reproductions on the walls. Only real horse people decorated their homes with equine art, the work distracting him temporarily as they walked down into a sunken living room. Cathedral ceilings towered above, sloping to sliding doors that opened onto a backyard patio. The midday sun reflected off a narrow pool. Claude motioned towards a large, soft, chair before seating himself on the chesterfield.

"Can I get you a drink?"

Nate's chair wasn't feeling so soft. "I'm fine, thanks."

Claude leaned forward, clasping and unclasping his hands between his knees. "Geai collapsed in the breeding shed this morning when he was bringing Just Lucky in to cover a mare. They called an ambulance..." Claude hesitated, gesturing helplessly. "He died on the way to the hospital. Cardiac arrest."

Nate stared at him blankly, the buzzing filling his ears making him think he'd heard it wrong. *This morning*...they bred the first mare at eight. In the last four hours, he'd carried on at the track unaware; getting on horses, joking with the rest of the crew, singing along with the stupid radio.

"Does Liv know?" It would tear her world apart.

Claude shook his head, looking down at his clenched hands. "I don't know how I'm going to tell her."

He needed to get out of there, before he suffocated, or screamed, or just broke down. "Let me know if there's anything I can do," he forced through strangled vocal cords, staggering to his feet.

"I'm sorry, Nate. I know you were close."

The fresh air outside did nothing to open his airway, his chest imploding, head spinning. There had been no final words—no chance to say goodbye. *I'm not going to be around forever.* He'd dismissed Geai's comment, joking it away. *Sure you will.*

How wrong he'd been.

The picturesque country church was probably a popular choice for June weddings, beautifully ornate with its heavy wooden pews, colourful stained glass filtering sparkling sunlight. A cascade of flowers filled the front, the sickening smell of lilies one he would forever associate with death.

All Nate saw of Liv was the long French braid trailing down her back, three rows up from him and on the other side of the centre aisle. The simple black dress she wore seemed particularly dramatic, almost severe, her neck and shoulders rigid, like a mannequin had been set between Emilie and her mother in her stead.

Geai's death brought up a lot of questions, questions he wouldn't get answers to in this lifetime. *For now we see through a glass darkly...now I know in part; but then shall I know, even as also I am known...*words he had memorized as a child. They weren't sitting too well at the moment. It wasn't the first time he'd struggled with admitting things were beyond his comprehension, but so far, it was the hardest.

After the service Liv blew by him without so much as a glance. He didn't know if he should feel sorry for her, or be angry she could close herself off so neatly.

Emilie trailed, but stopped when she noticed him, throwing herself at him. He held her tightly, and left his arm draped over her shoulders as they walked out into the inappropriately pleasant afternoon.

"How are you doing, Nate?" Her eyes were red, the bit of makeup she wore smearing even more as she rubbed away fresh tears.

"I'll be all right. Thanks for asking, though. How about you? Are you going to be okay?"

Her nod was slow, a controlled chin-drop. "It's not me you have to worry about."

Liv disappeared into the back of her father's Jaguar while her family lingered with the other guests among the trees.

"Any idea how she is?"

"Not a chance. She flew in late morning, and she's leaving tonight. I guess the plan is not to stay long enough for anyone to find out."

He should go over, drag her out of the car; shake her, or hold her. But who was he to tell her how to deal with this? Instead he went back to the apartment, skipping the gathering back at the Lachance house. He changed into running gear, because running away was what he did.

The trails were fully shaded and cool, and he forced himself to think only about his breathing, making the autonomic extending and contracting of his muscles a conscious thing—feeling the burn as they went anaerobic, pushing through. By the time he came to the clearing, he'd exerted himself enough to be drenched in sweat, endorphins flooding him, dulling the ache. He ended up where he always did—at Chique's paddock, where the yearling fillies that weren't being prepped for the sales spent their days.

The red Honda parked by the barn was Emilie's, but it was Liv's slender figure, still in the smooth black dress, leaning against the white stud rails as the fillies swarmed the fenceline.

He had to do this, whatever this ended up being. For Geai.

Chique had inserted herself squarely in the middle of the group, but her head shot up, ears forward, giving away his arrival. She gave a low, throaty nicker and unceremoniously butted the others out of the way, poking her nose through the rails and nibbling on his shorts until he produced a peppermint. He stole a glimpse at Liv, but couldn't read her eyes, see any softening there.

Her arms rested on the top rail, and she made no attempt to fix the strand of dark hair escaping from her braid. "Napoleon died last night, did *Émilie* tell you?" Her voice was flat, traces of a lost accent surfacing. "He had no reason to go on without his friend."

"Liv—don't..."

The thought of the poor old Lab was enough to pull him apart, break him out of his paralysis, but she recoiled when he stepped towards her.

"And this one, my little Chique, *p'tite Chique...c'est du chiqué.* It changes the meaning entirely, *avec l'accent, n'est-ce pas?* It's all just make-believe."

She stared at him now, all that icy grey in her eyes concentrated on him. "How could you not have known something was wrong?"

The accusation froze him on the spot, arresting any kind of response, slamming him because it was so totally justified, wasn't it? *I seem to be entrusting you with the things that matter most to me. Don't screw up, Miller.* But he had, completely. He should have known.

The yearlings startled at some imaginary predator, setting off across the field. Chique wheeled and raced after them, throwing in a few bucks as she caught up, cavorting with head tossing when they slowed. Nate looked back for Liv, but she disappeared into the car, driving away.

The sun glinted off something in the grass by the fenceline. He leaned over, picking it up—a small hand-painted medallion on a fine silver chain, with the image of a woman, and a horse that looked remarkably like Claire.

Liv stared at the window, the dim glow from the streetlights creating obscure shadows on the walls. A bottle Kenny had given her—sedatives or sleeping pills, she wasn't sure which—taunted from her bedside table, unopened but not forgotten.

Her resolve faltered as the hours went by. Sleep deprivation would affect her ability to ride proficiently—not that she was doing anything close to that at the moment, wallowing in the boggiest of slumps. She had to keep riding. It held her world together, if only by delicate filaments. Riding, and Claire. Riding Claire, whose own status was in question.

Another unopened bottle beckoned on her dresser, thanks to Kenny again—the wine he'd sent to her hotel room after the Oaks. If she were to resort to mood-altering substances, that was a safer option. It was time to develop a taste for the stuff. It went down easily enough, once she got past the initial burn. It didn't take much to numb her into an unsettled slumber.

Geai's living room. He was saying something, his words reassuring, even if she couldn't make them out. It didn't matter. Just being in his presence calmed her. The call from her father, the trip home for the memorial; it had all just been a bad dream.

The vision faded, receding like wisps through her fingers no matter how desperately she clung to it. The sadness that came with consciousness burrowed deep, the visceral agony of it jarring her awake, forcing her upright.

Her phone vibrated, startling her, the screen lighting up briefly with a banner before dimming. She'd forgotten to turn the damn thing off.

Missed call. Nate.

The sight of his name added another layer to her pain. She'd trusted him. He noticed things. If there was a hair out of place on a horse, he saw. He should have picked up on something—anything—that might have saved Geai's life.

But—she was the one who'd run off with the big dreams, accepting Geai's support like an endorsement. She was the one who'd made a mess of everything. She was the one who'd failed to call him in her shame since the Oaks. *Guilty, guilty, guilty.*

What was Nate doing up this time of night anyway? It was probably a mistake, some random middle-of-the-night fumble.

Then the phone pinged. *Voicemail.*

The only reason she kept her mailbox clear was to be sure she could be contacted if something happened to Claire. She had to listen to the message to delete it. She held the phone just close enough to hear, to keep him from getting too far into her head.

"Listen...I'm sorry...just...call me. Please? Anytime you want to talk...I'm here, okay?"

Her throat constricted, her next breath a gulp. She'd been so unfair to him. Maybe even cruel. All those afternoons last fall. He would understand this...what? Despair? Desolation? She should call. She couldn't, though.

She'd always relied on Geai. She'd been relying on Nate, for too much. She needed to be stronger. She deleted the message, then held down the button on the side, suffocating the device until it powered off.

She grasped at the medallion like she hadn't cast it aside so carelessly back at the farm, a phantom at her throat. *Silly religious trinket.* Now Ste-Anne mocked her.

How's that storm going? Because you are, so very, alone.

CHAPTER SIXTEEN

July

His first time coming to Canada's most prestigious race, the Queen's Plate, and Nate wasn't feeling it. Em, social convenor that she was, wouldn't take no for an answer, but where the hell in this insanity was she?

Nate leaned against the rail of the walking ring, taking in the spectacle of food trucks and overpriced alcohol, and finally picked her out, though she blended in with this crowd—cobalt blue dress, hair coiffed and topped with a fascinator. She sidled up to him and looped her arm through his, her heels making her as tall as he was. Not that that was saying much.

"Looking pretty classy there, Em."

"What about you? You could have made a little effort." She grinned as she dropped her eyes to the polo and jeans he'd galloped horses in this morning. At least they were black jeans. That had to count for something, didn't it? "I'm glad you came."

"Had to at least check it out."

The crowd was inflated with people who'd probably never been to a horse race—people who bought into the advertising that the Plate was a fun fashion fest, and probably couldn't care less about the horses running in the actual event, let alone its history. People Nate's age, but worlds apart.

"Do you think Liv would have come home if we'd had one make it?"

He hadn't meant to ask, or even think about her, but she kept popping into his mind, every time he thought of Geai—which was all the time. Last year, the whole reason he hadn't come was because he'd stayed home to watch it with the old man. That as much as anything had convinced him to show up. At home Geai's absence would have been way too obvious.

Emilie didn't answer right away, and he put an arm around her as she leaned into him.

"My dad went down for a few days, hoping maybe she'd come back with him. My mom is freaking out, but there's no point in her going, because she's never even gone to see Liv ride. Liv comes by her stubbornness naturally." She paused as the paddock judge called riders up for the current race. "Want to stay down here so we have a good spot to watch them come in for the Plate?"

"Sure."

"Faye is pissed." Emilie curled her program in her hands, returning to the topic Nate hadn't really wanted to get into at all, even though he'd introduced it. "Liv should know better than to shut out Faye. They met a few months after Faye and Dean lost their mom and dad and brother in a car accident."

At least he wasn't the only one being frosted, and of all of them, he had the least right to be hurt. He was, though. He really had thought that, like Geai's wish, they'd be there for each other. Instead, he was left struggling with the blame.

"That's quite the hat." Desperate to get his mind off of Liv, he pointed out a particularly flamboyant one that looked like a pink shrub.

Emilie laughed behind her program. "I'm going to have to up my game next year."

The walking ring was filling with the connections of the Plate horses, a more civilized display of traditional Plate pageantry: men in morning coats and top hats, women in tailored suits and chic headwear. Even some of the horses were dressed up, with quarter markers and braids, trickling up the walkway to the saddling enclosure.

When the field left for the track, outriders brought up the rear of the procession in red jackets, their ponies decorated with intricate plaiting jobs, colourful pom poms bouncing on top of their tails. The anticipation in the air did get to him then, a little; a buzz he'd noticed even on the backstretch that morning.

"Come up to the box and watch the race with us. You need to meet Faye."

"I'm pretty sure I'm not dressed for it, Em. I'll just stay down here with the other riffraff." He smirked as she rolled her eyes. "But thanks. Say hi to your parents."

"Catch up with you after?" She didn't wait for him to answer, swallowed up by the throng.

He headed trackside and found a spot on a raised part of the apron—it gave him a clear view, the start way down the mile and a quarter chute.

The favourite came through, emerging mid-stretch to win going away. He lingered long enough to see an outrider bring the victorious team back on the turf course, the jock leaning down to kiss the bubbling groom's cheek before they draped the purple and gold blanket of flowers over his knees.

See you at the winner's barn!

He replied to Em's message with his regrets, and made a dash for his car, hoping to beat the worst of the traffic.

When he got to the farm he drove to the yearling fillies' paddock. Chique, ever curious, ambled over with tail swishing lazily at the flies, coat bleached and mosquito-bitten; far removed from the racehorse she was supposed to become. She lifted her nose and snuffled softly on his face, then began to lip at his hair before he offered up a peppermint.

Chique was still the smallest in the bunch, but had the biggest personality—that was all on Nate, good or bad. He tried to offer a mint to one of the other fillies who had wandered over, muzzle stretched inquisitively next to Chique, but Chique pinned her ears and snaked her neck, the other filly backing out rapidly and thereafter keeping her distance.

"Ever the cheeky little bitch. Maybe that'll be you at Woodbine in two years."

Not all that long ago he would have snapped a photo for Liv, but what was the point? She hated him. He took the long way back to his apartment, past the paddocks with this year's mares and foals, behind the woods, to the stallion barn. One of the farm staff had stepped in to handle things for the final weeks of the breeding season.

See, Geai, we could have gone to Kentucky for the Oaks. They're managing without you. It goes on. We go on. What choice do we have?

CHAPTER SEVENTEEN

August

The alarm droned through Liv's throbbing skull. A shower didn't clear the fuzz in her brain, and the ball cap she tugged on probably did more to deepen the shadows under her eyes than hide them. She blocked out Jeanne's concerned looks when she walked into the barn at Saratoga. Don left her alone, no doubt trusting she would take care of herself. He didn't know she shouldn't be trusted.

*Just get through the next four hours...*only to spend another afternoon sequestered in her changeroom, on standby, in case one of the other jocks booked off or got hurt, and some desperate trainer plucked her out of the barrel she'd bottomed out in. No one wanted to ride a stone-cold bug.

The morning was a blur. Caffeine made the headache from the wine worse. She popped a couple of NSAIDs, and the way they inflamed her empty stomach did nothing for her already non-existent appetite.

"You gotta eat something, darlin'," Kenny said after her last horse, not even his now-rare use of the endearment getting a rise out of her.

She turned away from the hand he'd rested on her back, but gave in, selecting a yogurt cup from the track kitchen, and choked it down. It did settle her stomach, and the painkillers started to kick in to relieve her pounding skull.

"C'mon. We need to go see Don."

It was entry day for the Saratoga Dew Stakes, a restricted race for New York-breds; a softer spot for Claire after running in open company. Claire was her chance at redemption; the different venue was sure to change her luck. Don pushed back his chair from the desk when they walked in the office, his hard gaze levelling on her.

"I'm naming Ricky on Claire. You need to go home and get yourself sorted out. You won't be riding anything in this barn until you do."

Nate felt the sting of the whip like it was flaying his own hide, but it didn't keep Claire from stopping like she'd been hit by a Mack truck. *Beat the ambulance.* That's what they said about horses that finished that far back.

He watched Acosta bring the filly back to the grandstand, her bold blaze mired by dirt, then turned and scanned the crowd. Still no sign of Liv.

"Jeanne!" he called, seeing the assistant trainer walking back behind Claire.

She turned, and stopped, eyebrows arching. "Nate, isn't it?"

"Where's Liv?"

Jeanne's face fell into a frown. "She's been scarce since…"

Since Don fired her.

"You might find her at the house. She won't talk to any of us."

He wasn't sure he'd have any better luck, but he'd just spent six hours in the car because he had to try.

The split-level was on the outskirts of town. Liv's little Nissan sat in the open garage, the hood still warm. His gut had been right—she must have been at the races. The door from the garage to the house was unlocked, and he pushed it open.

A row of empty wine bottles lined the kitchen counter. He

caught Liv in his peripheral vision, in the living area to the right, a glass of wine balanced on her thigh, legs tucked underneath her.

She looked translucent, as if something had eaten away at her. Her loose t-shirt draped her rigid shoulders, the muscles in her arms too sinewy. When she tucked a piece of hair that had fallen from her messy ponytail behind her ear, his eyes got stuck on the tension in her neck, the severe hollow of her cheek.

"So what, did you lose the coin toss? Draw the short straw and get suckered into coming down here to check up on me?"

This had to be an alternate universe. She seemed as unconcerned about his arrival as he was stunned by the state of her. She was drunk, when he couldn't remember ever seeing her touch alcohol.

"You could have picked up the fucking phone and saved me the trip."

He wanted her to flinch, like the anger, and fear, and frustration in his words would be a slap in the face, but she choked back a bitter laugh.

"You're the last person I want to talk to. It's not my fault you made a stupid decision. Seriously, why are you here?"

What had he been thinking, driving all this way just to confirm she did, in fact, despise him? He should leave. Hop right back in the Mustang and head home. But this wasn't about him. He inched into the room, but her glare stopped him, the contempt in it demanding an explanation.

"I came because…if I did somehow let you down with Geai…I don't want to make the same mistake letting Geai down, with you."

"That's very noble, Miller." Her tone mocked him. "What ever gave you the idea you were responsible for me?"

How did he explain that, without sounding like he thought he was here to rescue her? Liv, who didn't need anything but her career and a fast horse to carry it. No wonder she looked lost.

"I can take care of myself." She raised the wine to her lips.

It was his turn to stifle a laugh. "Sure. You're doing a stellar job." He reached for the half-empty bottle on the coffee table, and swept it up. It burned in his hand, igniting memories, his lips falling to a frown. "I tried this, you know. Drinking to forget."

Her eyes flashed to his, fingers tightening on the stem of her glass. "Recently?"

"Two years ago. After my ex announced her engagement, actually—all of a few months after we broke up."

"Ouch." It was so soft he barely heard it.

"Yeah. Her wedding anniversary is next week, so I hit my peak right about this time. No two-year engagement for her."

"Help yourself." She inclined her head to the bottle.

It was tempting. While that time was far enough away he was supposed to be putting it behind him, layering Geai's death on top of it disrupted what little progress he'd made. Selfishly he'd hoped they could share their grief—but not by plunging to the depths of her misery. He set the bottle back down. "That's why I came to Ontario. To get away. You giving me that job probably saved my ass."

She snorted, reaching for the bottle and topping up her glass. "We needed someone to break yearlings because I was going to school. You were qualified. Don't make it sound heroic."

"But still."

Her face lost its edge, her shoulders sinking. She looked bereft, and all he wanted to do was peel her fingers off that glass and wrap himself around her to absorb some of the pain —but she wasn't letting down her force field.

"You've fulfilled your obligation, Miller. You can go back and tell them I'm not going to kill myself. You can't help me. Just like I can't help Claire."

"You saw the race?"

She stared into the wine, fingers clenching and releasing around the stem. "Maybe I should feel vindicated she ran so bad...but I can't."

"Of course you can't." He stared out at the treed backyard

on the other side of some sliding doors, then looked back to her, pleading, "Come back with me."

A beat of silence gave him hope, but she shook her head. "Please just go. You only remind me he's gone. I need to get away, just like you did. Get away from this whole soul-sucking business. If I'm not back by the time you start breaking Chique, go ahead without me."

I can't fix this. How do I fix this? He stood there, hoping the answer would come. It didn't, though. All he could do was leave, and pray she'd make it through.

The cottage wasn't what would come to mind for most at the mention of a chalet in the Laurentians. Calling it modest was generous. It did have indoor plumbing—that was something—and a charming wood stove, which she very well might need. Beggars couldn't be choosers, looking for a summer rental in August.

It was secluded, and after that, Liv didn't care. Just like those posts on social media, with a photo of a rustic cabin in the wild, asking *for a million dollars, would you live here with no TV and no internet for a month?*

A month? Piece of cake. How about forever?

She slipped her bare feet into running shoes and stepped outside, skipping over a path of roots and stones, coming out at a lee in the river.

This was the only spot she had a hope of getting reception, and she waited while her phone found a signal. The texts and call notifications were fewer and farther between now, but she responded to one, as if to acknowledge her existence. Something kept her from throwing the device into the river.

Maybe here she'd find peace, with the birds and chipmunks, among the trees. There was nothing she could do for Claire anymore; it was childish to think she shared some special bond with the filly. Even the owner's daughter could get fired.

She'd let Claire down. She'd let Geai down. And Chique deserved better than a has-been if she was going to make it to the Plate. But could she even call herself a has-been? Because

115

what had she even been?

CHAPTER EIGHTEEN

September

Chique rumbled, crowding the door as Nate opened it. He waited until he'd led her to the back wall before slipping her a peppermint, and snapped her to the rubber tie.

"Life as you know it is about to change, my dear," he said, plucking a hoof pick from his back pocket and running his hand down her left foreleg. Her foot popped up, but she pulled away, then leaned on him, testing the limits of the stretchy tie as she tried to reach his back with her lips.

"Hey, Miller."

He straightened abruptly, dropping Chique's foot without meaning to. *Wow.* Liv. She was back, liked she'd just teleported here—from wherever the hell she'd been.

"Hey." He tried to sound nonchalant, but it came out strangled. *Recover, damn it.*

Her steps were tentative as she walked past him to Chique's head. He stayed glued at the filly's shoulder, watching her stroke Chique's smooth, shiny neck before letting the filly nuzzle her empty hands. Chique threw her head impatiently when her investigation extracted no treats, and Nate was still too stunned to pull one of the mints out of his own pocket to give Liv to make up for it.

"How's she doing?"

Liv avoided his gaze, one hand on Chique's halter as the other straightened the unruly black forelock. Chique was still unconvinced there weren't treats somewhere, and grabbed the corner of Liv's t-shirt between deft teeth, flipping it up and down until Liv slipped a finger into her mouth to make her release it. The filly pawed and tossed her forelock, leaving it a chaotic mess around her ears again.

He couldn't even find his voice to answer—not that Chique hadn't adequately done so herself. Catching a glimpse of Liv's concave abdomen above her tightly cinched belt had reinforced his first impression—she didn't look a whole hell of a lot better than the last time he'd seen her. At least she was sober. He finished picking Chique's feet and grabbed the curry comb.

"Just pretend I'm not here." She slipped back into the aisle.

Like he could do that. She had, at least, checked in from time to time when she'd been AWOL, Emilie being her contact of choice. Logical, really, because Em was the hub of the network of people who needed to know. Not him.

Chique's tail lashed, hind foot cocked, and he realized he was currying too hard. He flashed an apologetic glance at the filly, then back to Liv, leaning silently against the doorframe. He finished currying more kindly, and knocked the dust off hastily with a soft brush.

"So just to clarify, you're not here, but you're here?"

Liv evaded his eyes, and passed him the navy surcingle and pad he'd left outside the stall, exchanging them for the brushes. She went to Chique's head and unsnapped her from the wall, attaching a long cotton lead.

It unnerved him they could go through these motions instinctively, without speaking, working in sync as if they'd been doing this together for years. Geai haunted his mind. How could he not? Liv had to feel it. Geai had been the one to show her how it was done in the first place. Did she find solace in the September ritual, or was it agonizing? He had no idea which, because her expression never changed. She just scratched Chique's forehead and carried on an unintelligible one-sided conversation in her soft voice.

He slid the surcingle off his shoulder and rested it on top of the pad, allowing the length to drop off Chique's right side as he held the roller at the top. Chique shifted her weight away from the strap as it hit her belly.

"Good girl," for caring less about that and enough about him not to step over. He rubbed her belly and reached for the dangling strap, drawing it up against her rounded barrel to buckle it first loosely, then up a hole—securing it just enough that it wouldn't move. Liv passed him the rope, and retreated.

With a flick he urged Chique forward, rewarding her first hesitant steps with lavish vocal praise, until she was circling around him.

"Ho-oh," he crooned, stepping in and rubbing her neck when she stopped. "What a good baby girl."

Snug up the surcingle, walk on again. Another halt, change direction, then repeat the process to the right. He'd expected more attitude, Chique being strangely good—not that he believed for a minute it wouldn't surface at some point.

Liv handed him the headstall, and he slipped the light bit into the filly's mouth, sliding the crown piece behind her ears and adjusting the cheek piece. He turned her loose, leaving her to get used to the feel of the equipment as she moved about the stall on her own.

"Who's next?"

Nate looked at Liv sideways, and moved to the adjacent box. "I don't know if this one ties—maybe you could hold her for me."

"Claire's coming back." Her comment dropped out of nowhere, just like she had. There was no discernible emotion attached to it.

He ducked away to hide his reaction. "Let me grab the surcingle from Chique." So was it the combined power of Claire and Chique that had pulled her out of hiding?

Chique stood in the middle of her stall, mouthing the bit, processing her first lesson. When he relieved her of the equipment, she shook her head, then shuddered, and followed him to the door like she was disappointed that was it.

"Real tack tomorrow, Cheeky." He scratched her forehead before backing out.

Liv was in with the next student, absently stroking her fingers along the bridge of the chestnut filly's nose.

"What's the plan?" That seemed a safe question.

"She could run at Woodbine, but I'm hoping she's done for the year."

"Why the hell isn't she?" So much for safe. His frustration seemed determined to surface.

"It's not up to me."

"Sure it is. Your father owns her. You gotta stand up for her. Do the right bloody thing and speak up."

He hadn't meant to let into her like that. He thought he'd dealt with his anger, for her checking out. For his own hurt, thinking *how bloody selfish of you, to withdraw, thinking you're the only one affected by Geai's death.*

"Sorry," he said quickly, but wished she'd throw the shank in his face for overstepping, and slink off. Anything to indicate she felt something.

"No, you're right." The filly was falling asleep under her repetitive touch, and it seemed to be bringing words out. "You still want to ride, right?"

He quirked an eyebrow at her as he lightly curried the chestnut. "Yeah." *Once more with feeling, Miller. Say it like you mean it.* The conviction he'd felt in the spring had gone missing, somewhere around the time they'd lost Geai, or maybe when she'd decided it was his fault.

"I've been doing a lot of thinking. You should ride Chique. It's obvious you've spent a lot of time with her already."

"Wait a minute—" He was pretty sure he knew what she meant, and it was delusional. This wasn't her letting him off the hook. It wasn't a peace offering. It was a business transaction, based on the lies she was telling herself.

"It'll be next summer, at least, before she runs," Liv continued.

"Hold on—"

"But I guess I'm looking for a commitment."

Last winter, he would have cracked a grin at that, wondering how it would sound to someone walking in on this conversation, but whatever they'd been then, they were miles away from now.

"No, Liv. I'm not—you can't—"

"Can't what?"

There was something there, finally. A challenge. But it wasn't one he liked. Maybe he should just take what she'd just offered him and run with it, but he couldn't. It felt like stealing her dream.

"You can't give up."

She went back to the methodical stroking of the filly's nose. "I just, *can't,* right now, Miller. So indulge me. Please."

He sighed. What was he supposed to say? "This isn't a permanent arrangement."

Liv didn't debate that, just offered her hand, the gesture awkward and formal. Her grasp was still as strong as he remembered last summer in Saratoga.

"I have one condition, though," he said, letting his hand fall. "You're helping me. Here."

Her eyes shifted, her despondent expression deepening to a frown. "Haven't you hired someone?"

"I'd rather have you."

He could see his declaration firing around her brain, inciting all sorts of conflict. *Good.* Let her figure that out.

Claire whinnied, like whoever was coming through the door had something better on offer than she did. Which was probably true; she didn't have anything good to offer anyone right now. She crouched next to the filly's foreleg to remove the flannel bandage and thick cotton, rising to stuff both in the feed tub before switching to the off side.

It wasn't hard to figure out her father had used Claire to

lure her home. It had worked, as much as she hated to admit it. Her parents were being so perfectly careful with her. Not trying to talk. Not pushing anything. *Good parents.*

"Welcome back, Amazon filly."

Nate's voice set her on edge like playing piano wire, his jean-clad legs pausing at the stall door before going to Claire's head. Claire's weight shifted as her head swung towards him, and she crunched his offering, the mintiness of it filling Liv's nose. He reached for the bundle of cotton and bandage Liv had just removed, and she relinquished it under the filly's neck.

Nate, though. Not so well-behaved. She didn't trust him not to push—but she'd opened the door. After deciding she relied on him too much, she'd gone and invited him back in. Just for Chique mind you. The filly needed more than she was capable of right now, when it was so hard just being here, where she saw Geai everywhere.

"I assumed she was going to Woodbine." He crouched opposite her at Claire's quarters.

"I asked if she could come here."

"Good for you."

She flinched at the praise, and her hands wavered as she made sure they didn't collide with his while they unwound the hind bandages.

"Why don't you throw the tack on her, and she can play escort for Chique's first adventure in the real world?"

"She just spent ten hours on a van."

"She'll be quiet then. C'mon, it'll be good for her to stretch her legs. She can tell Chique all about being a racehorse."

Like those would be good stories. "I don't have any tack here."

"That's okay, I brought an extra set from the track. Because you're getting on some yearlings, right? Come with me."

His rusty Mustang was parked beside her Nissan, and he strode between the two cars, extracting an exercise saddle, bridle and martingale.

"Shit...I don't think I brought an Amazon filly-sized girth."

"Why would you have? Yearlings don't wear fifty-four inch

girths." She might get out of this yet. It's not as if he could've been expecting to outfit Claire. But he deposited his armful into hers, and kept rifling through the front seat.

He emerged victorious and added the long girth to her collection. "Apparently I grabbed one by mistake. Must be fate. Bring her over to the training barn when you're ready." He walked around to the driver's side, flashing her his annoying grin, and ducked into the car before she came up with another excuse.

This was crazy.

Claire pinned her ears and swung her head as Liv started grooming. "I know. Stupid idea, right? I'm sure you'd be happier if I just left you alone." But the desperate void she'd felt through the six weeks she'd been separated from Claire was enough to make her long to be on the filly again, if only for a short hack around the farm. Claire began leaning into the pressure of the curry comb when Liv reached her withers, head torquing, lip contorted, and actually gave a happy snort when Liv tacked her up.

Her boots and helmet were in the car, where they'd stayed since the last time she'd been on a horse, in Saratoga—an unwanted reminder of her abject failure. The kerchief jammed under the helmet's harness was still knotted, stiff from dried sweat, but she tugged it over her head without bothering to untie it, smoothing it back over her hair before pushing her helmet on. The worn galloping boots were harder. Geai had given them to her years ago, her first summer getting on horses at Woodbine. Her feet had hurt for days from blisters on her heels before she'd broken them in.

Claire was dozing on the tie when she returned with bridle in hand. The filly was happy enough to accept the bit, her head curling into Liv as she did up the throat latch. Getting on would be the challenge—she should probably just lead Claire to the training barn and get a leg up there. But Claire was levelheaded, if a little too tall to just hop on.

Claire looked at her like she'd lost it—with good reason— but stood quietly as Liv climbed on a fence rail, draping herself over the tack before pushing her arms straight and throwing her leg over. She leaned down and threw both arms around Claire's neck like a kid on her favourite pony, burying her face in the filly's mane and breathing deep.

Nate was jogging Chique in the sand ring when they sauntered around the corner to the training barn. Chique's head flew up, and she propped and wheeled so fast Nate had no shot, dropping him unceremoniously in the dirt and whipping away with tail flagged. She did a neat one-eighty, landing with a stiff-legged thump and an emphatic snort.

"Well, that's a first, Miller. I don't think I've ever seen you come off before. You okay?"

Nate climbed to his feet and looked over his shoulder with a smirk, dusting himself off. Chique dropped her head, her nostrils fluttering with a big sigh as he approached. He grabbed the dangling reins and led her to the fence to get a better view of the big bay alien.

"I knew the Cheeky little bitch would show up sooner or later. See? Not a yearling-eating monster." Chique snuffled a greeting, admitting the intruder was equine, then Nate walked her over to open the gate.

Liv's eyebrows peaked. "You sure you want to do that?"

"Just stand over here and block the opening. We'll be fine."

With an effortless bounce he swung on, and to Liv's surprise, Chique didn't budge. He spent five minutes re-establishing *forward* before walking Chique over to where Claire remained posted by the gate.

"Lead on," he said. "Brave new world, baby girl."

Soon Chique was walking beside the older filly like she thought she knew where she was going, feeding off Claire's responsible presence.

"She's a bold little thing." Liv glanced down, Claire dwarfing the yearling.

"Bold and quick and smart. A lethal combination." Nate ran a hand down Chique's neck with an affectionate smile, his legs solidly hugging her barrel.

This crazy idea might have merit—the sun warming her

back, the roll of Claire's walk soothing her. Chique shied and side-stepped at the dancing shadows from the overhanging branches, bumping into Claire for security. Nate's knee brushed Liv's calf before he nudged Chique away, and it sent a current up her leg. *Damn it.*

His eyes followed the steady pulse of Claire's head. "She looks happy, at least. Are you back on her, if she runs?"

Liv glanced away when his eyes shifted to her. "I'm not sure. Maybe we're both finished."

"What are you talking about?"

"She bled through Lasix in Saratoga, Miller. What if we can't get her right?" It was bad when the anti-bleeding meds most Thoroughbreds were treated with didn't work—and Claire had been on more than just that.

"You convince them to give her the time off, I'll help you get her right."

Liv snorted. "So what's your magical plan? What do you know that Don and his vet don't?"

"She needs to be rebuilt." His eyes narrowed on her. "Kind of like you."

"We're not talking about me," she snapped.

His words were measured. "There's a school of thought out there, that if you build them up, long and slow, you make the capillaries stronger. Give her the time to let her lungs heal; support her with good nutrition. Maybe some interval training. A few equipment adjustments when she runs again."

"She's probably got scarring in those lungs, thanks to that virus she had last fall. She might well be a lost cause."

"What have you got to lose?"

That much was true. She looked at him sideways. "So much more than just a pretty face, aren't you, Miller?"

His eyebrow twitched and he pulled at Chique's mane with one hand, swallowing a broken laugh. *Loss for words?* For once she'd caught him off guard.

A circuit around the farm and they were back in front of the training barn. Nate dropped lightly to the ground, scrubbing Chique's neck, and Chique wiped the side of her face on his shoulder, leaving a frothy streak. The two of them were soulmates. Hashtag *relationshipgoals.*

"See you back here with the tack." He led Chique away.

Liv kicked her feet out of the irons and let her legs hang, sorry when they reached the barn. Claire stopped automatically. When she hopped off, the big filly curled her head around and gave Liv a nudge.

"Careful, I might think you liked that."

It hit her, at that moment—for the first time in what seemed like forever—she felt content. Back in the stall, she laced her fingers over the bridge of Claire's pink nose, kissing the softness of her muzzle.

"She's alive!"

Claire swung her head towards the stall door, knocking Liv sideways. Faye leaned on the doorframe, hand propped on one hip.

"You've been back for a week and haven't asked me over. What the hell is your problem?" Faye hugged her tightly.

"I'm sorry. I didn't realize you needed an invitation."

"Because you've been so open and welcoming lately."

Liv curried away Claire's saddle mark, and braced herself, her wisp of tranquility evaporating.

"You've got to talk, sweetie. You can't drop off the face of the earth and expect anyone to believe you're okay."

"Will it make it go away?"

"No."

"Then I'll just stick to what I'm doing."

"Which is…?"

"I don't know."

"Obviously it's working, then."

Liv pushed past her and pulled the door shut. "I have to go help with the yearlings."

Faye placed a hand on Liv's arm, her eyes lighting up. "Is that exercise rider still working for you?"

Liv pressed her lips together. "Nate? Yes."

"Then I'm definitely coming along."

"I can't believe you haven't met him yet."

"I know, it's tragic."

Liv sighed. "Let's go, then."

Nate was getting the next yearling ready when they walked in the training barn. Liv stopped in the doorway with her tack.

"There she is," he said. "You want to get Jay?"

Liv inhaled, and tried to be casual. "Hey, Miller. This is my friend Faye Taylor, Dean's sister. Faye...Nate Miller."

Faye stepped forward, recognition flashing over Nate's face as he wiped his hand on his dusty jeans.

"I've heard so much about you." Faye tucked her dark hair behind an ear, her hand lingering in his.

Nate eyed her with mock suspicion. "Uh-oh. From whom?"

"Oh, Dean, mostly."

"It can't be all bad, then. I was worried you'd been talking to Emilie."

"Well *that* goes without saying."

Liv was used to seeing men react to Faye, but this was different. This was Nate. He was handling Faye Taylor like he handled a horse that was testing him—with patient humour. She felt some satisfaction—Faye was definitely not used to meeting her match. The chemistry, however, was undeniable, and for some reason, it made Liv feel very small, and very unworldly.

"So what do you do, Faye?"

"I'm still working on my degree at Guelph—unlike a certain drop out." Faye cast a sideways glance at Liv, looking for a reaction, but Liv wasn't about to be drawn into the conversation. "Just started my final year."

"Didn't the two of you go to school together?"

"I took her in on her first day of high school here and looked after her. She could barely speak English then," Faye joked, then sobered. "Truth be told, that wasn't long after I lost my parents and brother, so she probably helped me a lot more than I helped her—as ironic as that seems at the moment."

Liv avoided Faye's pointed look before her friend turned back to Nate.

"I try to keep out of the horse thing—it seems to affect one's

127

common sense. I just help Dean with the books. But enough about me. They tell me one of these days you're going to be challenging Dave Johnson for the title of leading rider at Woodbine."

Nate shifted his weight, the amusement falling from his features. "I don't know about that."

"Look, he's modest too. There's obviously a lot about you they haven't told me." Faye smirked, her eyes flashing to Liv.

Nate glanced over his shoulder as the colt he'd left on the wall stomped. "On that note—I'd better get back to work. Nice to meet you, Faye."

Faye's head tilted ever-so-slightly. "Likewise."

"Are you going to stand there and gawk, or are you here to see me?" Liv hissed in Faye's ear before she spun on her heel to tack up Jay. She swore Faye giggled before scurrying after her.

"We need to talk about your friend Mr. Miller. Now I know there's something seriously wrong with you."

Liv tied Jay to the wall, thankful they were far enough away she was sure Nate couldn't hear. "Thanks. My self-esteem is shaky enough right now without your help."

"I'll bet he could help you get over it."

"Why does everyone think sex is the answer to everything?"

Faye looked at her sideways, her lips twisting wickedly. "Don't knock it till you've tried it, sweetie."

Liv glared, blood rushing to her cheeks. "He's not interested in me, Faye."

"You wouldn't know someone was interested in you if they fell on their knees in front of you professing undying love for all eternity."

"He's all yours."

"Just remember you said that."

Liv put on the bridle and turned the chestnut colt towards the door. "Are you sticking around to watch?"

Faye laughed low in her throat. "Absolutely."

Liv followed with Jay as Nate led his colt out into the ring, Faye trailing behind.

"You know how to give a leg up?" Nate's gaze leveled on Faye with a smirk.

If that wasn't flirting, Liv didn't know what was. Faye scuttled over. To her credit, she stopped to help Liv before breezing over to Nate, then retreated to the other side of the fence.

"That's the legend that is Faye Taylor, eh?" He gathered the lines and edged his colt forward.

"I didn't realize she was a legend," Liv grumbled as they walked the perimeter.

She forgot Faye was watching as she rode, letting the simple exercises absorb her attention. Jay was the best of the bunch, gentlemanly and quick to learn. He was also the most fashionably bred of the ones her father owned, a half-brother to Just Lucky, by a Kentucky stallion. The colt's barn name reflected Claude's intent to name him after Geai. She didn't know how she felt about that.

"Ready for a little hack?" Nate asked once they fell back into a walk.

Faye opened the gate for them. "I'll be going, then. Promise we'll get together soon, okay sweetie?"

"Wait—you're not going to stick around to call 911 when this colt sends me into a tree?" Nate called.

Faye fluttered her fingers in a wave.

"Guess we're on our own." He grinned at Liv. Always that grin.

Liv eyed him suspiciously as she bumped her heel into Jay's side to keep him from running into Nate's colt. Faye was wrong, of course. About Nate. He had some misguided hero complex because of Geai, but that was it.

But maybe it was best to be careful. She'd seen how things played out around the track. People worked together, then got together. Things went wrong, then blew up, leaving a big ugly mess. Innocent bystanders—like the horses—suffered. She needed him for Chique, period. She had to make sure that line between personal and professional remained precisely defined.

CHAPTER NINETEEN

October

Faye handed Liv the coffee cup, still looking skeptical she drank the stuff. She'd curtailed the wine on her little retreat in the Laurantians, but caffeine had stuck.

"How's school?" *Mmmmm, cappuccino...*the frothy warm milk was therapeutic.

"Midterms. Final year. You know. Oh wait, no, you don't." Faye set the cardboard tray on the kitchen table in front of Liv with a smirk.

"I'm thinking of going back. School is something I'm actually good at."

"What's that?" Anne Lachance swept into the kitchen, and Liv shriveled. "Hello, Faye. Where did you get that adorable sweater?"

Faye popped up. With her sensible educational path and fashion-conscious wardrobe, she would have been the perfect daughter for Anne. Anne accepted the coffee Faye offered with an air kiss, and magically extracted some croissants from the cupboard.

"That's not like you to give up so easily," Anne said, setting a plate of pastries on the table as Faye sat across from Liv. "And your father just bought a condo in the same complex as Roger and Hélène in Florida, thinking it would be there for you."

"He what?"

"It seemed to make sense, when he was assuming you'd be spending your winters there. It gives us a place to stay when we come down. I suppose the staff can use it instead." Anne picked one of the pastries for herself. "So nice to see you Faye. Have a good visit, girls."

"Well." Faye eyed Liv, tearing off the end of a croissant after Anne was gone.

"Was my mother actually just encouraging me to keep at a profession she made pretty clear she was dead set against?"

"Almost sounded that way, didn't it? Seriously though— she's right. It's not like you. I'm the last one who's going to tell you how to grieve, but at some point you have to accept you're the only one who can make things better."

"That's what I'm doing. Going to Florida isn't going to make things better."

"What's happening with Claire?"

"My father and Roger agreed she should have some time off while we figure out what to do with her. She's been playing pony for the yearling fillies."

"That's kind of below her pay grade, isn't it?"

Liv shook away the disappointment Faye's statement conjured up. *We were meant to be so much more.*

"She might just be retired." The two of them could slip away into oblivion. They could find something different. Something involving jumps, and dressage, and tearing around a cross-country course.

"I didn't realize it was that serious."

"It is."

Nate's idea was far-fetched, but it niggled at her. It wasn't a new concept to her, but she'd been scouring the internet for whatever information she could find, and had dug out and devoured Tom Ivers' *The Fit Racehorse*—the interval training bible, pretty much—from Geai's collection of books. It would be a longshot, a lot of work that might not pan out. She'd have to talk her father and Roger into that, too.

But it seemed she could have whatever she wanted right now, like they were catering to her every whim because they were worried she'd fall apart. It was embarrassing, and almost reason enough to reject their ploys. Except she owed it to Claire. And she owed it to Geai. Even if Nate's involvement complicated it all.

CHAPTER TWENTY

November

The weather sucked, the best racing of the season over, and the yearlings were off after their sixty-day start: it was officially the worst time of the year. Sure the horses were leaving for Florida in a couple of weeks, but Nate still hadn't heard if Chique was accompanying them...and he'd made a commitment, so if she was staying behind, so was he. This is what he got for making irrational promises. Limbo.

Instead of doing something productive like going to the gym, he was here in his apartment scrolling through his feed, scanning status updates—half from people he knew now, half from back in Calgary. Clicking on Cindy's profile, because he couldn't help himself.

Her cover photo was still from the wedding—so perfect in the white dress, the familiar smile next to her the one she'd deemed worthy, when he hadn't been good enough. Honestly, was there nothing else she could use from the last two years? More likely it meant she had better things to do than post something more current. Like he had better things to do than creep. Though, what, exactly? He was supposed to be moving on, but another year had gone by, and he wasn't really any farther ahead; stuck on whether this thing with Chique was because he was trying to make things right with Liv because of Geai, or because of Liv herself, or just because he was content to tread water. Because Cindy being right about *him* meant he'd been wrong about *them*.

A text notification interrupted his wallowing, but only for a second—because it was Liv.

Got a minute? I'm in the office.

Instead of answering, he put on his jacket and headed downstairs. Hopefully she had news. Good news.

It always felt like he was entering a shrine when he walked into that room: glass cabinets showcasing a scattering of trophies, the large oil of Just Lucky and Sotisse with Geai, hanging behind the desk. The sight of the painting stirred up his grief like sediment at the bottom of a pond, and he wondered what Liv had to do to be able to sit there beneath it.

She glanced up and held out a piece of paper. "We have names."

This better not be all she wanted to share. He scanned the list. "*Chiquenaude?*"

"It's a flick, like with your fingers." She demonstrated.

Geai'd done just that to his head on more than one occasion, but he couldn't bring himself to mention it. "I can see that from Sotisse. A little more civilized than *Cheekylittlebitch*, I guess."

Further down was Jay—now officially registered as Just Jay, which was just perfect.

Liv stapled name tags to foal papers and placed them in a file folder. "Chique's going to Payson. You still in?"

Hallelujah. "Absolutely. '*Love, honour and obey*', isn't that it? '*Till death do us part?*'"

"You have an odd sense of humour, Miller."

At least I still have one. "Have you made a decision about Claire?"

"She'll go too. If you're still willing to help with her."

This was encouraging. Maybe she was coming around. This

winter was looking decidedly better than it had five minutes ago. "Definitely."

"I realize I've kept you hanging with this, so you might not've made arrangements for a place to stay, but the room at Roger's is available if you want it."

Hmm, it was almost as if she was thinking about him. "Wait —you're not coming?"

There was a beat, an unsure flash of her eyes, before she answered.

"I'm coming. My father bought a condo so I'll stay there."

It wasn't exactly relief he felt—in many ways it might be easier, for him, if she wasn't around this winter. But it wouldn't be better for her, he was convinced of that.

"That's good, because I signed up for Chique—even if I don't really buy into your why—and I'll help whatever way I can with Claire, but she's your project. She needs you."

"I'm not sure I believe in that sort of sentimentality anymore."

"Then you need her."

She pressed her lips together but didn't push back, just swept it aside, probably before it had a chance to settle. "Roger and Jo are staying till the end of the meet—Sans Défaut's going to run in the Valedictory. Michel and Sue will go down a couple of days early to get the stalls ready. The horses are leaving on the twenty-sixth, so as long as you're there the morning of the twenty-eighth it should be good. I'll follow the van."

"You have someone to share the driving with you?"

She shook her head. "I'll be all right."

"It's twenty-eight hours with the van." With nothing more than brief stops every four hours to hay and water the horses.

"I know how long it is. I did it last winter. Alone."

Yeah, when you were in a lot better state than you are now. "The drivers are pros; the horses will be fine. Why don't you come with me down I-79? It saves you eight hours. You can stop for the night and still be there to meet them."

She tidied the desk and stood, putting on her coat and

zipping it. "I don't need you to take care of me, Miller. If you're feeling guilty because of Geai...I absolve you, or whatever." She made a vague gesture with her hands.

"Maybe you don't get to do that."

She brushed past him. "You can't replace him. You can't fill that void. I don't need you to, okay? Let it go. Lock the door behind you."

"Fine," he muttered, when it wasn't fine at all.

He could ask the drivers to keep an eye on her. It wasn't his job, trying to help someone who didn't want to be helped. He had to stop setting himself up. Like she said, let it go, Miller.

Sorry, Geai.

Nate's absence was obvious. He wasn't required to be there, but somehow she'd expected him to show up, to lead Chique off the van at Payson, laugh softly at the filly's fatigue. He was probably fast asleep, relishing his wiser choice.

"You okay?" Michel asked after settling the last of the horses.

Liv nodded, because words would make the lie more obvious. "See you guys in the morning. Eight is early enough."

She sat in the car for a moment, looking back at the shedrow, now in darkness. Would anyone really notice if she just slept in the car? The van had made an unexpected stop in the middle of the night in Tennessee, the drivers claiming the fog was bad in the mountains—but more likely they'd noticed her drifting. She'd slept like a rock until they'd come tapping on her window. It had put them two hours behind schedule.

She didn't remember the drive to the condo, unlocking the door, or falling asleep. Sitting up slowly, she waited for the haze to clear, glancing around at unfamiliar surroundings. Apparently she hadn't made it any further than the couch. Four AM. That gave her what, three hours rest? Her internal alarm had decided that was it, so she groped for her bag, and dragged it upstairs to the shower.

The icy water was a shock, but couldn't make up for what she really needed—another five hours passed out in bed. She braided her hair back wet, pulled on a clean t-shirt and yesterday's jeans, and popped a couple of caffeine pills with the last swallow of water in her bottle.

Payson Park was already alive at five o'clock—shedrows illuminated, grooms mucking out, some horses already tacking the shed in the surrounding barns. Turning on the lights triggered expectant nickers, heads poking over the screens, feet tapping in anticipation as she lugged the bucket of grain from the feed room. Claire pinned her ears and backed up, rumbling from her throat as Liv dumped a scoop in her tub. Chique was next, looking uncharacteristically meek.

She continued down the row until everyone was fed, returned the empty bucket to the feed room, and unlocked the tack room. Where in this mess were the thermometers? Stepping precariously through the crammed equipment, she planted herself on a foot locker to stare at the disaster before her. The day ahead was going to be a long one.

"Morning."

Liv jumped. Nate stood in the doorway with a box of doughnuts and tray of coffees.

"Sorry." He looked nothing close to apologetic with that grin. "Caffeine?"

"Thanks." She resignedly accepted one of the paper cups. Maybe she'd feel better after the liquid top-up.

Nate appeared decidedly cooler and more together than she felt, neat polo tucked into clean jeans. He found a place to set the tray and turned over a bucket to sit. "Doughnut?"

Still smiling—how did a guy who had grown up playing hockey get away with those perfect teeth? She scowled, but took one—chocolate, for good measure. He chose one for himself before putting the box down.

"Cheers." He lifted his coffee, taking a sip. "How was the drive?"

"It's over."

"When's everyone supposed to get here?"

"Eight."

"What the hell are you doing here, then?"

She shrugged. "Couldn't sleep."

"What, you weren't tired enough?"

She didn't know if he was being intentionally annoying, or she was just totally exhausted, but whatever this was was getting old. "Find a shank. You can start walking while I muck."

"Yes, boss. No rest for the wicked, eh?"

Liv ignored him and started looking for a muck sack, rake and fork, finally finding a thermometer in one of the wall boxes in the process.

"Take everyone's temp. Start with Chique. I think she's a little under the weather."

He nodded and accepted the thermometer from her, and she followed him to the stall, removing the feed tub and water bucket while he tied Chique to the back wall.

"Oh yeah." He held out the thermometer for her, confirming her suspicion.

"All right. We'll see if we've got anyone else to worry about before calling the vet. Take her a couple of turns, and I'll get the stall done quick."

By the time the others arrived, they were almost finished with the horses. It had been easy to fall into a steady rhythm of routine. They worked well together, she couldn't deny that.

Liv called the vet to treat Jay and Chique for shipping fever while the others started to set up the shed. The tack room gradually emptied out as the barn took order: stall plaques up, gates and bars and webbings in place, wall boxes and foot lockers positioned.

"You want to go to the kitchen and grab some cold drinks, Michel?" They were almost done. All she needed to do was organize the tack room.

Michel nodded, taking the bills she offered, and dragged Sue with him.

"Get some ice, buddy," Nate called, halfway down the shed, methodically levelling the surface with a landscape rake.

It was mesmerizing, something undeniably appealing about him leaning over, reaching, then drawing back the sand. She shook her head and grabbed the fan rake. Definitely overtired, letting things like that sneak into her thoughts. She started raking, the herringbone pattern she created setting her mind straight, like meditation—back and forth, breathe in, exhale slowly; the horses snuffling happily in the background behind full haynets better than New Age music. It gave her something to focus on other than his ass.

Michel and Sue returned triumphantly with a six-pack of beer. Liv took one, even though she didn't like the stuff. It was cold, the bitterness refreshing.

"Everything looks great," she said. "We can start clipping tomorrow."

"You're actually giving us the rest of the day off?" Nate eyed her.

"Hey Miller, there's a pool in the complex at Rog's place, isn't there?" Michel said. "How about inviting us over?"

"Oh no, forget that. I'm not going to screw up my invitation to stay there by having a party when they're not around."

"You're so responsible, Nate." Sue laughed behind her can.

"Remember Liv has her own place now. We can just invite ourselves over there." Nate's grin taunted her.

Liv shot him a black look. "Sure, come and raise hell at my place instead. I haven't even unpacked."

"Oh come on, Liv," Sue said. "We'll behave. And we'll take care of everything. You don't have to worry about a thing."

Liv sighed. "Okay. But just you guys, all right? I don't want half of Payson showing up at my door asking where the party is." They were probably all leery enough of her not to overstay their welcome. "I'm going to feed lunch. Just tell me when you plan to show up."

Back at the condo, she took a stab at unloading everything jammed in the back of her car, but after two trips curled up on the couch, fatigue sucking her in like quicksand.

A knock at the door dragged her back to consciousness. She stumbled over, rubbing grit from her eyes, fumbling for her phone. Four o'clock! Michel and Sue waited on the front step, arms full of snacks and drinks.

"Come in. I still need to change." Her attempt to muster some enthusiasm was failing. All she really wanted to do was go back to sleep.

Somewhere she had a one-piece bathing suit—but not in the overnight bag she'd packed for easy access. Obviously back in the cold of Ontario, maximizing her exposure to the Florida sun had been more of a priority than modesty. The cover up she draped over the white two-piece disguised the most obvious of her angles – not that she thought she was fooling anyone.

When she rejoined them, Sue and Michel were looking quite at home in the kitchen with more beer, a bag of chips open between them.

"Sorry about that."

"Where's Nate?" Sue asked.

"Oh, I'm sure he knows where the pool is," Liv responded dryly.

The pool area was deserted. Liv spread her towel on a deck chair, tossing her cover up over the arm and stretching out. She opened a magazine on her lap, but the sun's warmth lulled her, and she leaned back and closed her eyes. The splash of someone diving into the water seemed distant as sleep beckoned again.

"Not going in?"

She pried one eye open to see Nate settle into the chair beside her—with no shirt, looking ridiculously fit. Her nicely relaxing muscles tensed back up. At least he was as pale as she was.

"Not really my idea of a pool," she replied coolly. "Something about twenty metres would do, for a good sixty lengths or so."

"Snob."

He reached over and boldly took the magazine from her lap, leaving her feeling exposed as his eyes lingered a bit too long. She was sure he did it on purpose, and not because he was admiring her. She tucked her knees to her chest, wrapping her arms around them.

"What's going on with those two?" Nate nodded towards Michel, who beckoned Sue to join him in the water.

It hadn't really clicked earlier, but it was true—there was infatuation all over their faces, in every nuance of their body language. "I guess spending two days in a car can bring people together."

"That's the track for you—sooner or later everyone sleeps with everyone else." The smirk fell from his face as he glanced at her. "Present company excepted."

A flush crept from her neck to her cheeks as he continued flipping through the *Blood-Horse* he'd appropriated. Was her nonstarter status that obvious, or was it just a good guess on his part?

Nate stopped and looked at her sideways. "Sorry I've been such a jerk today."

His directness caught her off guard. "So that's what that was?" She made herself breathe. He was trying to be nice. "I probably deserved it. It was stupid to make that drive on my own."

"Yeah, it was. I'm just glad you got here safe."

Why did he keep trying to *care*? That she didn't deserve, with the way she'd treated him since Geai died. She wound a loose thread from her towel around her fingertip, fixating on it to avoid his eyes, leaving him to keep talking to the side of her head.

"Listen. I know you hate me, and I appreciate you gave me this chance with Chique anyway. I hope I don't let you down. I know you've had a rough year. It hasn't exactly been a cakewalk for me either. I just want us to get along, at least for the sake of Chique and Claire. Truce?"

They did have to get along for the sake of Chique and Claire. She needed to learn to be cordial while regaining her professionalism, which wasn't happening lying in a lounge chair in her bikini admiring his abs.

He shook his head almost imperceptibly, then stood, returning the *Blood-Horse* silently and tossing his shades on the chair.

"Wait—"

He stopped, eyebrow quirked.

"I don't hate you, Miller. Truce."

The corner of his mouth turned up every so slightly, and he nodded. "All right then."

CHAPTER TWENTY-ONE

December

Mouthwatering aromas wafted from the kitchen, making Nate's stomach grumble. Roger's wife Hélène flitted from the stovetop, to the oven, to the counter. A decadent-looking cake ' stood out amid a fleet of savoury dishes.

"What's that for?" he asked.

"It's Olivia's birthday. I know she wouldn't want anyone to make a fuss, but I had to do something."

Great. That should be extra-awkward. "What can I do to help?"

"Find Roger for me? I think he's in the office. Olivia should be here any time."

Hélène had put a kink in his original plan for the evening— an early night so he'd be functional to work the next morning —but refusing hadn't seemed to be an option, seeing as he lived here. Maybe the birthday celebration would balance out his bad association with New Year's Eve. Just like maybe Liv would be happy about the cake. *Not likely.*

He dragged Roger away from watching the races at Santa Anita on his computer, and Hélène put her husband to work with a bottle of wine and a corkscrew. When the doorbell rang, Hélène swept over and ushered Liv in, greeting her with air kisses on either cheek.

Liv's eyes darted to Nate, her gaze reverting to the floor as she padded behind Hélène in bare feet, tucking her dark hair behind an ear. He was so used to seeing it pulled into a ponytail, or braided, or hidden under a helmet and kerchief, not all long and shiny and perfectly straight. With the simple pale blue dress she wore, she looked like someone he barely recognized—pretty, petite, and these days, just a little bit lost— instead of a rider, or his boss, or whatever she was at work.

They took their places at the table, and Roger glanced from Nate to Liv. "Wine?"

Nate almost laughed when they both pushed their glasses towards him simultaneously. Alcohol was going to be a requirement for getting through this night. He imagined Liv didn't want to be here any more than he did, but her sense of propriety demanded it. Roger and Hélène had entertained the crew on Christmas Day with a traditional meal, DVDs of corny movies, and the inevitable American football—in true Canadians-wintering-down-south fashion—and Liv had made merely a token appearance before ghosting. Not into larger social gatherings, apparently.

Hélène raised her glass and smiled at her husband expectantly.

"Santé." Roger reached forward to clink his to hers, and Nate couldn't help but wonder what it was like to have a love like that, one that endured. Did that ever happen anymore?

Roger turned next to Liv, and as Hélène looked at Nate with her glass aloft, he sensed there was custom to this, distinctly aware of being the only anglophone. He reflected her smile as he returned her gaze, clinked, then shifted uneasily to Liv.

Her eyes locked on his with their icy grey before she proffered her glass.

She wasn't wearing makeup—not that she needed it, with her dark brows and lashes, her face with some colour now from the Florida sun. Their glasses touched, and he stared right back until she pulled hers away and tipped the wine to her lips. He stopped himself from sucking back half of his.

"*Bon appétit,*" Hélène said, lifting a bowl of root veggies and passing it to Nate.

"This is great, as always." He scooped some onto his plate.

Liv certainly didn't have to worry about her weight right now—and not because she wasn't back riding—but there was conscious control in the portions she served herself. He was the one who should be doing that. *New Year's resolution number one.* In three and a half months he was supposed to be riding at Woodbine. No more excuses.

After the meal, he jumped up to help clear the table, beating Liv—he needed to move, his muscles seizing from the tension. Hélène handed him dessert plates and forks, and followed him back out with the cake. Liv looked like she wanted to crawl under the table when Hélène set it in front of her, Nate placing the plates and forks next to it.

"Hélène said no candles," he quipped. "I was looking forward to singing."

That got at least one corner of her mouth to turn up as Hélène passed her the knife. Liv looked at Nate pointedly when she passed him a generous slice.

"I'm going to have to move out soon if I want to be able to make weight in April," he said, smiling at Hélène, then quirking an eyebrow at Liv.

She took a careful mouthful of her own piece, drawing her fork out slowly, holding his gaze. With anyone else he would have thought that was flirting, but with Liv? He was sure it wasn't. Taunting, maybe. Kind of hot just the same. He looked away.

Hélène gave him a strange look when he escaped to the kitchen again, blowing out a long breath, his jaw aching from too many forced smiles. She had to know things were weird with Liv right now. Instead of serving coffee, she handed him another bottle of wine. He looked at her sideways, and she patted his arm with what he took to be consolation.

"I'll leave the three of you to talk horses," she said once

Roger refilled her glass. "I hope you'll come for dinner again soon, Olivia."

Liv rose, reciprocating a hug. *"Merci, Hélène. Bonne Année."*

"Why don't we go sit on the patio?" Roger stood, reaching for the bottle.

Liv hesitated, reluctance seeping from her pores, but she followed Roger out the sliding doors off the dining area. Nate filed out after them, parking himself on one of the metal chairs under the awning. Why hadn't she taken that perfect opportunity to bolt? He glanced at his watch. His early evening was floating away.

"What are we doing with Claire? Are we going to run her this winter?" Roger placed the bottle on the round metal table between he and Liv, and sat back.

Nate laughed. "Aren't you the trainer?"

"I used to be. You two have been on your own project since September. I'm assuming you have a plan."

Nate exchanged a look with Liv. "You make it sound like some kind of conspiracy."

"Isn't it?" Roger smirked

Liv crossed her legs as she balanced her glass on a bare knee. "If I'm going to ride at Gulfstream, Nate's going to have to carry on without me."

It was the first she'd mentioned riding again. "Happy to," Nate said. "Is that happening?"

She shrugged him off.

"I'd like you on Sans Défaut in the Mac Diarmida, at least," Roger said. "Fountain of Youth Day, beginning of March."

Liv shifted. "Noted."

"We'll jog Claire and Chique tomorrow?" Nate looked over at her. She gave a short nod in response.

Roger watched with a wry expression. "Let me know if you need me to enter Claire or anything. Though you'd better have some breezes planned before that." He checked the time and rose abruptly, glass in hand. "I'm going to see in the New Year with my wife. No leaving before midnight, Liv." He pointed a finger at her. "I trust Nate can see you out."

Nate sat up quickly. *You're kidding, right?* He was pretty sure he read the same look of dismay on Liv's face as the trainer disappeared into the house.

He reached for the bottle, tilting it to gauge how much was left. "Guess we shouldn't let this go to waste."

Liv hesitated, her eyes shifting from the bottle, to Nate, to the door...but she held out her glass. Nate poured.

She took a demure sip. "Why aren't you at that party with the others, Miller?"

He grunted. "New Year's Eve is only enjoyable if you're drunk or in love." He slouched back into Roger's chair—he was halfway to the former anyway, maybe he should take a run at it. He'd seen another bottle in the kitchen.

"Well that's touching." She re-crossed her legs and brushed something imaginary off her knee. "You don't go home over the holidays." It was a statement, not a question.

"You didn't."

She turned her hand palm up in a gesture of concession. "Just making an observation."

Nate raised his glass. "Here's to avoidance. Who knew we had so much in common."

"So what are you avoiding, Miller?"

Bold question. "I'll tell you if you'll tell me."

She took another sip of wine. "You first."

Well...all right then.

"My ex, back in Calgary. I got dumped on New Year's Eve, two years ago. Thought she was the love of my life. Guess not." That wasn't the whole story, not by half, but he wasn't about to bare his soul tonight, no matter how much wine he'd had.

"The same ex that turned around and got engaged?" Her face softened slightly into what he could almost call sympathy.

"There's only one. Your turn."

"Now it's going to seem like I'm just feeling sorry for myself," she said. "This is part of it. I hate birthdays. And this year? My mother would be in full-blown overcompensation mode, trying to make up for Geai not being there. I don't want to be around during the holidays when everyone's supposed to be happy. All of them looking at me like I'm broken."

"Aren't you?"

He expected something for that—a scowl, a snarky remark —but she just looked down into her glass.

"It would be tough," he said, his voice softer. "Aren't you glad you're spending it with me?" He tried a grin, and she tried a smile back, but it didn't hold.

Five minutes to go, then he could go to bed. Time to queue up *Same Old Lang Syne*—his mom's favourite song, though playing it right before midnight was his New Year's ritual now. It fed his self-pity, and he wasn't alone in that department tonight. The first melancholy piano notes drifted from the tinny speakers on his phone, into the night, and he planted his glass on the table and rose.

"Dance with me."

Liv glanced up warily. "I don't dance, Miller."

"It's not hard. I'll teach you." He held out his hand.

"Forget it. I'm hopeless."

"Defies death daily on the backs of racehorses; can't move her feet worth shit on the ground," he cracked. "Make you a deal. I'll feel sorry for you, if you feel sorry for me."

He was about to give up when she set her glass next to his and reached out.

He could feel his pulse as his fingers closed around hers, her body tensing when he rested his hand on her ribcage. *This was a bad idea.* The fabric of her dress seemed far too flimsy a barrier to her skin.

"Dan Fogelberg?" She'd squared her shoulders, like she was making sure he knew she wasn't getting any closer. It pulled the corner of his lips up, just a bit, making him think of his mother again—dancing in the kitchen, her teaching him a proper ballroom stance.

That's it; keep thinking about your mother, Miller. "Don't judge."

A small smile from her, then. He inched closer, a little sway, his hand slipping to her waist. Liv braced, but didn't back

148

CHAPTER TWENTY-TWO

January

The lights of Nate's beat up Mustang cut through the darkness between barns, then extinguished next to her Nissan. Liv bent over the bucket, scrubbing furiously, as if she could rub out last night.

Why couldn't he be a typical racetracker and be a no-show after a night of drinking? Why did he have to be so *reliable?* She wanted to disappear. *I take it back. I do hate you.*

She was complaining about reliable help—in this business. But—that's all he was, right? The help. It was cold, but if she thought of him that way, maybe she could get through this. Everyone made mistakes. She'd made more than her fair share of them in the past year. Staying till midnight, letting him... *gah*...had been just one of them. Or was that two? Whatever. *Suck it up.*

He walked in the barn at the other end of the shed, hood pulled up over a Calgary Flames ball cap; one hand curled around a travel mug. The temperature had dropped drastically since midnight, a cruel joke at the expense of Canadians here to duck the cold.

"Happy New Year, Nate," Jo said, coming out of Claire's stall with a feed tub and water bucket.

He grunted. "You too, Jo. What do you want me to do?"

"Fill up the waters, then you and Liv can start putting horses out."

He dragged out the hose, pulling it to the bucket Liv had just cleaned, and threw her a sideways glance.

"Red wine is the devil. Whose idea was that?"

She let out a shallow breath. "What did you do, open another bottle after I left?"

"Clearly you have a much greater tolerance for the stuff than I do."

Or an agent who'd shared a great hangover remedy with her. Whatever.

"I don't know if there's enough ibuprofen in the state of Florida for the headache I have," he added.

"Sucks to be you."

He smirked and moved to the next bucket. They finished the row in silence.

Liv handed him a shank after he rolled up the hose. "Grab Paz. He can go out with Jay."

They walked the horses the wrong way down the shed, outside over the sandy path that led to the track, on through the crabgrass to the paddocks beyond.

Liv closed the gate, Paz going straight to his knees in the sand and flopping down flat, rubbing the side of his neck up and down before righting himself. He climbed to his feet, then dropped right back down on the other side. Jay stood at a distance and snorted, lowering his nose and pawing twice before nibbling at the scrubby grass, one eye locked suspiciously on the pony gelding.

"Watch and learn, buddy." Nate turned away from the paddock. "Who's next?"

"Gemma and Miracle. Then Excursion and Sans Défaut can go individual. We're getting on Claire and Chique, right?"

Nate grimaced. "I said that, didn't I?"

"You most certainly did."

She could overhear him singing *Happy Birthday* to Chique in the next stall while they got the fillies ready, and while it replaced the Fogelberg song that had been running through her head non-stop, the softness of his voice just reminded her she'd fallen for that last night. The kiss...the kiss had just been him feeling sorry for her. He'd said that up front. Stupid girl. She slipped the bit into Claire's mouth, snapped on the martingale, and pulled the filly into the aisle.

"Throw me up, Jo?" She sounded like she was pleading. *Get me on Claire so I can think straight.*

Nate joined her outside, Chique strutting next to Claire, the sun sparkling at the horizon of a postcard-blue sky. "Turf course?"

Liv nodded, Claire strolling on the knot. Nate had his usual ready-for-anything grasp, one hand holding a long cross, the other floating on the right line. Chique's head bobbed a steady rhythm, ears alert, scanning. Liv wished Claire were more of a handful, so she had something to distract her muddled brain.

"She's wondering where the other horses are," Nate said.

"Who trains on New Year's Day?"

"Us, apparently."

Payson's turf course wasn't a typical racetrack oval—more of a European-inspired, random shape. Liv posted quietly to Claire's daisy-cutter trot, the big bay filly stretching her neck down with a happy snort. She'd never actually said it to Nate, but she loved this approach they were taking with Claire, the science behind it feeding her need to feel in control.

"Jog, jog, jog. Nice and slow, Cheeky," he dictated to the now-two-year-old filly. Chique pushed against his cross—jaw clamped, nose wrinkled, toes flicking out in front of her in a clear display of what she thought of *slow*.

He stood loosely in the irons, knees absorbing the bounce, his lean frame angled over the filly in perfect balance. No one could blame her for being drawn to that: his uncomplicated smile, clear blue eyes glancing from Chique's swiveling ears to the way Claire's flopped on either side of her head, relaxed. Or his laugh when Chique popped into a rocking canter before he brought her back; the way he reached forward to stroke the length of her bunched neck, encouraging her to unwind. That voice again, gently singing *I Got Spurs* in the filly's listening ear as they jogged along. It seemed to settle Chique, but it was having the opposite effect on Liv.

Wine or no wine, she'd let her guard down last night. She'd let herself think she wasn't the only broken one, when she was just that awkward, shy girl, dancing with the hottest guy in school at the high school formal. There was a reason she'd never gone to those things. She needed to get herself back; get Claire back. New year, fresh start. No sympathy required.

"So where do we go with Claire from here?" She forced her mind to things she understood. Six weeks of building miles, long slow distance; it was time to move on.

"Assuming the goal is to get her back to the races, I guess it's time to start throwing some speed at her. Just not the way we're used to. Starting longer. Intervals. Stuff like that."

"Okay, Tom Ivers. But you get to sell that to Rog."

By the third circuit Chique had given up hope there would be galloping involved today, resigning herself to a slow jog without Nate having to constantly remind her. They turned in near the gap.

"How's the headache?" Liv asked.

"I think between the drugs and the caffeine and the company..." he drawled, grin surfacing, "...it might actually be gone." Chique pawed, but he stopped her when she tried to take a step forward, his eyes settling steadily on Liv. "Sorry about last night."

Her stomach flipped, and she nudged Claire away. "Already forgotten," she lied.

Liv was gone, and that was just fine with him. Off to Gulfstream, or Palm Meadows, while he put in miles on Claire. Doing the grunt work. Though that was kind of what Liv was doing too—getting on whatever horses Kenny scraped up for her to work, hoping some of those trainers would put her up in a race.

It was okay. Putting in miles on Claire was good for thinking. Time to ponder life's great mysteries. Like what the hell had possessed him to do what he'd done New Year's Eve.

It was fine. It was too cold for the beach, so not too hot to train later in the morning. They had the track to themselves. Hotwalkers were probably already back in their dorm rooms, or drinking in the kitchen. Grooms doing up the last of their charges. Vets making their rounds.

It was great. Just him and Claire out here, round and round, doing a crazy long jog warmup. No one even looked at him strange anymore.

Why had he done it?

It wasn't because that's what you did New Year's Eve at the stroke of midnight. It wasn't that he'd drunk too much wine. It wasn't because, for once, she'd made herself vulnerable. Maybe it had been his own self-pity, trying to erase the bad association that night had. Was there more to it than that?

He thought *gallop* and Claire transitioned into her easy, ground-covering stride. He eyed the heart rate monitor on his wrist. Each day he had to let her go a little stronger to maintain the same numbers. Round and round.

Tomorrow was interval day. Liv would be back, and he'd pretend he wasn't aware. Aware of her presence, of the pull, of that memory of her being right there, his lips on hers.

He didn't know why he'd done it. But given half the chance and a bottle of Merlot, he'd do it again.

CHAPTER TWENTY-THREE

February

Chique stomped a foot impatiently.

"All right." Nate slid his free hand up her neck, under her crazy mane. The filly responded with a snaky toss of her head and a step to the side, and he let her start off.

"You let her get away with too much," Liv chided as she jogged Claire up next to them, the pair breaking into an easy gallop. The air current sent ripples through the quarter sheets covering their haunches.

"It's too cold to stand still for long." Not that they didn't already have windburn from galloping the earlier sets. Liv's presence made it an easy day from a work perspective, at least. She'd do Claire's intervals later; babysitting was just part of the older filly's warmup.

Chique grunted, rocking against his hold, her hind end swinging sideways and bumping Claire. Claire pinned her ears in warning, but Chique didn't look the least bit chastised.

"Try and keep her going straight, will you?"

That was a pointless request—only going faster would make that happen. It seemed to take every ounce of Chique's self-control to comply with his request to go this slow. She was just putting up with him, humouring him. *More, give me more,* she begged with each bouncy stride. Claire's wary wall eye watched her the whole way around.

When they came into the lane the second time, Liv let the lines slip through her fingers, Claire eating up the freedom. Chique eagerly lengthened her stride to keep pace as they flashed past the eighth pole, ears laced against her head. *You think you're so tough.*

Just past the wire, Liv stood in the irons, the big filly responding to the shift in her posture, and Nate talked Chique into easing, managing not to inspire a fight. They pulled up on the backside, Roger cantering Paz up to join them as they turned to face the infield.

"Just like that." Nate slapped the filly's neck, and Chique tossed her head with a happy snort, for once standing still.

"Did you catch a time?" Liv asked.

"You knew about this?" Nate stared at Roger.

Roger nodded, waving the stopwatch cupped in his hand. "But I don't think you need me to tell you, do you?"

"Twelve. Pretty damn close to flat, I should think," Nate snapped, then glared at Liv. "And here I thought you'd finally done something spontaneous." Maybe agreeing to that dance New Year's Eve had been spontaneous, but that was forgotten, right?

Chique bounced through the off-gap, proud of herself after that first taste of speed. She skittered across the pathway, Nate dropping his irons as she tried to pitch her head, shaking it back and forth as a squeal built inside her, humming just under the surface.

Roger sidled up with Paz, grabbing a line, and she sighed in resignation, not quite flat-footed the rest of the way back to the barn.

"Take her a turn for me while I get my boots off, Jo, and I'll walk her," Nate said, depositing the tack on the rail. None of the horses had been bathed since before the cold snap. He was done for the day, so he was in no hurry. This wasn't exactly beach weather.

He took the bridle with him and hung it on the tack hook, then pulled off his helmet, running a hand through his hair.

Liv came through the door. "That was easy for her."

He tugged his boots off and kicked the jack aside. "Ridiculously. She's going to be impossible to live with now."

"Maybe she'd better not walk tomorrow."

"Agreed. Otherwise I might not live to see her breeze a quarter." Chique's head bobbed past outside the door, but he had Liv captive for a rare moment. Jo could take her a few more turns. "So do I just wait and see when you decide to spring the next one on me? Guess I had to know one of these days we'd get to gallop along a bit after you x-rayed her knees."

Liv returned his look carefully. "She reads you too easily. You wanted that as much as she did. I don't think we could have slipped it in if you'd known."

"Obviously you either think I'm incompetent or don't trust me."

Liv sighed, sweeping a loose strand of hair out of her eyes and tucking it behind her ear. "You know we have to be careful with her. It's not just me being paranoid, saying that."

"Yes, it is. So like what, we might get her to the races by the time she's four? That rules out the Plate, doesn't it?" He smirked. "I'm thinking more like June."

"That sounds an awful lot like counting chickens, Miller."

"Gotta have goals, right?" Even if it was a little soon to be getting excited. It just felt good to have something to be excited about.

CHAPTER TWENTY-FOUR

March

Sans Défaut had run huge, beaten less than a length his first time on the turf. On a more selfish level...Liv had ridden a good race. She'd dragged her heels about riding at Gulfstream —she would have been perfectly happy spending the winter hiding at Payson, except for the whole weirdness with Nate she couldn't entirely put behind her—but she'd had to dive back in before Belmont, for Claire.

"Would you like one of our cheap, virtually tasteless American beers?" Jo stood, pushing Nate off the cooler they were parked on so she could open it. The colt was back from the test barn, tearing at his haynet in the receiving barn behind them.

"With that glowing endorsement...I think I'll pass." She'd made herself a rule. No more drinking with Nate Miller.

Nate took a swig, then looked deep into the can. "This is pretty sad."

"You bought the beer Nate." Jo sat back down. "You had choices."

They looked at each other and laughed.

"Roger been back?" Liv pulled her coat more tightly around herself. Would it be wrong to just head home and leave those two to their party?

"He's staying over there to watch the rest of the races."

"You wanna sit down?" Nate asked, popping up again to offer his spot on the cooler.

"I'm fine thanks."

"You guys should go over. I'll get the colt done up." Jo rose and drained the last of the beer onto the pavement.

"You sure?" Nate said.

"Go. This is my job. That's going to be yours soon."

Nate glanced warily at Liv. "Drive, or walk?"

Was she doing this? Really? She should have bolted when she'd had the chance.

"Walk," she said, turning on her heel and flipping up her collar to protect the back of her neck from the cool breeze. "Parking is a nightmare."

The front side was packed, nine stake races on the card, highlighted by the Derby-prep Fountain of Youth. Liv didn't know where to go, feeling exposed out here. She fished the phone out of her pocket and stopped in her tracks, Nate wheeling to a standstill beside her with a question mark on his face. Thank goodness Kenny was quick to return texts, at least from his rider.

"This way." She set off again, needing to keep moving.

"Hold up a second." Nate grabbed her arm and dragged her to a halt.

Liv pursed her lips, shooting him a dark glance. He laughed, no apology in his grin, lifting his hand and tilting his head to the side.

The girl standing there was tiny, maybe twelve, bright eyes fixed on Liv with a hopeful expression. Those devoted few who still sought her out confused her. She didn't understand why anyone would look up to her, and was more than a little surprised to be recognized in street clothes.

"C'mon," Nate said quietly, nudging her with his elbow. "You'll make the kid's day."

away. Then relaxed, just a little. *A really, really, bad idea.* He should let her go. But he didn't.

The sound of fireworks obscured the soprano sax at the end of the song. Liv's head turned, searching the sky above the privacy fence that enclosed the little yard.

Midnight.

His eyes traced her delicate profile, the sweep of her hair, aware of the warmth of her hand in his, the way she moved when he inched his fingers to the small of her back, how very near she was. When she looked back to him, her mouth was a breath away. A tilt of his head, the softest brush, longing for just a taste....a taste that sent tremors through him, his blood running simultaneously hot and cold as their lips touched. Inching back, he found her eyes, wide and dark.

"You should go." It came out wheezing, his vocal cords not cooperating with his lungs, and he dropped his arms, stepping away, when he wanted to dive back in. He grappled for his phone before the next song began.

She stood frozen, then shoved past him, darting for the sliding doors.

He stumbled after her, finding her toeing into her flats before diving through the entrance. By the time he reached it, she was halfway down the driveway.

"Happy New Year, Liv," he called, his voice gravel.

She glanced over her shoulder, closed expression blocking him out.

Why did he have to be so *nice?* But he was right. Liv forced a smile, and stepped forward to take the offered pen.

"You going to be a rider one day?" Nate asked, and the girl nodded with a smile bigger than she was.

They had no idea—this wasn't a life to be lauded. It was hardness, and pain, and constant scrutiny—by the trainers, the owners, the horseplayers in the grandstand, the deadbeat hotwalkers in the track kitchen—all of them sure they could ride a horse better than her.

"Good luck," she said, returning pen and program, hoping it didn't sound ironic.

Kenny was in one of the bars. Liv weaved her way through the bodies, muttering *excuse me* and *sorry* until she spotted him. He chased away his neighbour to free up a seat, and Nate deferred to her.

"Kenny, this is Nate Miller. He's been galloping for us the last couple of years. He's going to start riding at Woodbine this spring."

Kenny reached for Nate's hand. He didn't give Nate any feedback on his grip.

"You kids want something?"

Liv balanced on the edge of the chair, Nate close enough behind her to push a current of awareness through her. *Damn it.* "Water, please."

"The same." When Kenny looked disappointed, Nate added, "She doesn't like me any better when I'm drunk."

Kenny roared and waved over the bartender. "Glad it's not just me."

Of course Nate hit it off right away with Kenny. Everything that was hard for her was easy for him. At least it meant she didn't have to talk to either of them. She focused on the television monitors, hands clutching her coat, once again feeling very much the odd one out.

Kenny tapped the side of her knee. "See darlin', you could learn a thing or two from your friend Nate here."

Nate's face contorted. "You let him get away with that?"

"I've given up." She turned back to Kenny "And I have.

Learned a thing or two."

Pulling out her phone, she snapped a photo of the two of them, opening up a long-unused app, and posting, *I think Miller might be trying to steal my agent.* She showed them the screen, and went back to watching races.

"Are you any good?"

Liv peeked over as Kenny spoke. Questions like that seemed to always make Nate squirm.

"Guess that remains to be seen."

Kenny leaned forward and swatted at Liv's knee again. "Is he?"

Liv shrugged. "Probably. Looks good on a horse, anyway." She glanced over her shoulder at Nate with a smirk.

"Maybe you should come to New York."

"Sorry, Kenny," Nate said. "My girl's going back to Toronto, and I think it might be serious, so I'm going with her."

Kenny's eyebrows twitched, and Liv melted. That, there, was both the solution and the problem. The reason she had no doubt she'd been right to give Nate Chique; what made all the awkward worth it. The reason it needed to stay that way, so she didn't screw it up. His devotion was straightforward; she and Nate were anything but.

CHAPTER TWENTY-FIVE

April

Nate tried not to breathe, half-standing in the irons in an attempt to convince Chique they weren't really doing anything. Liv crouched low over Jay's neck. *An easy half.* Those were Roger's instructions.

The wind droned past his ears as they rounded the turn, and he focused on keeping still—not on the problem he was going to have when they hit the quarter pole. It flashed by, Chique's ears pricking forward, and she might as well have been speaking English—very clearly telling him to go screw himself.

"What the hell are you doing?" Liv yelled across at him.

The filly eyeballed Jay, and the colt faltered, Chique pushing her nose in front. Liv reached back with her stick, left-handed, and Jay jumped back up beside the filly. That just drove Chique on again.

Nate cursed. So much for an easy half. He was going to hear about this.

Chique still fought him, dragging him to gain half a length on Jay before she decided that was enough—just in time to pass under the wire. The challenge off, she came right back to him, and galloped out fluidly beside the colt.

Jay was blowing when they pulled up and turned in halfway down the backstretch. Chique snorted triumphantly, and Nate glared at the back of her head. He tried to read Roger's face. He didn't dare look at Liv.

"Who's *that* one, Rog?" somebody called as they started towards the gap. "Forty-five and two!"

"Holy shit," Nate muttered, and felt like he was going to be sick.

Roger glanced at him. "You okay?"

He made a face in Liv's direction. She still hadn't spoken. Her face was grim as she stared him down.

"Well Miller, I guess we've got ourselves a racehorse."

He stood silently at the end of the shank, Liv hosing the remains of poultice off the filly's forelegs. Chique didn't like the cold running water, her hind legs alternating kicks as it splashed. She lipped at Nate's arm, weight shifting from side to side.

Liv kinked the hose to stop the flow and squeezed the water from each foreleg. She ran her hand more carefully down the left one, probing the ankle before standing.

"Hose her when she's done walking. We'll take pictures of it later."

Chique wasn't sore on the ankle, but there was pressure in the fetlock joint....and none of her usual squealing and bouncing as they rounded the shed. He pulled his hat low over his eyes and started turning left. Liv set him up with the hose when they were done walking, then disappeared back into the barn.

Michel walked up to his elbow, cleaning a halter.

"You look good on the end of a hose, Miller. Nice to know you have the whole hotwalker thing to fall back on, if the pinhead thing doesn't work, eh? Though I think you've got the pinhead thing nailed. Just sit there and hang on."

"Shut up, Mike."

"Breaking down the star two-year old, I don't know. You and Liv haven't been getting along so great lately. I hate to tell you, but this ain't gonna help."

It was a good thing his hands were occupied. He really, really, wanted to smack the guy.

"It gets even better. Jay's tendon ain't looking so good. Great work. Looks like maybe you took them both out. Maybe singing hotwalkers make more money than normal ones. What do you think?" Michel finally walked away, and Nate resisted the temptation to turn the hose on him.

He kept the stream on the middle of the filly's left shin so it flowed around the ankle. He knew they'd gone too fast—the filly had just done it way too easily. It hadn't helped when Liv had sent Jay after them—that had only fired Chique up more—but what was Liv supposed to do, let Chique dust the colt?

The alarm on his phone let him know when he was done, and he dropped the hose in the grass, leading Chique over to turn off the water. He put the filly in, hanging her bucket and haynet, and went to do his tack. And wait.

Liv held Chique when Doc Benson came, the filly standing like a champ while the assistant positioned the plate this way and that. The vet captured a series of angles, peering at the images as they popped up in succession on the laptop.

"Right there." Benson pointed out a chip on the front of the joint.

Nate skulked back to the tack room. He heard the vet's SUV rumble off, then Roger's voice outside the door.

"Some time off will let her grow a bit."

"I'll let you make the arrangements for the surgery when you get back."

Liv. She walked in, Roger behind her, and glanced at Nate as she went to the back of the room to pick up her keys.

"Guess you'll have your girl back at the farm for a bit, Miller. I'm going to the beach."

The ocean was commanding, rhythmic as it crashed up on the shore, leaving abandoned shells and glittering stones in its wake.　Distant clouds stretched across the horizon of an otherwise perfect blue sky, a hot breeze carrying the salty smell of the surf across the sandy beach.

Liv gazed beyond the waves to the faraway point where the neverending blue-green of water dropped off to meet the heavens. She loved the ocean, the mesmerizing roar, and the sound of the seagulls calling and sweeping overhead.

She didn't know if she believed in God, but here she felt a presence that made her feel foolish for doubting. *Everything happened for a reason* Nate had said after she'd broken her arm, and with things like Chique's injury, she could agree. The filly scared her a little, she was so precocious. That word was thrown around liberally with young Thoroughbreds, but it seemed particularly appropriate in Chique's case. A few months off would be good for her.

It was losing Geai she couldn't figure out. Life had gone on, despite her pain and confusion. She didn't think Geai was up there somewhere, beyond the expanse of endless sky, watching her as she struggled—but she knew if he was, he'd be telling her to get on with it, life was too short. She had no real concept of that, still believing she was invincible. She tested it every day she got on a horse. But life had certainly been too short for Geai, even though he'd lived his years fully, so his death brought the idea a little closer to home.

Claire was her constant, but whether this winter's methodical program would get her successfully back to the races remained to be seen. If it didn't, it was something else she had to figure out how to accept. Claire would be retired. Would her conscience let her take the mount on Chique back from Nate, after all the work he'd put into her? For now, Chique was his.

She pulled her eyes away from the hypnotic waves and scanned the stretch of sand extending north. Something about the figure walking in her direction attracted her attention, then the casual walk became familiar, the understated confidence and athleticism Nate's.

She boldly watched him, knowing he wasn't aware of her

yet. The wind tousled his blond hair, his t-shirt in his hand, the sun deepening the tan on his bare back. He was the skinny one now—reducing evidently in progress in preparation for riding back at Woodbine.

He hesitated, spotting her. But he came over, spreading his t-shirt on the sand next to her and sitting cross-legged.

"What a disaster of a winter," he said.

She had to laugh. "Well it's over now."

"You seem nicely back on track."

He glanced at her, his eyes sweeping from her face to her arms, wrapped around her shins. She pulled her knees closer to her chest and looked away.

"But now it's back to New York," she said. "I got chased out of there."

"You'll fight back. With your dragon." One corner of his mouth twisted up.

Claire was training like a monster, but Nate had done most of the work, so the question of her own competence still lingered in her head.

"Rog says he's going to put you on Gemma for your first mount."

"Guess I can't put it off any longer, eh? Too bad I broke my secret weapon."

"You'll be fine. You're way better prepared than I was." She watched him as he stared out over the water. "You know I don't blame you for Chique's injury, right? She's hard on herself. It was probably in the cards."

"It was too fast."

"Just the proverbial straw."

He shrugged her off.

"I don't blame you for Geai, either. It wasn't fair, to suggest that."

He was silent a beat, still staring at the waves. "I wracked my brain, trying to think what I missed. Maybe he didn't know. Typical horseman, neglecting his own health when the horses get the best care. Did he ever even go to the doctor?"

"I should have been around. It's not like I've been setting

the world on fire down here."

"But that's just it. He never would have let on. He wouldn't want to worry us. He wouldn't want to hold you back."

"You're right, he never would have let on, if he even knew anything was wrong." She looked down at her toes, pushing them into the sand, her voice faltering. "I still can't believe he's gone."

"Stubborn old man." Nate picked up a handful of beach; let it fall through his fingers.

"I do blame you for getting me drunk on New Year's Eve, though."

She'd said it to lighten the tone, expecting his default grin, proving to herself she was past it. Instead the look he gave her was like throwing kerosene on embers, her intent blowing up in her face.

"I apologized for that."

"I realize you were just feeling sorry for me."

"What if I wasn't?"

She searched the ocean desperately, calling on the waves to calm her, without success. Then she forced herself to meet his eyes again, beating back the flames the only way she knew how.

"It's never going to happen Miller. You and me? I'm not your rebound girl."

After three years of killing time, buying time, *wasting* time...it was time. Nate almost felt guilty, it came together so easily.

With Chique on the farm and Liv in New York—out of sight, out of mind, her point driven home—he had no excuses not to be laser-focused. At least she'd been honest. Saved him the embarrassment of pining over someone who didn't want him —again. Been there, done that, wrote the song about it.

He didn't intend to have the ten-pound bug for long. He'd worked hard to lay the groundwork, and it was going to pay off.

And it did.

CHAPTER TWENTY-SIX

May

Nate parked his tired Mustang behind Johnson's shiny BMW. It would take several hundred more winners before he'd be driving a car like that. Johnson surprised him by waiting, and they walked into the barn together.

"Excursion ran huge, eh Dave? He looks good for the Achievement Stakes."

"Sounds like you're trying to take the credit there, Miller," Johnson replied.

"You rode him all right." Even though Nate had galloped the colt all winter, and breezed him more than once leading up to the race when Johnson was busy elsewhere.

Liv stood halfway down the shed with Emilie and Faye, looking like she'd stepped out of an office in a black pencil skirt and white blouse. She'd flown up to guide Sans Défaut to an easy win in the Eclipse Stakes. Just in case Nate had forgotten: he might be the hot bug at Woodbine, but he was still second—or maybe third—string at Triple Stripe.

"Gentlemen." Liv looked from Johnson to Nate, eyebrows slightly raised in amusement.

She looked good. Healthy. Dare he say content? Definitely good. *Nope. Not your rebound girl.*

"Isn't that nice, Woodbine's top two riders gracing us with their presence," Faye interjected.

"What's the occasion, boys?" Trust Em to come right out with it. "Christmas isn't for another seven months yet."

Johnson kept a straight face, enduring the wisecracks, but Nate didn't imagine he'd joined this group to be made fun of by three smart-assed women, regardless of how attractive they were.

"Everything going well in New York?" Johnson homed right in on Liv.

"Yes, thanks."

"How's that two-year old doing on the farm?"

There it was. Cut to the chase.

"Which two-year old is that?"

"You didn't have to be at Payson this winter to hear about the Just Lucky filly. Sounds like she's going to be a runner. She outworked Just Lucky's half-brother, didn't she?"

"Something like that."

"When's she coming back in?"

"I don't know. You'll have to ask Nate. She's his project."

Nate smothered a grin. He could've—no, thinking about kissing Liv just got him in trouble.

The clench of Johnson's jaw was brief but unmistakable. "I'm sure I'm not the only one looking forward to seeing if she lives up to everyone's expectations. Nice seeing you, Liv."

He shook her hand and stepped away, stopping at the office to check in with Roger.

"I don't think he much liked our company," Faye said, a smile toying with her lips.

Nate glanced at Liv. "Thanks."

"Just stating the facts. How is our filly?"

"She's good. Even if she doesn't think so. I can't wait till she can start jogging, though I fear for my life, getting on her after her little vacation."

"You have the time?"

"I'll make the time."

Between not trusting anyone else to do it and considering it his penance, he'd taken it upon himself to walk Chique every day, as per the post-op instructions. On dark days he walked her in the afternoon, on race days—every one but Wednesday, when they had night racing—in the evening. The staff at the farm thought he was crazy, but no one complained about not having to deal with the cheeky little bitch.

"You're off to a quick start." Liv crossed her arms, her manner as professional as her outfit. "Good things come to those who wait?"

"Where have I heard that before?" He matched her pose, but the corner of his mouth tipped up. "I can't complain. Claire still on track for the big comeback?"

There was a little shift to her eyes, her posture, as she nodded. "Guess we'll find out if the same holds true for her."

Faye was following the conversation with more interest than Nate would have expected for someone who claimed not to care about the horses. Emilie looked like she'd pulled up a chair and a bowl of popcorn. He felt like he'd missed a memo somewhere.

Johnson left the office, and Nate saw his chance to escape whatever was going on here. "My turn to check in with the boss. Catch you all later."

Roger was preoccupied with the condition book, like every other trainer who'd run a horse today, when Nate opened the door.

"Looks like you had your work cut out for you out there, Miller." Michel eyeballed him, sprawled on the couch. "Faye Taylor, Liv Lachance, and Emilie. That's my idea of pain."

"Shut up, Mike."

"I'm really surprised Faye hasn't taken a run at you yet. Hot bug riders are her thing, you know."

Was that what that had been about out there? He kicked Michel's legs out of the way, and parked himself on the other end of the sofa.

"I'm thinking the Steady Growth next time out for Sans

Défaut," Roger said. He hadn't lifted his eyes from the book. "What do you think?"

"Sounds like a no-brainer. Do I get to ride him?"

"Not likely."

No surprise. "Johnson was sniffing around. He say anything to you about Chique?"

Roger shook his head.

"I'd still put money on Liv coming back to ride her when the time comes," Michel goaded.

"Probably." He couldn't disagree, because the thought crossed his mind every day. "I'll cling to the fantasy in the meantime."

"Of course, she may turn out to be no good."

Nate laughed. "There's always that. They're all champions until they get a chance to prove otherwise, right?"

CHAPTER TWENTY-SEVEN

June

It had been almost a year now, Geai had been gone. She could still feel the pain like stitches pulling at the edge of a wound, but it finally felt like she was coming to terms with her loss—both of Geai, and her sense of self. It wasn't on Claire to restore her, but an encouraging performance in today's comeback sure wouldn't hurt.

As she walked into Belmont's paddock, Liv's eyes went automatically to the tall filly—that flash of blaze, the three white legs, the glint of gold in her coat—before she located Don, and the cluster around him. Jeanne, her father, Emilie and…her mouth fell open.

"*Maman?* You came!" She choked up, blinking hard as she gave her mother a hug. "Thank you."

"She's here, but no guarantee she'll actually be able to watch." Emilie grinned.

"True," her mother said, squeezing back. "*Bonne chance.* Come back safe."

This was the Belmont Gold Cup Invitational, two miles on the turf—which seemed an insane choice for the filly's first race in nearly ten months. Some thought running on the grass was easier on bleeders, but the air quality worried Liv—the mugginess suffocating, like breathing pure New York smog.

After the post parade Liv broke Claire away from the pony, the breeze cooling her face as they zipped through their new pre-race routine, leaving the others behind. None of them probably broke out of a trot—it seemed common sense to conserve every ounce of energy, and she fought the doubts that crept up. She had to believe—all or nothing, right down to the aggressive warmup.

Claire had a healthy sheen of sweat on her neck as they loaded into the gate. *Check*—internal cooling systems functioning as they should. The doors sprang open, bell rattling Liv's ears, and she let Claire fall out and settle into her stride, the filly relaxing in her favourite spot, at the back of the pack.

It wasn't until they came into the backstretch for the second time that Claire started picking up horses along the rail, the distance weeding out the pretenders. She snuck up the inside, Ricky Acosta's mount, a big grey named Eureka Moment, rolling now on the outside. They wheeled around the turf course's tighter turn, the leader tiring. Liv pulled Claire out and into Eureka Moment's slipstream.

Claire's ears flipped forward as they turned for home, and she started closing the gap between her and Eureka Moment before Liv even started to ask. The filly inched her nose to the edge of his saddle cloth. Acosta looked back, going to the whip, left-handed, and Eureka Moment began to drift out.

Not that she'd expected anything different from Acosta—it wasn't a surprise he'd float her to the middle of the course if she let him. She gauged Claire's reserves, and took a chance. Asked the big filly to back off, getting an ear flick in response. Eureka Moment jumped ahead.

Liv glanced over her shoulder to make sure no one had moved up the rail, and fired Claire back up—on the inside. The filly dragged her to Eureka Moment, ears laced against her head. Acosta let the grey horse drift back in, and Liv reached back left-handed, hitting Claire for three strides...then drove with her hands, pushing with each thrust of the filly's neck. Claire's ears snapped forward, bounding past her rival, drawing clear.

Galloping out, Claire powered on, and Liv laughed as she tried to pull the filly up. All those crazy long miles of jogging and galloping, the methodical reintroduction of speed, the intervals—just old school training, no drugs. It was madness, impractical, but it had worked.

Jeanne met her with a bucket of ice water, sluicing it over Claire's neck, then passed the sponge to Liv so she could douse the filly between the ears while Jeanne undid the tongue tie, peeled off the nasal strip, loosened the noseband—all little pieces of the puzzle. A cooling spray with the hose, then on to the winner's circle, the coveted space that had eluded them far too long.

Back in the room she sat in front of her locker; let it sink in, let herself feel all of it. There was a tightness around her heart, knowing she couldn't call Geai. The wound prickled, and wept a little.

Her phone buzzed, the screen coming to life, the message from Nate just the most recent in a stack of congratulations.

Annnnnnd...she's back. Mother of dragons.

She wished he were here. Then again, it was probably a good thing he wasn't, because her resistance to him—to them—might've gone out the window.

"Hi Nate, it's your mother..."

Like he wouldn't recognize her voice, always and forever; like it didn't always make him smile, the only thing about Calgary that could do that.

"I just wanted you to hear before you saw it on Facebook...Cindy and Phil are expecting. Call me okay?"

He blew out a long breath, and disconnected.

It didn't sting as much as he'd thought it would. Time and space. He was living the dream now, right? Battling Johnson at the top of the standings. And in the shadow of Geai's death, it seemed almost benign.

He fired off a quick text. *Thanks for the heads up. I'm good. Going upstairs for a drink—had an especially nice winner today. Call you later.*

He didn't make a habit of it, but it felt justified after piloting Dean's promising two-year old colt, Touch and Go, to an impressive maiden win this afternoon. Dean waved him over from a table off to the side, sitting across from his sister Faye. Dean had already ordered.

"If we can keep his shins under control, what do you think of the Victoria Stakes?"

"Sounds like you read my mind," Nate replied, taking a careful sip of his beer and stealing a look around. "I say go for it."

One sure bet at the racetrack was someone was always watching. There were no corners here in the grandstand's fourth floor lounge, and Nate was aware his every move was likely being monitored for bad behaviour.

"Would you be free to ride him?"

"Absolutely."

"Have to take advantage of Triple Stripe's bad luck this spring, because if those two of Roger's make it to the races this fall, we might not have it so easy. Is that going to happen?"

"Hopefully. We brought them both in from the farm this week, but it's kind of early to be making predictions."

"Right. From what Emilie says, you're pretty high on that filly." Faye used the leafy stalk of celery in her Caesar to stir, the bracelets on her wrist jangling softly.

Nate ran his eyes from the bangles to her tanned, bare shoulder before reaching her eyes. "She's a long way from running yet."

"So cautious." Faye peered at him slyly over her drink.

"I've already been accused of counting chickens," he countered, with another swallow from his glass.

Conversation centred around the afternoon's races, he and Dean running through the standouts and disappointments while Faye looked bored, until Dean glanced at his watch and drained the last of his ale. "I'm beat, kids. You ready to go, Faye?"

Well that was good. Dean didn't seem to be a big drinker either.

"Already?" Faye flipped her dark hair off her shoulder and locked on Nate. "Maybe if I offer to buy Mr. Miller another drink, he'll agree to give me a ride home."

He gulped the mouthful he'd just taken, Faye's perfect eyebrows arching at his hesitation. She'd made it awkward for him to refuse. "Sure. But just water for me."

"So responsible." She plucked out the celery stalk and crunched off the bottom.

Dean left some bills on the table, apparently unfazed by his sister's forwardness. "We'll see how the colt is in the next few days and talk about the Victoria again."

Nate nodded. "Thanks Dean."

Faye used her smile to summon their server. "Another Caesar for me. And a glass of water for my driver." She tipped her chin towards Nate, and picked up the bills. "My big brother. Guess he's paying for that drink."

"He's a good guy."

"Yes, he is. He's taken care of me for a long time."

"I kind of doubt you need much taking care of anymore."

Her eyes lingered on him until the arrival of the drinks interrupted her perusal. Nate took a deep breath, and almost wished he'd opted for another beer.

"So what's your story?" Faye picked up the fresh Caesar and pushed the celery stalk out of the way, closing her lips over the peppery rim.

"My life isn't that interesting."

"You didn't leave Calgary because you were running from the law or got some girl in trouble?"

"Nothing that exciting, trust me. Dean's a bit older than you, isn't he?"

Her eyes flashed suspiciously as she registered the subject change. "Eight years. There were only three between my brother Shawn and I, so we were a lot closer." She fingered the coaster under her drink. "I didn't really get to know Dean till he came back to help settle things after the accident. He gave up finishing his masters to take over training my dad's horses. I was only fifteen."

"That must've been tough."

"It's hard to believe it's already been ten years." She shrugged. "Life does go on."

"But no boyfriend?" Her boldness was catching.

"Not currently. I haven't found anyone who holds my interest." She smiled coyly. "What about you? How have you managed to keep your nose clean all this time? You're Woodbine's mystery man."

"Please." He rolled his eyes, then frowned. "There was someone back home. It didn't work out."

"Oh, he's *wounded*. I like that in a man. Sounds like it's time to get over it." She placed her elbows on the table and rested her chin on the backs of long, intertwined fingers. "Don't worry, I don't need your relationship CV. I certainly don't intend to give you mine."

Well. No need to wonder what was on Faye's mind. He sucked in some water and checked the time. "We should get going. Some of us have to be up at four in the morning. You can finish your cross-examination in the car."

She didn't look nearly as disappointed by that suggestion as she had the similar one from her brother, promptly shouldering into her cardigan. Her dark lashes swept at him sideways as they walked to the escalator.

Faye watched him carefully after he opened the Mustang's passenger door and made sure she was settled before walking around and slipping behind the wheel. He turned the key in the ignition. "Don't look at me like that. What can I say, my mother taught me right."

One thing was certain, there would be some new rumours flying in the morning. He'd bet the moment they'd left Champions the first text had been fired off.

"Emilie says you're musically inclined as well," Faye resumed, shifting in her seat so she was angled towards him.

"Not your average bug boy, are you?"

"What all has Emilie told you?"

"Everything she knows. Which isn't nearly enough."

She obviously liked this game, and played it effectively. By the time they reached the Taylor's Northwest Stud—down the road and on the opposite side from Triple Stripe—he felt as if he'd been vetted and deemed worthy of acquisition.

A short lane led to an old Victorian red brick farmhouse, and Nate pulled in beside the two vehicles already there. Faye made no attempt to let herself out.

"You're going to make me do this, aren't you?" he said, one hand resting on the wheel.

"I am." She smiled at him unrelentingly. "You've given me expectations."

He started to sweat as he walked around the car. *No one's watching you now, Miller.* Assumptions have already been made. *So?* Maybe she was right. *Time to get over it.* It was a short walk to the back door, and she turned to face him.

"Thanks for the ride home."

Before he could reply, she laced her fingers behind his neck, drawing him closer. It was easy to yield, their lips meeting as he caught the subtle scent of her perfume; his hands slipping around the curve of her waist, the way the warmth of her moulded to him messing with his self-control.

She broke off slowly, her mouth still close, dark eyes luring under those lashes.

"Well?" she murmured, tracing fingers from his neck to his chest. "Perhaps we should continue this discussion inside."

Cindy was having babies. Liv just made him crazy. Faye had been clocking him since the day they'd met, and might as well have been holding up a sign in bold letters: *REBOUND GIRL HERE.* Would it be such a bad thing, to go for that? But he wavered, his heart pounding against her palm.

"I'd better get home. That four AM thing."

Her head tilted slightly, then she kissed him again, soft but brief, and backed out of his hold with a meandering smile. "Some other time, maybe."

He'd sleep on that. In his own bed.

"Monsters!"

Nate laughed as Chique leapt into a canter, skittering to the side when a car drove past them beyond the tall chain link fence to the left. He eased her back to a jog, reaching forward to stroke her neck with one hand.

Taking a two-year old to The Field without company wasn't necessarily sensible, but it got her out before the main track opened, one horse taken care of before his day took off at its usual torrid pace.

Chique was used to galloping in the dark. They'd done it at the farm until she shipped in—early enough none of the staff were working so he'd have been SOL if they'd parted company—but at least the training track at Triple Stripe had proper rails. There were none out here. Every day he expected her to take a shortcut through the infield, deposit him in a heap, and head home without him.

Next time around he let her pick up a slow gallop, still travelling the wrong way. Chique's ears swept forward when headlights came towards them, her head flying up with a snort that bounced off the trees.

"Goblins!" He chased her forward until the car went past. "We do this every single day, Cheeky." But every day was a new day, when you were an opinionated two-year-old filly.

They went a couple more times around, finishing with a jog past the gap. He turned her in. Both of them exhaled. *Lived to tell.* Except sometimes the walk home was the scariest part.

So far the sun was just making the clouds pretty colours over the city to the east. Chique did her fire-breathing dragon impersonation when the silhouette of a horse grazing on the lawn outside one of the barns lifted its head. The horse whinnied. Chique whinnied back. Nate smiled. This was the best part of his morning.

"One of these times you're just not gonna come back," Jo said, ready for him when he steered Chique into her stall.

"It's all part of the adventure."

Safely back on the ground, he ducked out of the stall and set the saddle in front of Jay, pulling out the saddle cloth and girth cover to add to the laundry and leaving Michel to tack up the colt. Gallop Jay at six, then off to Barn Twenty-five to work one. And so on, all morning long.

Emilie's head popped up from pulling on her boots as he walked in the tack room.

"Hey Nate." Oh, that grin. She knew.

"Hey Em. What's up?" Might as well at least try to feign innocence.

"You'll never believe what I heard in the kitchen this morning. Apparently you were seen leaving Champions with Faye Taylor last night."

Yep. He'd called that right.

Emilie straightened and leaned back against the cupboards, crossing her arms. "So?"

"So nothing."

"Ha! Why do I not believe that?"

"Okay. Maybe I drove her home after Dean left early."

"And?"

"Maybe she kissed me, and I didn't see any reason to fight her off. But that's all."

"Really."

"Come on, Em, I've been good to the point of monkish since I came out here."

"Fools rush in, Nate."

"Yeah, yeah. I didn't get her number or anything."

"What does that mean?"

"That I need her number? I could just show up and throw stones at her window, but..."

Emilie pressed her lips into a hard line. "Are you sure about this? She has a pattern."

"That's cute, you looking out for me. I'm making an informed decision. I understand Faye doesn't like to get attached. Sounds perfect."

Emilie's frown poked at his conscience. "I didn't think you were like that."

"You don't know everything about me, Em."

She scowled as she picked up her phone, and seconds later he heard his chime with Faye's contact info.

"Promise not to hold you responsible." He tapped her on the shoulder and went to get on Jay.

CHAPTER TWENTY-EIGHT

July

The hardest part of coming back to New York was returning to Saratoga. Her demons lurked here, in the eaves of the old barns and seats of the fabled grandstand. The association was strong—a dark time she never wanted to go back to—so it made Claire's win in the Bowling Green Handicap that much sweeter.

Two for two.

Nate's text had a thumbs-up tacked on the end; the congratulatory message less personal, his influence on the result more remote. She was the one carrying out Claire's unconventional training regime now, day in day out. He was busy with his own career, and his shiny new relationship.

Hot bug riders were Faye's go-to—but for some reason Liv had thought Nate would be immune. Which was silly, because Faye was beautiful, and confident, and experienced. And he was just a man, after all. It was a relief, really. It let her off the hook. She was happy for them. Really.

Never mind. She had Claire—Claire, back on track.

* * *

Faye's expression said what she didn't verbalize. *A picnic? Are you serious?* Yet she followed him along the path, negotiating rocks and glancing up at the overhanging trees.

"I must trust you," she said wryly.

"What, you think I'm going to take you captive?"

"Obviously not. You are quite captivating, however."

He glanced over his shoulder, catching the mischievous look in her eyes.

He slid the backpack to the ground when they reached the clearing, and pulled out a blanket. Faye helped him spread it, then sunk to her knees—digging into the bag for the bottle of wine, nodding as she appraised the label.

"Plastic cups, though?"

"The bottle's already too much glass out here."

"Were you a boy scout too?"

He smirked, sitting next to her to pour the wine, and she leaned in, kissing him.

"Is this where you propose? Because I'm starting to think that's what it's going to take to get you in bed."

Of course she didn't mean to be cruel, but it was as if her nails had dug into his old wound, making it bleed all over again. He stared at his chest, expecting to see it oozing through his shirt.

Faye frowned, her brow wrinkling. "I'm sorry, I was kidding."

He set his wine down, biting his lip and focusing on the clouds drifting overhead. "Listen, Faye...this really isn't how I thought this would go, either. It turns out I'm not that guy. That girl back home...she really did a number on my head. I don't want to make that your problem." He shifted his gaze back to her. "I get you didn't sign up for this, so I won't take it personally if you want to move on."

Instead of the sassy comeback he expected, her head tilted to the side, eyes mellowing. She rested a hand over his heart, her lips gently touching his. "This is unfamiliar territory for me. I've never had a guy not be up for sex, let alone take me on a...picnic."

"I didn't say I wasn't up for it." He was still fixed on the curve of those lips, and dragged his eyes back to hers. "But sex is easy, Faye. It's the other stuff that's hard. If we can halfway figure that out, it'll be the icing on the cake, right?"

"There might have to be real cake to get me through this, but okay."

There she was, the Faye he was used to, but the hand still on his heart somehow slowed the bleeding.

CHAPTER TWENTY-NINE

September

Chique danced, outfitted in a bright white shadow roll and matching polo bandages. Jo had a death-grip on the shank, and despite Sue on the other side, both women were red-faced as the filly dragged them into the saddling enclosure. When Jo stopped in front of the identifier and lifted Chique's upper lip —exposing the new tattoo, imprinted just last week—the filly tossed her head and swung her hindquarters sideways, her compact body vibrating.

"Put them in, please!"

The paddock judge's voice rang out, and Liv ducked through the gap in the middle of the saddling stalls. She slipped into the number one slot, rubbing sweaty palms on her black slacks as the two-year-old fillies gradually filed into their assigned spots.

Jo spun Chique to face out, Chique gawking at her surroundings. It was as if she could tell the people were studying her, glancing at their programs and *Forms* and trying to figure out where she fit in this group of maidens.

"How is she?" Liv asked as she crouched opposite Sue, the

two of them quickly unwrapping the polos.

"How does she look?" Jo snapped, holding the filly steady and monitoring all four feet. "You'd think we'd never schooled her over here. Watch yourself!"

Liv skipped out of the way as Chique kicked, skittering over the rubber bricks. "If she hadn't given you a hard time, I'd be wondering what was wrong with her."

"Everybody still alive?" Roger slipped into the stall and ran a hand over the network of exposed veins on Chique's neck.

Chique was rigid from her poll to the tip of her tailbone, Liv holding her breath as Roger and the valet worked. Before Roger managed to buckle the elastic girth to the billet of the saddle, the filly erupted, scattering the tack in a heap behind her and launching away from it, taking Jo with her.

"I'm going a turn!" Jo growled over her shoulder.

It seemed, more accurately, Chique was taking her a turn.

"We'll do her on the walk," Roger said when she came back around, handing his jacket to Liv.

Sue quaked next to her, face pale. "Okay! Breathing! You?"

Liv dipped her chin with a jerk and peeled herself off the wall of the stall, trying to catch a glimpse of Roger and the valet putting on the tack as Jo led the filly around. Roger waved away his jacket when Liv offered it back as he rejoined her, pulling the collar of his shirt from his flushed neck.

Someone grabbed her elbow, and she dragged her gaze from the filly. Nate, oblivious to the shenanigans.

He reached across and shook Roger's hand, then turned to Liv. "Are you allowed to be here? How's our girl handling everything?"

"She's sharp," Roger answered flatly.

Sue started to laugh, a little shrilly, and Nate quirked an eyebrow. "What did she do?"

"A very impressive kite demonstration?" Sue quipped.

"It was ridiculously athletic," Liv agreed.

"So, nothing I haven't seen before?"

"Hold up, Jo." Roger motioned her into the stall when she came back around. "Let's get the halter off and put her blinkers on."

Liv stepped around the corner to be safe, Nate following her lead.

"Any instructions?" he asked.

"Ask the trainer."

"Don't let her run off with you." Roger's voice reached them from the other side of the wall, and Liv didn't think he was kidding.

"*Bonne chance,* Miller," she said as the paddock judge called for riders up. "Don't fall off."

She caught the grin he flashed as he hopped up from Roger's legup, Chique jigging away. They disappeared behind the outrider, her sense of helplessness growing the further they were away.

Emilie—who had stayed outside of the saddling enclosure —caught up with her as she weaved through the crowd to the escalator, Roger trailing with less urgency. The horses were on the track by the time they reached the seats.

Liv fumbled for her binoculars. "Is he still on?"

Nate looked perfectly relaxed, standing in the irons as they jogged to the front of the grandstand for the post parade. He chatted to their new exercise girl, Nicole, who had also taken on afternoon pony duties with Paz. Chique's neck glistened, lather forming between her hind legs, but she was moving forward, not sideways, or backwards, or up. That was a win in itself.

Liv didn't even hear the announcer as he rattled off the names and connections of the six fillies, the lack of control eating at her, nausea rising in the pit of her stomach. Chique jumped into the warmup—bumping Paz, nose flipping up— but she gradually settled into a rhythm, galloping around the clubhouse turn in stride with the pony.

The view of the gate was obstructed, set down the seven-furlong chute, and Liv dropped her binoculars and focused on the infield screen once the horses disappeared from sight. They were leaving Chique for last, despite her inside post position. *Problem child?* When the assistant starter took the filly from

Nicole—leading her towards the metal barrier, away from the security of Paz—Chique froze, her legs braced. *Yep.*

"Did you forget to gate school her?" Liv muttered, tension gripping the back of her skull.

"She's been there practically every day." Roger gave Liv a long-suffering look.

Two more of the gate crew joined the effort, locking arms around the filly's quarters, and Chique fired out, scattering them, then reared and spun away from the man at her head. Nate stuck like it was an afterthought, calmly steering her around to face the gate again, but the camera shifted away.

"Oh, come on!" Liv stared at the screen, then futilely across to the chute, cursing the massive, inappropriately-placed building that blocked the view. Her eyes flashed back to the screen to see a head-on of the gate as Chique's head finally bobbed in.

"She comes out like a bullet," Roger said.

But the starter wasn't releasing them. "What's the hold up?" Then, "Where'd she go?"

Muffled words she was sure weren't kind came out of Roger's mouth before the intelligible ones. "Nate's off her. He's on the frame."

Blood rushed in Liv's ears, seconds dragging with no way of knowing what was going on before she caught movement. "I see her. I think he's back on."

With a jolt they were off, Chique catapulting from the barrier like she'd been fired from a cannon.

"You weren't kidding," Liv mumbled.

Nate let her fly, and Liv clenched her jaw, knuckles white as she gripped the binoculars. This was not the good experience she'd had in mind. She glanced at the tote board to catch the first quarter fraction and quelled a moan.

"Make it stop, Rog. There's no way she can keep this up."

"Try telling her that," Emilie cracked, and Liv shot a dark glance in her direction before turning back to the spectacle unfolding on the track.

Chique opened up a lead with her little game of catch me if

you can, still showing no sign of letting up. Nate wasn't trying to rate her, but he wasn't working on her either. Chique just kept rolling, and he really didn't have much say in the matter. At the head of the stretch, she had to have five lengths on the others.

"Now we'll see if she's got any stamina to go with that speed," Roger said.

"She should," Emilie interjected. "With the three miles Nate gallops her every day."

"What?" Liv gasped, the binoculars falling as she stared at Emilie.

"I'm kidding. But look. He's riding her now. If you can call it that."

Mid-stretch Nate picked her up, throwing the lines at her— and Chique responded by drifting right, then left, running like she was drunk, so he resorted to pushing with hands only, his body still. She was tiring, and now the other fillies were coming at her. That zippy pace she'd laid down set it up perfectly for the closers.

"C'mon Chique, hang in there. Come on, Miller!" Liv screamed.

Emilie joined in, even Roger, the three of them on their feet hollering at the staggering filly, as if they could help Nate carry her to the wire. Someone was charging up the rail, into all that room Chique had left in her erratic drive.

"Don't fall over, Chique!" Emily dissolved into laughter, and Chique held on by half a length before letting the field eclipse her as they galloped out.

Jo and Sue were already waiting on the turf course when they got down there, mirroring expressions of disbelief.

"Maybe she's going to be worth all the aggravation," Jo said.

"Show's not over yet!" Sue pointed towards the clubhouse turn. Chique balked as Nate pointed her at the gap from the main track onto the grass.

"It's ironic an outrider escorts the stake winners back, but not lost maiden winners, don't you think?"

Emilie made a good point.

Nate finally threaded Chique through, and she travelled in an irregular serpentine towards them: head up, ears fixed forward, questioning every step of the route. Nate dropped his irons for better control, and Jo intercepted to lead them the rest of the way.

The smile Nate turned on Liv as Jo walked them into the winner's circle looked a little unhinged. "I don't even know what to say."

"I didn't think I was going to live through that," Liv said once he was safely back on the ground, Jo and Sue leading Chique away.

"What about me?" Nate chortled. "I didn't dare get in her way."

"I kind of got that."

"If the race was any longer, they would have caught her," Roger said.

"It's her first start." Nate was ever Chique's champion. "She's got a lot to learn."

He weighed in, and Liv walked with him down the stairs and through the tunnel under the grandstand.

"What happened in the gate?" Though it crossed her mind maybe she didn't want to know.

"She laid down! I thought she was going to crawl out of there. The bridle broke when they were trying to hold her, then she popped up and stood like nothing happened, so they just put another bridle on. I never knew they kept one back there, did you?"

Liv rubbed her forehead, trying to smooth out the wrinkles. "Never had reason to know. Why didn't you have her scratched?"

"She wasn't even fazed. All we need is for her to think she can get away with that."

"Still a little risky, don't you think?"

They came out the door by the paddock, Nate waving at someone. "See you back at the barn."

Liv turned, and the sight of Faye next to Emilie made her

pause. She put on a smile, strolling over and giving Faye a squeeze.

"Congratulations! That was...ah..." Faye gave up. "How are you?"

"More importantly, how are you? Three months with the same guy?" Liv gave her an exaggerated eyebrow arch. If she stayed detached, she could joke about it. "You coming with us? You know he'll be going back to the barn when he's done."

"When are you heading back to New York?"

"Tonight—but we're coming back soon. Me and Claire."

Claire stepped off the van and stopped, Liv holding the shank loosely while the tall filly stood, statuesque, taking in the Woodbine backstretch. Chique's whinny reverberated from the first stall, head bobbing, forelock flying. She disappeared, squealing, the solid thud of aluminum shoes on rubber-matted wall making Nate wince.

"Easy, filly."

He stepped back next to the door as Liv led Claire by, the leggy filly outfitted in bell boots and white flannel shipping bandages, the top of her hindquarters decorated with fancy red and blue kinesiology tape. Chique charged the webbing and Nate ducked.

"She all right?" Liv called.

"*Reunited and it feels so good...*" he crooned, giving Chique a wary eye before he looked in on Liv and Claire. "She's a little excited."

Liv crouched in the straw, taking off the bandages, Claire tied to the back wall. "Hang that haynet for me, would you?"

He picked up the rope net, shaken and stuffed into a perfect nest of timothy and alfalfa, and hauled it over. Chique reached for it as if Claire's was better than her own as he secured it and gave it a flip.

Liv was removing the last bandage when he peered in again. "Good to have you back."

She looked at him sideways. "Let's see if you feel that way when I start stealing wins from you."

He scooped up the bandages she'd left on the mat and shook them out, draping them over the rail while Liv turned Claire loose. Claire followed her to the door, diving into her hay as Liv snapped the webbing in place.

"So how is our little freak show?" she asked.

Nate scowled and reached up to cover Chique's ears, drawing her head into his torso. "Don't listen to her, Cheeky." The filly grabbed the edge of his polo shirt, and he extracted it from her mouth.

Liv watched, arms crossed. "Rog nominated her for the Mazarine Stakes. Ambitious maybe?"

"If she runs like she did first time out, nothing can touch her."

"Don't hold back on the confidence, Miller. It's two turns, a stake race, against open company. If she runs like she did first time out, she'll get beat."

"She'll get a lot out of that first race."

"You mean more than just a sense of entitlement?"

"Come on, Liv, a little faith." He cradled Chique's head again until she latched on to the end of his belt and started tugging.

She was right, of course. A furlong and a half farther, a Grade Three stake with no protection for being Ontario-sired, or Canadian-bred. Liv always had to be so damned practical. "Rog promises she'll be better behaved, so she should have some energy left for the extra distance."

"Like maybe you'll be able to rate her a little?"

"It could happen." He grinned. "The gate crew is sick of seeing us, so she might even load this time."

Liv turned to Claire's bold-blazed face, and Claire shifted her focus from the haynet, ears swiveling forward and head tilting as she stretched out her neck. Liv pulled a peppermint from her pocket, and it disappeared from her palm.

"The E.P. Taylor Stakes for this girl." She drew the hairs of Claire's black forelock together, her lips set in a line. "Time to move up."

"Not tempted to go for the International? Turf plus distance,

Claire's favourite thing." The Canadian International was a quarter mile longer—but it wasn't restricted to fillies and mares like the E.P. Taylor. Both races were often stepping-stones to the Breeders' Cup, but he wasn't bringing that up. Yet.

"Tempted, yes. But even the E.P. Taylor will be a tough race for her, after the company she's been keeping."

"The company she's been toying with, you mean."

Liv dropped her hands and stuffed them into the pockets of her jeans. Claire kept one white-rimmed eye on her, in case another mint appeared.

"I really wasn't sure we'd get her back. But your little one-rat study worked, Miller." She met his eyes. "Honestly, a year ago?" She shook her head slightly, and fell silent, her gaze turning back to Claire.

"Well, you know what they say about time…"

He wasn't sure he'd meant it to be deep, but it was out there now. Her expression suggested the significance wasn't lost on her.

"Thank you."

It wasn't a sarcastic comment to deflect his sentiment like he might have expected. He tried to laugh it off anyway. "For what?"

"For pushing, when everyone else backed off. Which is exactly what I wanted, of course—for everyone to just leave me alone. But you didn't. I may have considered it insensitive at times. But someone needed to do it. So thank you."

The word dumbstruck was meant for moments like these, his mouth falling open for words he couldn't find.

"Life goes on," she said, eyes still steadily holding his.

"It certainly does."

Not that he could ever get a read on Liv—most times it was like there was so much conflict bouncing around in her brain, it was no wonder wires got crossed—but he would have put money on that being about Faye, and the last time he'd been alone with Liv, on a beach in Florida.

CHAPTER THIRTY

October

The second start of a young horse's life usually went one of two ways: either they were better behaved, because they'd adapted to the routine, or the exact opposite, because of the anticipation.

"She is being better so far." Liv watched Jo circle Chique beneath the huge old willow in Woodbine's walking ring.

"She thinks she's got it all figured out." Nate smirked, his arms crossed.

"Let's hope she's right."

"Oh, I don't know. Chique thinking she's in charge is a dangerous thing."

Liv touched his arm as the paddock judge gave the call. "*Bonne* chance, Miller. Come home safe."

She stayed next to Emilie as Roger tossed Nate up, Chique dancing along with calm focus. A little calcium, a little ACTH —both legal pre-race treatments that had a settling effect— *better living through chemistry.*

"There's Faye," Emilie said, following Liv through the crowd. "Faye! Come watch the race with us."

Liv had been too intent on getting upstairs to notice. She managed to slow down enough to give Faye a quick hug. "You'd better keep up."

"I don't know if I can deal with the tension."

Emilie grabbed Faye's arm and steered her forward. "If we don't keep moving, my sister will self-destruct."

They rode the elevator to the fifth floor, and Liv went straight outside to stand next to Roger. The view was panoramic, the sky so clear she could see downtown Toronto, but she focused her binoculars on Chique and Nate as they went through the post parade. Chique was perfectly composed.

Liv glanced at Roger. "She's actually behaving like a grown-up."

"You're welcome," he responded.

They broke into their warm-ups, Chique galloping next to Paz the wrong way around the turn. "I hope you didn't give her too much."

Roger peered at her sideways with that long-suffering look she'd accepted as part of every discussion about Chique.

Emile and Faye rushed out and joined them with the tote board reading zero minutes to post, and Liv felt Faye's fingers wrap tightly around her arm as she kept the binoculars locked on the gate, backed into place at the sixteenth pole. The schooling paid off—the crew still left Chique till last, but she filed in quietly, and stood until the latch was sprung. She popped out perfectly, with none of the frenzy from three weeks ago. She even let Nate take her back, running mid-pack on the outside as the field raced into the clubhouse turn.

"You sure that's the same filly?" Emilie quipped. "Look at her, being all professional."

Chique maintained her position, through the backstretch, and past the half-mile pole. Liv glanced at the time, waiting for Nate to set her loose. Turning for home, she saw him pick her up, imagined him chirping to her...but Chique's stride didn't change. A filly flew by them on the outside, but Chique didn't take up the challenge. Finally he hit her, once—then when she

Linda Shantz

didn't react adversely, he smacked her a second, then a third time. But Chique showed no interest in going on no matter what Nate did to rouse her. The pace-setters faded behind her, but Liv didn't try to count the lengths Chique finished behind the winner, watching her gallop out like a pony.

"I hope she's okay," Faye said carefully, like she was afraid things were about to blow up.

Liv glanced at Roger. His face was blank. "I'll go talk to Nate," he said.

Liv was right on his heels. She frowned at Faye and Emilie.

"We'll catch up," Emilie said.

Chique was on her way back to the barn next to Jo when they made it down to the apron, Nate walking across the turf. He stopped in front of them, threw his hands up, and flopped them back to his sides.

"Do you think she bled?" Liv asked.

"I guess it's possible." He looked Liv in the eye. "I'll talk to you back at the barn."

Liv turned to Roger. "You'll scope her, right?"

Roger nodded, and took out his phone, calling the vet as he walked away.

Emilie inched up, Faye beside her. "What did Nate say?"

"Not much. You want to come back with us, Faye, or are you waiting for him here?"

"I'll come."

There was no flare to Chique's nostrils as she toured the shed back at the barn, walking with a casual sway, stopping the hotwalker to gaze out the end of the barn before carrying on. The vet pulled up, and Roger waved the hotwalker into the stall.

The vet handed Liv the twitch, and Chique did her best to evade her fingers as she grasped the filly's upper lip and twisted the rope snug. She passed the handle to the hotwalker and stepped out of the way. Chique shoved her head sideways, knocking the hotwalker off balance, but he held tight. She huffed, dropping her head in resignation. The filly's eyes shifted as if she thought they were the only things safe to

196

move in her current state of restraint, the vet slowly guiding the scope through one nostril. She inched it along the filly's airway, then offered the eyepiece for Liv to see.

Removing the tube carefully, the vet nodded at the hotwalker to release the twitch. "Not a speck," she said. "She's got a beautiful throat. Sorry?"

"Take her out for some grass, Marc," Jo said as Roger followed the vet to her SUV.

Liv wandered out to the picnic table where Emile and Faye waited, both of them watching her expectantly. She sat next to Emilie and shook her head. "No excuses."

"Don't you just love horses?" Emilie said.

Chique dragged the hotwalker over the lawn like a dog taking a kid for a walk as she searched for the best spot, settling on a patch of dirt. When Nate's Mustang pulled up, her head popped up, dark eyes drawing him like a magnet.

Faye rested her chin on the heel of her hand and drummed her fingers against the wooden table, and Emilie laughed. Liv swung her legs away from the table.

"I'll spare you the pain of having to listen to us, Faye. You can have him in a minute." She patted Faye lightly on the shoulder, and met Nate in front of Chique.

Chique gobbled up a peppermint, then smeared her muddy lips against the arm of Nate's suit jacket. "Good thing I love her more than this suit, isn't it?" He took a step away, and Chique went back to licking her patch of dirt. "You scoped her, didn't you?"

Liv nodded. "If we'd been betting, you would have won."

He smirked. "Now what?"

"She's your project, Miller. You figure it out."

His eyes levelled on her. "You want to know what I really think?"

She choked back a laugh. "Of course."

"I think the pre-race took away her crazy. She needs her crazy. We just have to find a way to work with it."

Liv sighed, glancing at Chique, who'd finally settled on some grass. "As ridiculous as that sounds...I think you're probably right."

She looked back to him. "So what are you going to do?"

He gave her a twisty grin. "Leave it with me."

"Can the four of us maybe go somewhere, so at least Em and I can eat?" Faye called, interrupting.

Liv walked more slowly as Nate strode over, sitting next to Faye. His arm went easily around her shoulders as he turned her face to his and kissed her.

"Come on, Faye, you know better than that. We're not going anywhere till the filly's back in her stall and done up."

Faye rolled her eyes, but her lips melted into a smile. "Here I thought Roger paid people for that. Maybe Em and I should go, and you two can join us when you've got the little princess all tucked in."

Emilie reached over from the other side of the picnic table and patted the back of Faye's hand. "Better get used to being second to a horse, sweetie."

Nate plunked himself next to Liv, putting his feet up and stretching with his hands locked behind his neck. Though he was pretty modest most of the time, he did, on occasion, act as if he owned the place. Which wasn't entirely inaccurate.

"It's beautiful out there today, isn't it?"

"Enjoy it while it lasts," Liv responded, refocusing on the novel in her lap.

"You're such a pessimist."

"I prefer to see myself as a realist."

"Oh yeah?"

"Yeah. And you will too, when the cold and snow settles in for the last part of the meet."

He laughed, his current expression making it obvious those days were far from his mind. "You could stay and make it interesting."

"No thanks. I'd hate to take any more wins away from you." Not that she was putting any kind of a dent in his hot bug rider lead. "The girls and I will be heading to Florida end of November, as planned."

"Rub it in."

"If you keep winning races at the rate you're going, you'll be in the running for the Eclipse Award for top apprentice. That would be a big deal."

He sobered, sitting up and dropping his arms to his thighs. "It would. It's only October, though. It could all fall apart any day now."

Liv tipped the book down. "Who's the pessimist now?"

"Realist, you mean." The grin came back.

Would she trade places with him, for the kind of success that had eluded her that first year? It wasn't as easy as it looked. Part of it was luck; most of it was hard work. Nate just happened to have a magic balance of both.

"Speaking of reality..." Liv placed her bookmark in the pages, closing the paperback. "I'm assuming Dean is planning to run Touch and Go in the Coronation."

"Last I heard."

"Roger's nominating Chique."

He straightened. "Why would he do that?"

"Just keeping Chique's options open."

"Isn't the Princess Elizabeth more appropriate?"

"Or maybe a non-winners of two?"

"Really. Well, it's nice he thinks that much of her."

"Or whatever your plan is to deal with the crazy." The corners of her lips drifted up, then settled back into a line. "Unless you choose to ride Touch and Go."

He met her eyes, shifting uncomfortably. "Is this where you step in and ride Chique?"

"I will, if that's what you decide. But you have to pick."

His gaze was unwavering. "I made you a promise last year."

It was more than his word; it was the kind of commitment he joked about, when Liv had no doubt he was utterly serious. Loyalty that touched her in a way she still couldn't let herself feel, stirring an attraction she wouldn't allow.

Dave Johnson sauntered out dressed in the Triple Stripe silks, a curious smirk on his face, like he knew he was walking in on something.

"Excursion has a good shot, Dave." Liv commented pleasantly, forcing herself to switch off. The Triple Stripe colt was one of the favourites for the next race, an undercard stake.

"Yeah, I think he does." Johnson turned to Nate. "Quiet day today, Miller?"

Nate looked up, and Liv could tell he really wanted to snap back at that dig.

"Yeah, Dave," he said. "Pretty quiet. Good luck. The colt's training great."

Liv suppressed a smile. *Very good, Miller. Very controlled.*

She could see him simmering, pondering the reality behind Johnson's taunt. It was Canadian International Day, second only to the Plate in hype at Woodbine. Riders had flown in from France, England, California and New York; it was easy to feel insignificant in a place he ruled the rest of the time.

Claire made up for any insignificance she might feel herself. When it was time for her to head to the walking ring for the E.P. Taylor, she tucked her whip under her arm, leaving her nerves behind.

The fitness and power Claire radiated bolstered her confidence. Claire was impeccably turned out, black mane falling in a neat line over her almost-metallic bay coat, a perfect quarter marker pattern accentuating her hindquarters. Once Liv was up, she concentrated on each step; heard each footfall on the rubberized walkway until they met the pony at the tunnel and headed to the track. Claire's extensive warm up routine wouldn't look so out of place amid the European contenders.

The gate was positioned out of sight of the grandstand. Claire broke sharply, but Liv convinced her to settle and drop back, ready for the sharp left-hand turn ahead. From there it was a long straightaway, the whole field travelling like a cohesive unit, the drumming of their hooves and rhythm of their breathing filling her ears. She imagined this was what it must be like on the gallops overseas, except for the layers of white rails separating three different track surfaces here, the stable area to the right, and the jet overhead, taking off from the International airport next door. Claire loved it too, loping along with her ears flopping like she could do it all day.

The next turn was huge and sweeping and carried them downhill, momentum building with it. The action started to unfold, Claire's ears sweeping forward, then swiveling back, waiting for her cue. With the final turn still seeming forever away from the finish, Liv remained motionless, weighing the distance remaining against the stored energy beneath her. Then she pulled Claire off the rail and sent her on.

Claire joined the charge, four-wide, ears laced as she flattened into an all-out drive. Liv pushed with each extension of the filly's neck, the spring of the turf sending power back up Claire's limbs. She reached back with her whip, one, two, three, then pumped again with her arms as they hurtled to the wire in a blanket of horses. The stewards would need a photo to separate them.

She pulled Claire up, scanning for the outrider's red coat, but he picked up the dark bay favourite from France. Liv reached forward and stroked Claire's neck, still thrilled. These were some of the toughest turf distaffers in the world.

Nate was waiting to go out for the next race when she got back to the room.

"So freaking close. The way she galloped out ... you should have gone in the International. She wanted that extra quarter-mile."

"Maybe." She gave him a wistful smile.

"Gotta go. Some of us have to stick around and ride the in-between races." He tapped her arm as he turned away.

Liv showered and changed, then stole past the crowd waiting for the International horses to arrive. She stopped at a monitor to watch the ninth race—another winner for Nate. Of course he wanted to ride in these big races, but he was doing a good job of paying his dues in the meantime. As the horses galloped out on the screen, she ducked away against the flow of traffic.

It was quiet back at the barn, Claire already cooled out and tearing at the grass on the lawn with the hotwalker. The filly lifted her head in aloof acknowledgement before returning to her mowing.

"I'm going to watch the International from the bleachers, Jo," she called, and walked across the road towards the bank.

"Wait up!"

Faye flagged her down, climbing out of her car and skittering across the road in her heels. She followed Liv up the steps.

The bleachers overlooked the lengthy backstretch of the turf course, the faint hum of the buzzing crowd drifting across the infield. Faye kept silent, and Liv could hear the track announcer giving the play-by-play as the starters entered the gate. *They're locked up...*but not for long. The horses were off before the sound of the starter's bell reached them.

It wasn't the best vantage point until the field entered that long straightaway and came thundering past, forty hooves thrumming along the green. They swept by and around the turn, rolling down the incline to the homestretch. The finish was obscured, the announcer's call drowned out by the roar of the crowd, the result a mystery.

"Why'd you come here to watch?" Faye asked.

"Probably so I couldn't see the time, compare it to the E.P. Taylor and go through all the coulda-shoulda-wouldas." She'd hear about it either way, eventually. "What are you doing here?"

"I came to see you. We haven't really talked in ages."

"You can't blame it on me this time." Liv looked at her sideways. "You're distracted."

"Guilty."

Faye beamed with genuine happiness Liv had rarely seen, and definitely never relating to a man. It irked her, then irked her more that she was bothered.

"I'm sure you don't want to hear it, but he just doesn't stop being amazing."

Faye was right, she didn't want to hear it. She knew it already. And she had, like some kind of mutant girl, pushed him away. But she rolled her eyes and smirked. "You're making me nauseous."

"Sorry. So not me, is it?" Faye laughed lightly.

Liv eyed her. "It's concerning. Have you considered asking for an MRI?"

That earned her a swat. "You don't mind, right? I warned you, remember."

"Of course I don't mind. As long as you don't distract him from riding Chique." She paused, telling herself it was true.

"It's so weird. He's so old-fashioned, but...it's kind of nice. Not that I won't jump his bones the second I get an opening, but, it's sweet, you know?"

Liv's eyebrows shot up. "You mean you're not—?"

"I know, right? So not me."

That just churned her gut more. How did Faye, who made no secret of her fondness for sex, land, then fall head over heels, for the one remaining guy on earth who didn't single-mindedly want to get a girl in bed?

You had your chance.

She ploughed ahead. "Seriously, Faye, it's a good thing. You never let anyone get to know you. It's about time you found a nice guy, one who's more than a passing amusement. You both deserve to be happy. He's been through a hard time too."

Faye tilted her head. "How do you know about that?"

"It was New Year's Eve, there was wine." She waved her hand through the air. "He didn't give me details."

"Why are you just telling me this now?"

"Because it was nothing." Even if it wasn't. "Nothing happened." Even if something did. It didn't matter anymore.

Faye sighed. "I didn't mean to suggest anything had. You two barely even tolerate each other most of the time. How have things been since you got back?"

Liv rose, glancing at Faye. "We're managing to be civil. We have Chique as our mediator."

CHAPTER THIRTY-ONE

November

Chique flipped her head, froth flying. *That was close.* It'd be embarrassing to blow the chance to prove his theory by getting knocked out in the post parade of the Coronation. Roger was going with it, but Nate was sure he'd only get one shot.

"Let us go."

Nicole gave him a look he was well familiar with—that *you're crazy* one—but she turned the filly loose.

Chique sprang forward, the horses warming up around the turn in her sights. The only thing that stopped her from running off with him was probably the direction—she was unsure enough galloping the wrong way to display a modicum of caution. It was still quicker than anyone else was going, and she caught up with them, passing them and dragging Nate into the backstretch. If she decided to head back to the barn he was sunk. But though her attention narrowed at the wide straight in front of her, she let him pull her up and turn her to face the infield, the grandstand in the distance. She even stood a moment, frozen to a statue as the faint hum from the crowd reached her. Nate stroked her neck, and they shared a deep breath before they set off, back towards the gate waiting for them at the eighth pole.

"That probably put the final nail in the coffin for anyone thinking of betting her, eh?" Nate said when Paz met them, Nicole looping the leather latigo through the bit. Chique snorted and dropped her head, trying to rub it against Paz.

His eyes settled on Touch and Go, disappearing into the metal barrier. Johnson had picked up the mount. No regrets. Even if the colt was the better option on paper, his heart was with his little wild child.

They were the last ones in, the doors slamming shut behind them, and before Chique had time to think about doing anything bad, the starter released them.

Nate almost laughed, because she was caught off guard, breaking at less than her normal mach 10—though it only fed her determination to make the lead. Trying to rate her might have seemed a reasonable choice, but when she'd won, she'd been in front, so he let her go on. Chique threw herself into the plan, her strides coming short and quick as she built up to cruising speed. When they were clear, he let her drop to the rail, and they led the field past the grandstand and into the clubhouse turn.

No one challenged, perhaps lulled into the reasonable assumption that Chique was only a speed horse, even though they weren't going that fast. *Perfect.* Chique wasn't running like it was the zombie apocalypse this time. Maybe that warm up had taken the edge off, though it might come back to bite him. He'd see if the longer morning gallops had done enough to build the stamina she'd need for the extra distance. Along the backstretch, she stayed a length up.

At the head of the stretch, he chirped, and Chique's ears flicked forward as the next gear kicked in. Nate grinned when he felt it. She might be more than a sprinter after all.

They were alone in front, and he resisted the temptation to look back to see if anyone was coming. Finally, he could feel Touch and Go closing ground; isolate the sound of the colt's hoofbeats behind them. Chique didn't need any encouragement to hold the colt at bay, Nate simply cocking his whip and flashing it before going to his hands. They still had a length and a half advantage when they hit the wire, and she had no intention of letting the colt pass her as they galloped out.

He was still laughing when the outrider picked them up. Chique tried to bite the pony, her attempt cut short as the outrider popped her head straight and growled at her.

"Stop that, we may need him one day," Nate said, but the rub on the neck he gave her was all affection.

Touch and Go galloped past, on the way back to be unsaddled. He didn't feel the triumph he thought he would, besting Johnson. He had nothing but respect for that colt, and in a rematch Johnson wouldn't let him get away with another steal. That rematch might not come until the Queen's Plate. *Chickens, Miller. Stop counting them.* It was a long way off.

Liv met them before Jo, lips twisted into not quite a smile, apparently lost for words as she reached up to grasp his hand.

"What did I tell you?" He grinned, squeezing so hard she should have flinched. "Just relax and embrace the crazy."

The sun slipped below the horizon in the west, reminding Liv in just a couple of weeks, they'd be packing up the shed and heading to Florida. Roger had organized a little stake party, as much to commemorate the approaching end of the season as the unlikely event that Chique would win. Liv had declined the sparkling wine, even though the post-race buzz that had kept her warm on the frontside had worn off.

She saw Chique's head pop up, then noticed Nate's Mustang rolling to a halt. The filly watched every step as he approached across the lawn. He offered her peppermints, said a word to the hotwalker, then rubbed her face before heading towards the barn. Chique continued to track him.

He squeezed in through the door, pulling it shut—not that it was a whole lot warmer inside than out—and sidled up to Faye, slipping an arm around her and kissing her quickly. Liv glanced away.

"Where's mine?" he said, eyes running over Faye's and Emilie's drinks, then quirking an eyebrow at Liv's lack.

"Go see Rog," Emilie said.

Nodding, he left them, walking down to the office and coming back with two glasses. He held one out to Liv.

"Oh come on. Drink up. To the big filly! An appropriate coronation, don't you think?"

She met his eyes, and shook her head, still convinced it wasn't safe to consume alcohol when he was around, despite his thing with Faye. She still didn't know what to say about Chique. When the filly was good, she showed so much talent it was scary, but her performance in the Mazarine Stakes still lurked in Liv's mind, feeding her doubts.

"It wouldn't kill you to believe a little," he said.

Liv laughed then—it was impossible not to be just a little bit affected by his conviction.

"So it's true, eh?" His mouth leveled into a line. "They're switching back to dirt at the end of the season."

"I guess there was too much pressure." Nearly all the tracks in North America that had invested in synthetic all-weather surfaces had reverted to dirt.

"What do you think?"

Liv shrugged. "I think it doesn't matter what I think. They're going to do it anyway. We'll find out what she thinks this winter, I guess."

Hopefully her opinion was favourable.

CHAPTER THIRTY-TWO

December

Nate drove up to the farmhouse at Northwest and parked the Mustang, stepping out onto the packed snow. There were about six inches of the stuff on the ground, King Township's rolling hills a bloody winter wonderland, but he didn't mind. For the first time in three years, he was getting Christmas the way Christmas was supposed to be.

Faye met him at the door and he wrapped himself around her. She pressed against him and kissed him, sliding the coat off his shoulders.

The Woodbine meet had passed tolerably, despite several cold and miserable days, but he'd made it worthwhile by beating Johnson in the standings to finish on top. Spending time here at Northwest had gotten him through it. Faye—he'd never expected her to stick with him, to be that understanding. This was more than he thought it would ever be—even without the icing.

She had wine poured, and handed him a glass. The iron wood stove warmed the small kitchen, filled with the incredible smells of a holiday feast that had never felt right in

Florida.

"Merry Christmas," she said, holding his gaze over her glass.

"Merry Christmas." He slipped his arm around her and kissed her again before they sipped. "Where're Dean and Gus?"

"Watering off. They'll be back soon."

She curled her hand into his and led him to the living room. He felt a tiny bit homesick for Calgary as he sat on the couch next to her, taking in the tree, sparkling with lights and tinsel, the fresh scent of spruce and citrus reaching him. It was the first time since he'd left home he'd felt part of something, these past few weeks—something like family—though the thought of family still brought traces of pain.

He set his glass on the coffee table, and dug out the envelope stuffed in the shirt pocket under his sweater. "Here. While we're waiting for Dean."

Faye's eyebrows arched as she took it. "What's this?"

"Your Christmas present."

She ripped it open with her thumb, and unfolded the paper. "A plane ticket? To Fort Lauderdale. At the end of January."

"It's a pretty safe bet I'll be nominated for the Eclipse Award for top apprentice. I thought maybe you could come down. Break up the winter at least a little."

Four months he'd be gone. While he was excited about Chique, and what lay ahead there, the separation would be hard. On him. On the relationship. One that was still in its infancy, thanks to the turtle-slow pace. Faye wouldn't go along with it forever. He'd have to figure out what was next. This winter would be a test.

"That would be incredible."

She leaned into him, pulling him close as she kissed him, and he reached around her and kept her there. He heard the door open, the click of nails over kitchen tile, but Faye didn't stop, so he saw no reason to either—until a wet Golden Retriever nose inserted itself between them.

"Gus the chaperone." He laughed, breaking away and

slapping the Golden's ribcage.

It was all just right—the food, the wine, the crackling fireplace and candlelight, the festive music playing softly in the background, Faye at his side. He almost felt whole. Like this could be his life, if this was who he chose to be.

CHAPTER THIRTY-THREE

January

Paz's strides quickened to match Claire's, and Nate loosened his hold, releasing her. He zeroed in on the mare as she set down to work—the early morning sun hitting her gleaming coat, Liv's slender form poised low and motionless over her withers.

Mopping the sweat from his eyes with the sleeve of his t-shirt, he glanced at the stopwatch clutched in his hand. Claire approached the sixteenth pole of Gulfstream's main track, Liv still unmoving as they flew down the lane.

The siren wailed, and every muscle in his body tensed.

Loose horse.

Paz's head flew up, feet dancing as they both went on high alert. Then he saw it, on the far side of the track, barreling wildly in the wrong direction.

The warning cry that escaped his throat was futile—there was no way Liv could possibly hear—but he couldn't stop it, any more than he could stop the danger coming at her. He spun Paz into action, the old sprinter taking off, flat out.

The wind rushing past his ears didn't mask the deadening

thud—a head-on collision, flesh on flesh; the force of a thousand pounds from each direction crashing, then crumbling into a treacherous heap of thrashing legs. Nate drove with hands and voice, pushing Paz still faster. The stretch seemed endless, like a nightmare where he'd never reach the disaster waiting just beyond the wire.

Paz's hocks dropped as Nate sat back, hind feet leaving a trail in the sandy surface that would have made any of the rodeo horses back in Calgary proud. Nate was out of the saddle and running in a single motion, leaving the pony like he knew how to ground tie; nostrils flared, ribcage heaving.

Both racehorses were on their feet. Claire stood by the rail, left hind held gingerly off the ground. Someone held her bridle, though the mare didn't look as if she intended to move. A murmuring group gathered around Liv's unconscious form.

"The ambulance is on the way."

He barely heard the words, pushing in and dropping to his knees beside her; hesitating. He wanted to take off her helmet and straighten her body, somehow make her crumpled form seem more comfortable. Reaching out, he touched her face lightly with the back of his hand. Her cheek was cool and clammy despite the heat, shock taking over with uncompromising stealth.

"Where the hell are they?" He stilled his fingers enough to find her pulse, rapid but weak, just below her jawline.

The ambulance was parked trackside during training hours so it wasn't long before it arrived, but it felt like hours. Nate answered questions and gave information as best he could while the paramedics worked, but jerked away when the vet arrived. Someone had stripped the saddle from Claire; another man had rescued Paz from where Nate had abandoned the blowing stable pony and walked the gelding in an irregular circle. The vet filled a syringe. Nate felt like he was the only one not doing anything.

Liv was on a backboard now, and the medics carried her to the ambulance. Nate took a step after it as it departed, lights flashing but silent. The emergency horse trailer pulled up, and his head snapped back to Claire. He pushed himself towards her, feeling like he was moving through deep sludge, and took over at the mare's head.

Claire followed him slowly up the low ramp. Her breath blew warm on his arm, eyes distant with sedation, and he placed a hand at the origin of the long white marking on her face as they were closed in, feeling as numb as she looked. He wanted to follow the ambulance, but Liv would never forgive him if he didn't wait to hear the status of her beloved Claire. She might be unconscious, but when she came to—assuming she did—Claire would be the first thing she asked about.

The trailer stopped moving, the doors opened, and the team at the backstretch surgical clinic took over. Now, at least, everything happened quickly, radiographs taken immediately to assess the damage. Nate hung over the surgeon's shoulder, focused on the images.

"It's good news, all things considered." The vet indicated a line, just above the fetlock joint. "Incomplete lateral condylar fracture of the third metatarsal. We'll realign it surgically, do an internal fixation—just screws. We can do it standing up. If everything goes right, she should be okay."

At the hospital, news took longer. He perched on the edge of a chair in the waiting room, alone amid the others there. Scrubs and a lab coat appeared, scanning the room. Nate rose, straightening his shoulders. That had to be the doctor. The man offered his hand; grasped Nate's.

"You the boyfriend?"

Nate laughed abruptly. "Ah, no," though that might have been what he'd led the nurses to believe in order to get this far. "We work together. We came down from the training centre in Indiantown to work a horse at Gulfstream this morning. Her family's in Canada. I'm as close to next of kin you're going to get at the moment."

The doctor waited out his rapid explanation. "She's stable. She's conscious. No head trauma, no internal injuries, no spinal injuries as far as we can tell. She's broken a couple of ribs but her lungs are okay. The worst of it is a fractured left femur. She'll need surgery, but because the femoral artery is involved, she's lost a lot of blood. She'll need a transfusion first."

Nate exhaled. It was a miracle she'd gotten off that easily. "So when will you do the surgery?"

"Once we have her blood back to where it needs to be, which is what the transfusion and fluids will accomplish."

"Can I see her?"

A nod. "Come with me."

The doctor pushed a door open and held it, waiting for him to go through. Nate walked in hesitantly, the door swinging shut behind him.

Her consciousness was relative. He didn't want to disturb her, and stood rooted, observing silently. Fluids hung from the drip feeding into her left hand. Her eyes were closed, her face ashen, and he assumed the medication coursing through her system did more to dull her reactions than to deaden the pain.

She must have sensed someone there, because she turned her head and opened her eyes, so he walked forward to the edge of the bed. He found himself reaching for her hand but stopped himself because of the intravenous needle, lightly touching her elbow instead.

"Hey." He tried to smile.

"Miller," she said, faintly. "What happened? Is Claire okay? I don't remember anything."

His answer came out slowly. "A loose horse ran into you."

"What about Claire?" The crease in her brow deepened, worry building on top of the pain.

He told her, watching her concern recede.

"I guess we should be thankful."

"Absolutely." He'd feared it was so much worse, when she'd been lying there on the racetrack. People died in wrecks like that. "Just so you know, I had to tell them we were married to get in here."

Her face contorted as she feebly tried to lift her free arm towards her torso. "Don't make me laugh, please."

"Oh, shit, Liv, sorry. The ribs, right?"

She was weak, and fatigued, and had to be in agony, but relief rushed to the tips of his limbs and back to his heart.

"What?"

Her tiny smile sent a surge of something he was afraid to identify through him. "It's just really good to see you. You had me pretty scared."

"Sorry about that." The way her eyes crimped threatened to pull them closed, her lids heavy. "Will you stay?"

How could he leave?

The haze of the anesthetic cleared, leaving a monumental headache, aching ribs, and a fierce pain in her left leg, pinning her to the mattress. Liv pulled her eyes from the ceiling, registering a regular hospital room—curtain drawn on her left side, a wall on her right—and Nate dozing in the chair beside the bed. He stirred and sat up, rubbing his eyes.

"How long have you been here?" Her throat was so dry and sore, it came out somewhere between a whisper and a croak.

"I told you I wasn't going anywhere."

"You did? That wasn't real bright, was it Miller?"

His blond hair was mussed and his t-shirt rumpled, a smear of dirt on the sleeve, and beyond the antiseptic hospital smell, she caught the faint scent of leather and horses. She had no right to want him here, but wished she could put into words how much it meant that he'd stayed.

"*Thanks* would do, you know."

Such a simple response seemed wildly inadequate for so many of the things he'd done for her.

The door clicked and Nate looked over, Roger shuffling in next to him. "What did you do, stand in front of a train?"

"Just about." Nate leveled his gaze on her.

She glanced away, the warm blue of his eyes feeding too much emotion, and forced hers to Roger. "How is Claire? Have they done the surgery?"

"Everything went smoothly. She came out of recovery with flying colours. She'll be fine. We're going to have to miss that race though."

The comment was meant to be light-hearted, no doubt, but an empty hollow formed in her gut as the reality struck her. That was it—Claire's career was over. A flicker crossed Nate's face—like he'd noticed, when she thought she'd kept the sadness inside.

"You should probably send Nate home, or you're going to have to gallop the barn yourself tomorrow." More reality. He'd done beyond enough, staying this long.

Roger rested a hand on Nate's shoulder. "You heard what she said. I don't think it's safe to give Chique another day off. She'll tear the place apart."

Nate pushed himself to his feet, touching her arm gently. "I'll see you tomorrow, all right?"

"Thank you." It wasn't enough. It was never enough. But it would have to do.

Roger didn't stay long, leaving her to drift back to sleep. She was plagued by broken visions of a scene she couldn't actually remember —the flashy bay mare's brilliant turn of foot in the lane, the dark form of the colt bearing down on her in the wrong direction, a collision, the clash of tangled legs. Then Claire was gone, Liv couldn't find her, the anguish waking her. In the darkness it became merely physical, and she embraced the pain, reminding herself Claire was fine, injured but recovering, just like her.

It was some sort of sick joke on Jo's part that she left Chique for last, the filly as fresh as Nate was tired by the end of the next morning. Chique was too close to running for any lapses, so he mustered his last bit of strength to hold her, much to the filly's disappointment.

"I'll get one of the hotwalkers to do the tack if you want to get going," Jo offered when he came back.

"Thanks." He slapped the filly on the neck, grateful to be back on the ground unscathed. "You're exhausting me, Cheeky."

He grabbed the keys for the farm truck, and for the second day in a row, made the trek to Fort Lauderdale. Roger was picking up Liv's parents, so someone had to bring Paz back. Of course he was going to stop by to see Liv while he was there. It was just the right thing to do.

He picked up yesterday's work sheet and the *Form* for Wednesday's races when he was at the track. At the hospital, Liv was sitting up, the bed cranked as far as it would go. She looked brighter and happier to see him than he'd expected. He presented the papers and dropped into the same chair he'd fallen asleep in last evening.

"Claire got the bullet yesterday." He hadn't known himself until he'd picked up the work sheet, the mare's final breeze the fastest of the day for the distance. "Not that you probably want to hear that."

"At least she went out with a flourish," Liv responded quietly. "How is she? You went to see her, right?"

"Yes, I did. She's doing great. I guess they'll keep her there for a while."

"At least until she's able to travel." Liv bit her lip, turning the work sheet face down and smoothing it with her hand, her face clouding. Nate could almost see her pushing through the darkness before she forced a smile and looked back to him. "How was Chique today?"

"No surprises—she hauled my ass around. Took everything I had to hold her."

"Still going to breeze her tomorrow?"

"I'd better. I don't think she's going to put up with me much longer."

"I hope I'm out of here and recovered enough to see her run." Dejection surfaced again as she glanced down at her leg.

"Sure you will be. Might not feel like it today, though."

"You have no idea."

He was sure he didn't, but avoided dwelling on it. "Faye says she wishes she could be here, and made me promise to talk you into FaceTiming her when you feel up to it. And Rog should be here any time with your parents."

Before the words were out of his mouth, there they were, huddling into the room. He pressed his hand to Claude's, then was caught totally off guard when Anne Lachance wrapped him in a tight embrace. She pushed him back, still clutching his shoulders, and mouthed *thank you* before sidling past him to Liv.

Geai might as well have been whispering in his ear, *you're already like family.*

Like a brother, right?

CHAPTER THIRTY-FOUR

January, continued

Nate sat on the other side of the living room, guitar in his lap--playing absently, sometimes singing—undisturbed by her scrutiny. She tucked the blanket around her legs, propped against a series of cushions, book abandoned in her lap.

He'd come to see her faithfully each day in the hospital, an hour and a half away, after galloping in the mornings—which she hadn't expected any more than she'd expected his visits to continue after she'd been released yesterday. Yet here he was.

If his intent was to distract her from the inevitable—the crutches lying on the floor beside her which would be her primary mode of transport for at least two months, and the orthopaedic surgeon's instructions to keep off the back of a horse for longer than that—then his mission was futile. She had enough time left to herself to dwell on it, lying awake at night when the discomfort still kept her from sleeping. The medication they'd sent her home with, when she actually took it, only did so much. But he was easy company, and the fact that she'd become so comfortable with him was the very thing that troubled her.

"You're very talented."

He glanced at her, but kept playing. "Thanks. Just another one of those things I've been blessed with that it's hard to make a go of."

The songs sounded vaguely familiar, and he played the notes like old friends, telling stories hardly unique in their tales of love that didn't work out, and freedom that remained elusive. The words obviously held meaning, like he was exposing his soul, but he didn't seem the least bit self-conscious—while the sound of his voice made her skin burn, blood roaring through her veins, pulling her back to New Year's Eve a year ago. He'd been down by then this winter, after staying in Ontario to spend Christmas with Faye, but it was no coincidence—on her part, at least—that they weren't in the same place this time around.

She batted those thoughts back where they belonged. "You thought about it?"

"Sure. Another cliché, group of teenage guys forming a band in a garage. Kind of fell apart after my dad kicked me out for quitting school." He stopped and set the guitar flat on the floor beside him. "Can I get you anything? Water?"

"That would be good, thanks."

He came back with two glasses, handing her one before returning to his seat. Liv wrapped her arms around her good leg, vision narrowing.

"What?"

"You quit school to start a band?" More stuff she didn't know about him, and didn't need to know, but he was here, so...

"No, I quit school because my girlfriend turned me down when I proposed, and I kind of fell apart."

"You *what?*"

She hadn't meant to spit out the words with such force, but there they were. He ducked her stare, placing the guitar back in his lap, though his fingers stayed flat and still on the strings.

"New Year's Eve Girl? You'd proposed? What were you thinking?"

He shrugged. "She was older—"

"Like Mrs. Robinson older?"

He shot her a look. "She wanted all that. To get married, have kids. So did I."

"Like normal people."

"We already know where you stand."

She didn't correct him; it was a fair assumption, but she didn't know herself.

He grabbed his glass of water, looking at it like it was inadequate, and set it down again. "It was a bit of a blow to realize she just didn't want it with me. She said she was holding me back, that I needed to leave Calgary if I wanted to be a rider."

"Obviously she was right."

"You suck as a friend."

"Is that what I am?"

"I'm still trying to figure that out."

The way his eyes leveled on her knocked her off stride, like he'd invited a massive mammal with a long trunk into her living room, and it was sucking up all her oxygen. She glanced down, pulling at the edge of the blanket, wishing she could hide underneath it.

"You don't have to be here, you know. I may be an invalid, but I don't require twenty-four hour supervision."

He smirked, recognizing her retreat. "You could be a flight risk. You do have a history."

"I'm not highly mobile at the moment."

"Still wouldn't put it past you."

Not a time she cared to remember...but it did remind her she'd managed to find her way back. And, reluctantly, that he'd been part of it.

"Maybe I just feel sorry for you." He strummed a random chord.

"Bastard," she retorted, one corner of her mouth curving up. "I definitely feel sorry for you,"

"Do you want me to stop coming?"

She should say yes. This terrified her. She'd only ever had

this kind of connection with Geai—mentor, practically a grandfather figure, safe. For it to come wrapped in the guise of a guy her own age—serenading, good-looking, *nice*, and quite possibly just as broken as her—was dangerous. Then there was Faye, and that niggling sense that such feelings, no matter how hard she kept trying to deny them, betrayed her only real friend. *Not a threat*, she told herself. She would never be a threat.

She met his eyes, pursing her lips. "No...but if this is about job security, I don't think you have anything to worry about. If we get Chique to the Plate, you'll be on her." Maybe it wasn't entirely impossible that she'd be sound enough again to ride, but she could never take the filly away from him now.

His fingers clenched the guitar's neck as he stared her down. "That crash scared the hell out of me, Liv. I know this sort of thing happens around us all the time, and it's bound to hit closer to home eventually—and I know one day it'll be my turn. But it has to make you take a step back and think about what's important."

"Do I want to know what that means?" It came out slowly, because she wasn't sure she did.

"I'm here because I want to find out. Because all that shit I left behind in Calgary was about more than me coming east to ride, and being here feels like it's about more than just riding horses."

She reached for her phone, a way out, fumbling. "When does Faye get in?"

His eyes shifted. Was that guilt, or was she just transferring her own?

Her mother burst in the front door, bearing groceries and calling a cheery salutation. Nate sprang over to help, disappearing into the kitchen. When he came back, he put the guitar away in its case.

"I'll see you later. Take it easy."

Then he was gone. Liv blinked. She jammed in her earbuds, blindly hitting play on the phone.

Damn Nate Miller, threatening to topple walls she'd so

carefully constructed. He had some nerve, coming here, saying things.

Not saying things.

Oh, shit...

The lights flashed in his rearview mirror, but he didn't hear the siren until he turned down the music, pulling over to the shoulder of the highway. There was no debate. He'd been flying.

No, I actually don't know how fast I was going.

He mumbled thanks to the officer as he took the ticket, even if he was going to have to start back riding to pay the damn thing. Not that it didn't serve him so, so right.

His eyes stayed on his side mirror as the officer climbed back into the cruiser, and he made himself take a deep lungful of air, pushing it out slowly. How about some calming tunes for the rest of the drive, Miller? Something to ease the frenzy. There—the playlist he'd made up of his mother's favourites; one he called on when he missed her most. Thinking of her would keep him sensible.

Or not. Even those lyrics chased him, called him out. *Living in a house of cards...*

It was getting to him, that was all—the driving back and forth; galloping the barn until Rog got things organized for Nicole to come down and help. He was on overload, his brain conjuring warped things about Liv that weren't there. Faye would set his mind straight.

At the Fort Lauderdale airport travellers emerged from the gate, and he saw her before she spotted him—her hair loose around her shoulders, wearing a flowy skirt and white blouse, a sweater over her arm. She glanced from side to side trying to locate him in the crowd, her face lighting up as her gaze finally reached him.

He enveloped her, his lips searching for reassurance as his mouth closed over hers, breathing her in until she pushed him back.

"It's almost like you missed me."

"You have no idea. I got a ticket driving down." He cracked a grin, letting go and grabbing her bag, and took her hand to lead her through the surrounding crush.

"How's Liv doing?"

His chest tightened. *Stop that.* State the facts. "She seems to be handling it all right so far."

"How are you holding up?"

"My blood pressure has dropped ten points in the last five minutes." He squeezed her hand. That was all that mattered.

At the condo, Anne welcomed Faye with a hug and air kisses before Faye caught sight of Liv, still on the couch like she hadn't moved since he'd left. Faye leaned over and gave her a gentle squeeze, then carefully sat on the end. Nate shoved his hands in his pockets, eyes drifting from one to the other. It wasn't supposed to feel like a mess, but it did.

"I guess you're not coming with us to the Eclipse Awards."

That was relief, not disappointment in the smile Liv gave Faye. "I'm heartbroken."

"The lengths you'll go to, to get out of an awards dinner." Nate tossed a smirk more or less in her direction.

"I'm looking forward to seeing you in a tux." Faye peered at him, then swiveled back to Liv. "I'll send pictures. And you can watch online."

Anne poked her head from the kitchen. "Can I bring you kids anything?"

"I should probably get going, but thanks." Nate sauntered to the couch, pulling Faye to her feet and slipping an arm around her as he kissed her. "I'll give you a heads up in the morning to let you know when I'll pick you up."

Liv glanced up at him before pasting on a fresh smile for Faye. "I'm counting on you both to make sure I get to the races next Saturday."

"You'll be there," Nate said. "What are friends for?"

Congratulations, Miller. Well deserved.

The message from Liv pinged onto the screen. Nate let it fade to black, and started the Mustang.

224

"Which one of your fans is congratulating you now?" Faye's smile teased, bronze statue cradled in her lap.

"Liv." He caught himself before he frowned, and held up the phone to snap a shot of Faye, writing *Thanks* and sending the photo in response. "I'm sure she's sick of you sending her pics of me in a tux."

"I agree. She'll appreciate this shiny trinket more." Faye stroked the trophy.

"Right you are." He powered off the phone.

None of it felt real. Not the perfect girlfriend in his passenger seat, not the fancy award. Not the feelings beyond simple gratitude for the opportunity that had led to it, aroused by that last text. Feelings that had to stop.

"Where are you going?"

"It's a surprise." He headed north, but not via the highway.

Faye's eyebrows peaked when he pulled into the hotel parking lot, and again when he mentioned *reservation* at reception.

"Well. Quite the surprise."

As she walked into the room, she dragged the shimmery shawl from her shoulders, dropping it on the bed. He set the trophy next to the television, eyes following as she kicked off her shoes and wandered to the window to peek out at the dark ocean beyond.

She turned, eyes meandering over him with a look that offered to give him what he'd brought her here for. What he'd made her wait for. "I hope I'm not making assumptions here."

His life had become a heap of self-restraint. Controlling what he ate, controlling what he said, controlling how he felt. This one thing, right now, he could run with.

The cool evening hadn't taken away the lingering flush in her cheeks from the wine—wine he'd skipped, in keeping with the image of straight-laced apprentice for his fifteen-minutes-or-less in the spotlight. He met her halfway, catching her lips as she laced her fingers behind his neck. Her hands roamed, knocking the jacket off his shoulders, tugging his bow tie free, her other palm resting on his pounding chest.

He hooked his hands around her waist and pulled her against him, pushing into her mouth.

"If you're sure about this, get me out of this dress."

Reaching behind her, he found the tiny metal pull of the zipper, and edged it down.

Faye waltzed in the door with fresh bagels Liv could smell from where she was sitting, and disappeared into the kitchen. Resurfacing, she marched over and pulled the cushions out from behind Liv.

"It's a gorgeous day. The sun is shining. I didn't come to Florida to sit inside."

"You already look like you have some colour."

An impish look transformed Faye's face. "So maybe we went to the beach this morning."

"Wasn't it kind of cold?"

"Not when you've just come from Ontario, let me tell you. Come on. You could use some colour yourself."

She helped Liv get settled on the patio, retreated into the house to retrieve the bagels, then stretched out on her own chair.

"Where's Nate?" Liv huddled in her sweatshirt, winding the blanket around the bottom half of her body.

Faye sloughed off her cardigan to bare her shoulders, her legs already exposed mid-thigh below her sundress. "Your mom invited us for dinner. He's going to pick something up so she doesn't have to cook."

"So? How was it?"

Faye's smile was far too self-satisfied as she dropped the sunglasses over her eyes from where they'd been propped on her head. "Oh, you mean the awards dinner. Silly me."

The heat crept up Liv's neck, a knot settling in her stomach. Even she, naïve as she was, could put the pieces together. She'd known they were staying in Fort Lauderdale overnight after the awards, but she could be forgiven for assuming it was a foregone conclusion, couldn't she? It had taken them long enough to get to that point.

So that was it, then. So foolish, to think the conversation with Nate the other day had meant more than it really had.

"You can spare me those details, thanks," she said, grabbing the bagels, and shoving too large a piece into her mouth.

"You're no fun. Sweet twenty-*six*? And never been kissed."

Not never. Not forgotten, as hard as she'd tried. It felt it like it was yesterday. She clamped her lips shut and let Faye believe the flush persisting on her face was because of just that.

Liv felt him before she saw him—it unnerved her as she realized it, glancing over her shoulder, catching him wavering at the door. How long had he been there?

He slid open the screen, fingers gripping a coffee cup, his gaze shifting like he knew he'd been caught. "Why didn't I think of this? Much better than sitting inside."

"Apparently I had to come all the way from Toronto to sort things out around here." Faye bent her legs enough to make room as he sat on the end of her lounger, and poked him with a bare toe. "Where's mine?"

"Your ability to sleep till ten AM means I need it more than you." He looked at Faye sideways, smirking, shoulders slouched as he rested the cup on his knee.

"Sorry to have messed up your sleep schedule." She reached for the coffee, took a sip, and handed it back. "What's for dinner? Are you going to cook for us?"

It was like watching a foreign film, a story Liv could never imagine starring in. She would always be on the outside, trying to understand the players, passing silent judgement as she attempted to interpret the scene.

Nate's eyes isolated her, making her gut clench again. "You look tired. Maybe I should have brought a coffee for you."

She adjusted the blanket, forcing herself to return his gaze while she pushed away the thought of him and Faye in a hotel room. "I'm always tired these days, Miller."

His expression morphed from self-pity to concern. They all still looked at her like that—like she had a torn "handle with care" sticker on her forehead. Claire, her big mare, came flooding back to her mind, both of them brought to a standstill.

"You'll get to see her next Saturday."

She didn't know how he'd understood exactly what she'd been thinking. She had to push through the darkness when it seeped in; prove to everyone, including herself, she wasn't going to succumb to the despair lurking at every corner. It got old, feeling as if her mental health was at risk.

Nate dropped his eyes back to his coffee, lifting the cup to his lips. "Dean's sending Wampum down—that three-year old of his. He's going to run down here."

Liv rejoiced silently, grateful to him for getting the conversation to more neutral ground. "He broke his maiden at the end of the Woodbine meet, didn't he?"

Faye nodded. "Nate rode him."

"Nice colt." Nate pulled his phone from his back pocket and checked the time. "I'm going to go help your mom get things ready."

He shook his cup, looking disappointed it was almost empty, and tipped it back. When he walked by, he touched Liv's shoulder, hesitating when she looked up at him and smiled with determination. She was sure now he was struggling with some crisis of conscience, and hated that he felt that way. Even more, she hated she could see it.

CHAPTER THIRTY-FIVE

February

Ouf.

Liv caught her breath, jabbed in the ribs as she raised her arms to shimmy into the slip-on dress. She tugged it to her midriff with merely a twinge, and pushed herself up, balancing on her good leg to ease it the rest of the way down. The skirt was long enough to cover her scar without being annoying with crutches.

She stared into the mirror, and reached carefully for her brush. Gingerly, she pulled it through the wet tangles with her right arm. That wasn't going to work.

"You need any help?" Faye's voice came from outside the room.

"No!"

Faye laughed, and opened the door. "That was mildly snappish. Here, if you let me do it, we might actually make it to the race on time." She extracted the brush from Liv's grip.

Faye was right. Liv sat on the end of the bed with a sigh, Faye tucking behind her and pulling strands of damp hair into a braid. She was done in probably the same time it would have taken Liv to do a simple ponytail.

"Elastic?"

She rolled it off her wrist, and placed it in Faye's waiting palm.

"There. Ready to get your picture taken."

"Might be best not to jinx us by saying that." She gave Faye a sheepish grin. "Thank you."

Her mother locked the condo behind them, and Liv stepped and swung herself to the car. The sky was clear and blue—the track would be fast for their little speed freak. Liv lowered the window and pushed out her arm, letting the rush of air against her fingers distract her from thoughts of this afternoon's race. She felt so out of touch, despite regular updates from Nate and Roger. It wasn't the same as being in the barn every day.

Decelerating off the interstate ninety miles later, her mother pointed the Nissan towards the massive complex of Gulfstream Park. "I'll drop you two off. Straight up to the seats." She looked pointedly from Faye to Liv.

An order, not a suggestion. Liv smiled her most agreeable smile. "Thanks, Maman." She'd pick her battles today.

The Forward Gal Stakes was in the middle of the card, so at least there wouldn't be too long a wait. Liv tuned out the conversation between Faye and her mother and went from reading the *Daily Racing Form* Nate had brought her yesterday, to checking the minutes to post for the next race, at which point the fillies in the Forward Gal would head over to be saddled. She didn't even watch that race when it went off, turning instead to Faye.

"Go down to the paddock, Faye. I promise not to hate you for it."

Faye wavered. Had her mother not been there, Liv would have gone too, regardless of how tired she was already.

"Tell Nate *bonne chance* for me. Tell him not to fall off and to not get run off with." She hoped she didn't look too miserable.

"Got it." Faye gave her an apologetic pat before dashing off.

Liv turned back to the *Form*, glancing over the picks and comments. They didn't discount Chique—her runaway maiden victory last September boded well for her here, the Forward Gal the same distance at seven furlongs. *If regular rider, apprentice Nate Miller, can rate her here, she deserves a look.*

"Who does she have to beat?" Anne asked.

"All of them." Liv's laugh was as automatic as the thought. "The favourite is Longstreet. She was second in the Eclipse Award balloting for last year's two-year old filly. This is her first race since the Breeders' Cup. She prefers to go long, so we have that in our favour. Nothing in here has Chique's speed. If Nate can control the pace…" What a big if that was.

A brief view of Chique in the paddock on the tote board jumbotron grabbed her attention—there was no mistaking the big white shadow roll against her smudgy-dark face; the curl of her neck as she pushed into Jo's hold. Why hadn't she thought to ask Faye to FaceTime her, to give her a private video feed? Gulfstream's cameras seemed to feel the need to show the other starters, damn it.

There, at last—riders up—and one more quick shot on the screen of Nate on Chique, legs dangling at her sides as he knotted his lines. Liv twirled the neck strap of her binoculars around her fingers, toe on her good leg bouncing as she waited.

Chique danced onto the track, a sheen of sweat darkening her neck to black, Nate resting a hand on her crest where her unruly mane spiraled. Faye squeezed Liv's arm when she slipped back into her seat, and Liv gave her a tense smile in acknowledgement before turning to Roger, settling on the other side of her mother.

"How was she?"

"She didn't take anyone out in the walking ring."

"So far, so good," Faye agreed.

Nate took Chique off on his own to warm up, the filly free-wheeling around the clubhouse turn, leaving the others jogging and hobby-horsing with their ponies. He insisted it kept her better settled—and their performance in the Coronation backed up that assertion—but Liv still had visions of Chique going for a joy-ride down the backstretch. She didn't breathe again until he had her pulled up and turned around, Chique jogging to the gate with head down, toes flicking.

"She seems to have her gate issue sorted out," Roger commented when the filly filed into her position without complaint.

"A two minute-lick for a warm-up probably took the wind out of her sails." Liv bit her lower lip so hard she tasted blood.

The doors flew open, and Chique catapulted out a jump ahead of the rest, Nate with plenty of room to capture the rail. It was where the filly wanted to be, and there was no sense arguing with her in a sprint. Liv glanced at the time when the first fraction popped up. Surprisingly reasonable.

Chique was four lengths clear at the half-mile pole, Nate like a statue on her back as he held her. Her ears went straight up midway around the turn, and it was like centrifugal force took over.

"What the hell—" Roger leapt to his feet, binoculars locked on the filly as Chique blew the turn, heading to the outside fence. Longstreet, stalking tight to the rail, dragged her rider to the lead.

"Oh come on, filly!" Liv couldn't take it, hopping up on her good leg. Faye's arm threaded around her waist to steady her, watching just as keenly, while on the other side her mother tried to pull her back down.

Nate got Chique back on course, more or less—she was in the middle of the track, but at least headed in the right direction—but his attempts to re-engage her were coming up short. Then her ears flattened and she made a beeline for the other filly, swooping in with such single-mindedness Nate had to wave his whip alongside her to keep her from barreling into Longstreet. Finally straight, Chique locked on and fought back as they yelled themselves hoarse.

When the two fillies hit the wire, Liv couldn't tell who'd won.

She slumped into her chair, eying Roger. "What do you think?"

"No idea. I'll go see what the rider has to say."

"I'm coming down."

"Don't be ridiculous," her mother snapped.

"It'll be all right." Faye smiled sympathetically at Anne, and set Liv up with the crutches.

Once trackside, they waited on the apron while Roger strode out with Jo to meet the returning filly, just as the tote board broadcast the result.

"Yes!" Faye bounced and threw her arms around Liv, threatening to knock her off balance. "Come on, Anne! Picture time!" Faye looped her arm through Anne's and left Liv to swing herself to the winner's circle.

Liv edged forward when Nate dismounted after the photo, and the strength with which he grasped her upraised hand reminded her how weak she was. Her thigh throbbed, her ribs ached, but she was determined to ignore both, waiting for him to weigh in.

"You look wiped." He passed his tack to the valet, rubbing sweat from his eyes, though Chique's front-running trip had kept him clean.

Liv waved it off. "That was...what was that, Miller?"

"That was Chique taking offence to the Pegasus monster. Or wanting to go commune with it, I'm not sure which."

She raised her eyebrows, not buying the excuse, but Chique didn't miss much. "She's been here before. She worked here. She schooled here."

"Maybe she was lonely, up there all by herself. At least once the other filly went by, she decided to run again. We just have to have it figured out by June, right?"

His offhanded confidence managed to disarm her, the corners of her mouth creeping up. "Before that would be nice."

Nate turned to Anne. "I know you're wanting to get her home, but you'll make a quick visit to see Claire at the clinic, right?"

Anne nodded wearily, and Liv's smile grew, for a moment forgetting her fatigue. If Nate's charm worked on her mother, she was all for it—though her appreciation was tempered when Faye wrapped herself around him for a lengthy congratulatory kiss before coming along to assist.

Claire's whicker of recognition reached her before she even saw the mare, melting Liv's heart, and she shuffled to the stall.

"Be careful, Liv," Anne sighed.

"It's Claire, Maman. We'll be fine. Poor Claire," she murmured, letting the soft muzzle explore her hands, apologetic for the lack of tidbit. "What's going to happen to us?"

Nate dropped down on one elbow, running a hand from Faye's shoulder, down her back to the curve of her waist. She rolled over, and he kissed away her sultry smile.

"What would it take to convince you to stay?"

"For you to be making enough money I wouldn't have to go back to my job? I've never been a kept woman, but I bet I'd be just darling at it."

"I see." He grinned. "You could get a job walking hots or something in the meantime."

"Oh no. I'm happy to leave those crazy horses to you."

Faye pushed herself up, eyes hidden behind her sunglasses. "It'll be at least April before you're home, won't it?"

He sighed, and sat up next to her. "At least. I don't know what will happen with Chique, but I have to go wherever she goes."

"Here I'm thinking I'd follow you anywhere, and you're following a bloody horse."

"Easy now, don't be using that horse's name in vain." He tried a grin, pulling her against his shoulder. "She's crazy and erratic, but she just might be my ticket to the Queen's Plate."

As, more or less, was Liv.

He could do this friends thing with Liv. He could balance that, and Faye, and Chique. This was him, having it all.

Liv stuffed her water bottle in the tote along with her book—catching up on her reading was the only good thing about all this. With the bag slung over her shoulder, she set off with the plant-swing stride that was second nature now, the soreness from overdoing it on Saturday just starting to ease. She reached for the handle on the screen door, pushing it the rest of the way open with the end of one crutch, and eased out onto the patio.

Solitude was like an old friend; it was the loneliness that was strange, even if the letdown after the last week was inevitable. Faye was back in Ontario. Chique was oblivious to the ruckus surrounding another unorthodox victory. She hadn't seen Nate since he'd come to take Faye to the airport. Their lives went on without her, while she was left trying to sort it all out in her head.

Did Nate's absence mean he'd decided his visits were a problem, especially now that he'd gone the next step with Faye? He had to do what he thought was right to preserve that. But it didn't make it better. It meant there was something to be avoided.

So, she was back to this, striving to keep it all professional, which she never should have let go in the first place. The anesthetic from the surgery had obviously messed with her brain chemistry, left her vulnerable, flooded with angst like some woebegone teenager.

She heard a light tap, the screen door scraping open, and there he was, like her brain had conjured him. The little surge in her chest was temporary, quickly fading to sadness, leaving her frustrated she couldn't control either the rise or fall of her fickle emotions.

"Sorry I haven't been by." He held a booklet in his hand, but didn't offer it to her.

"That's okay. How's the freakshow?" A problem she could tackle head on.

He smirked. "Great. Got on her this morning, because she was starting to wreck the barn."

"Well you're here, so she didn't kill you. That's good. What's next?"

"You're the boss."

"You're the custodian of the crazy. Besides, no one's given me a stakes schedule."

He tossed over the booklet. "Though I'm pretty sure you know what the options are."

"So what do you think?" She flipped through the pages until she reached the first weekend in March.

"Rog wants to run her in the Fountain of Youth."

"I'm sorry, what? Clearly the crazy is contagious."

"The Davona Dale is only a mile. The Fountain of Youth is a mile and a sixteenth. We want to run a mile and a quarter at the end of June, right? Chique can sprint a mile; she needs the practice going longer." His grin finally showed up.

"Or you need the practice rating her?"

"That too." He swung his legs onto the lounge chair, and leaned back. "Your mother out right now?"

"Yes. Apparently I don't need constant supervision anymore. What does that have to do with figuring out where to run Chique next?"

"How do you feel about the beach?"

"What?"

"You know, that sandy bit by the ocean? You plan on staying cooped up here for the next two months?"

"You saw me Saturday. I'm not exactly strong yet." The excursion had made her aware just how weak she'd become... though she was determined to turn that around. One thing she knew—she needed to get back to the barn, just to be there, or her long-term sanity was in jeopardy.

"It's not hard," he insisted. "You lie there, catch a few rays, plan the path that gets Chique to the Plate. I'll make it even more attractive by taking you to see the horses first."

He knew her weak spot. "My mom's going to kill you."

"Aw, she loves me. I can do no wrong."

"That's what you think. Just when she's decided it's safe to leave me alone."

"I'm just going to run home and have a shower. Be back in twenty."

When he returned he looked like the shower had washed away the tension he'd carried earlier, his hair damp, the bright blue Gulfstream t-shirt he wore making the colour of his eyes that much more vivid. He picked up her bag and held the door open.

"Trying to escape, are you?"

Her mother. Thank goodness. Just in time to get her out of this ridiculousness.

Anne smiled, too suspiciously for Liv's liking. "Have a nice time!"

Liv glanced at Nate. "Conspiring with my mother now?"

He shrugged. "Like I said, she loves me."

What's not to love? she thought wryly, but wasn't about to say it out loud.

She didn't know exactly what was happening; wasn't sure it was right, but couldn't seem to stop it. For once she decided to relax and go with it—not that she was particularly good at that.

Chique's head popped out when he pulled up to the barn— Liv swore the filly recognized the sound of the Mustang's tired engine. Nate helped her out, and she swung to the first stall and blew into a nostril when Chique lifted her soft nose.

"You have no idea the stress you cause me."

Nate leaned on the rail, watching. *And you, too.*

"Beach?" he said.

She nodded. "Beach."

The weather was perfect, which wasn't necessarily a given for Florida in February. He'd brought one of those little chairs, and set it up on the sand for her, standing by while she got organized.

"So...friends, then." She peered up at him over her sunglasses. "Just so we're clear."

He chuckled. "Yeah. Crystal."

He left her there, pulling off his t-shirt and wandering down to the surging water. Part of her yearned to follow him, and she pretended the draw she felt was nothing more than the pull of the waves and a longing to taste the salt on her tongue.

CHAPTER THIRTY-SIX

March

Just over five weeks since the accident, and Liv still woke well before dawn, her internal alarm prodding her to consciousness. This time, she pulled on jeans, zipped a hoodie over a long-sleeved t-shirt, and parked herself on the bed with her book to wait.

Stairs creaked around seven—her mother up now—and she thought about where they would be at in the routine at Payson. Nate liked to take Chique out first, so the filly would be back in her stall enjoying her haynet—six days away from her next test.

Emilie stirred, peeking around the door.

"There you are." Liv shuffled her hips over to make room. "Sorry I didn't wait up."

"I wasn't expecting you to." Emilie crawled onto the bed beside her and looked down at Liv's book. "I forget what it's like to read a novel."

"I remember that world. Research papers and textbooks. Hope you left all of them at home."

"Much too heavy for travel." Emilie nodded. "I'm mostly

238

caught up, so semester break can actually be a break."

"Did you see Maman?"

"Not yet. She told me last night I'm supposed to take you to Payson this morning though."

"Good." Liv gave her a shove. "Go get dressed. We can catch the last set."

The training centre was still busy, the grooms on the Triple Stripe shed ready for the current pair to return from the track while preparing the last two horses. Liv negotiated past the first stall, ignoring Chique's tap-tap-tap, and stopped to meet the bold blaze pushing out over the webbing. Claire pressed into her chest.

"Would someone please give that woman a peppermint?"

Nate's voice reached her at the exact moment Claire shoved her with her nose.

He pulled his horse to a halt and dropped his feet from the irons. "You're late, Em! We're almost all out. Grab this horse's halter, will you?"

Emilie scowled, picking the halter up from the rail. "Where's Michel? I'm supposed to be on vacation, you know."

"You're cuter. Get out here."

Liv backed into Claire, letting the mare nuzzle her neck from behind, and inhaled, drinking in the surroundings as she listened to their banter. *This is home.*

Roger tucked Paz away in the end stall and strode down the shed. "I thought you might show up this morning."

"I'm so glad she's back." She kissed Claire's pink muzzle and moved to let the mare go to her haynet.

"If this is going to be a regular thing, just do me a favour and stay off the horses for a while yet." Roger patted her lightly on the shoulder. "I have to go find Doc Benson."

When Liv was sure he was gone, she swung down to the end of the shed. Nate was setting his saddle in front of his final horse after sending Emilie walking with the one he'd just returned on.

"Come with me, Miller."

She ducked into the last stall where Paz stood, still tacked up.

"What are you doing?" Nate asked, his tone matching his suspicious expression.

"Get in here."

His eyebrows rose when she dropped the halter from the gelding's head. "Oh come on. Forget it."

"Throw me up."

"No way."

"It's Paz, Miller. Come on. Rog is gone. Throw me up." She leaned the crutches in the corner and hopped back over, gathering the reins. Nate shook his head, but stepped in behind her, Liv looking over her shoulder at him. "Okay, just easy now."

She couldn't completely mask her grimace as pain shot up her leg, but as soon as she transferred her weight to her arms, all she felt were pokes from her healing ribs. She quickly swung her good leg over and eased into the tack, taking a deep breath, then reached down and patted Paz's neck, grinning like she was four again.

"I'll get your helmet," Nate grumbled, turning to drop the bar.

"Thanks, Miller."

"Yeah well, if I get fired, it's your fault."

"No one's getting fired," she said, still beaming as she neck-reined Paz to the door. "Besides, if you haven't been fired by now, I don't think you have to worry."

Paz took her to the tack room, where Jo already waited with her helmet, then held up her safety vest. "Better put this on, too."

Nate met her outside on a plain bay horse she didn't recognize. "Is that Dean's colt? Wampum?"

He nodded. "Guess he's our competition on Saturday. The down side to Chique going in the Fountain of Youth instead of the Davona Dale is I don't get to ride them both."

Liv could think of other downsides, like the possibility Chique would get dusted by a bunch of colts, but she kept her mouth shut.

She parked Paz by the clocker's stand until Nate disappeared the wrong way around the turn, backing up, then nudged Paz to the right, restraining her impulse to canter him to the off-gap. Wampum zoomed past, galloping strongly.

"You look good on the pony," Nate said when they met up again. "You should get your trainer's license."

His expression was totally serious. It hadn't even crossed her mind. Why not? She needed something to occupy her mind—not that the object of the prospective job title wasn't already doing that. All the license would do was make it her official responsibility.

"Rog and I have already talked about it. We're a team, right?" Nate said, eyes steady on her as they walked off the track. "Maybe you won't be riding her in the Plate, but your name needs to be in the program. You deserve credit for your part."

"A one-horse stable?"

"But what a horse, right?"

"Temperamental, wildly unpredictable? Yeah, what a horse." But she matched his grin.

Emilie took over Paz when she got back, bathing him and letting him graze the coarse grass outside the barn. Roger was in the tack room, and Liv sheepishly rested the crutches against the wall, and settled into a chair.

He didn't look up, completing the morning's training record. "Someone said they saw you on my pony. I said that was impossible."

Liv grinned. "Really. They'll say anything around here, won't they?"

Chique's ears flattened, sticking out from her head like handlebars, and she pressed her face into the pony rider's lap as if hoping it would shield her from the driving rain. Nate hunched his shoulders, but otherwise tried to ignore the unrelenting downpour quickly threatening to turn Gulfstream's dirt track into part of the Everglades. Chique made no such effort, the look on her face almost comical—

except that he feared for their chances of success with her display of disdain.

The veteran pony wrinkled his nose and glared at the filly, but said no more. Paz had stayed at home because they needed the stall on the Triple Stripe van for Wampum, who was looking far less concerned about the weather a couple of spots up in the post parade.

He sent Chique away from her new best friend to warm up, but the filly lacked her usual zeal, her gallop mincy as she picked through the swamp. They wouldn't prolong the start with this deluge, so Nate didn't take her far, turning back towards the gate with the others and finding the solace of her pony pal to wait for their turn to load. Good thing it was a mile and a sixteenth today; maybe she'd get over herself in time to make a respectable showing. Chique butted the pony with her head, velcroed to the grumpy gelding's side.

"Sorry," Nate muttered at the pony rider, nodding thanks at her before she transferred him to the starter's assistant.

The filly walked into the outside stall and sighed, relieved to finally have shelter. Nate weaved his fingers through her mane, looking out at the murky stretch of soup in front of them, trying not to let her contempt for the conditions wear off on him.

She broke flat, a beat behind her rivals, popping out with the same caution she'd shown in her warmup, then veered for the outside rail as the rest of her opponents battled for position. Nate scrambled to refocus her, grateful they'd had no one to their right to interfere with. She'd sacrificed lengths with that move, and Nate had to hustle her to make up ground. It was such a short run to the clubhouse turn they got stuck three-wide, but he was pretty sure getting mud slung in her face on the inside wouldn't have gone over well anyway.

She tried to climb over her own splash, her head too high and her stride horribly inefficient, burning valuable energy. The splatter and slap of hooves ahead of them was unrelenting, and did nothing to invite her to join in. She drifted even wider before they straightened into the backstretch, just to be sure she was clear of the assault, and swapped leads so dramatically Nate almost laughed.

On the far turn, a couple of horses started moves, and he glanced to his left and saw Wampum. The colt looked like a clay sculpture, bay coat covered in a layer of uniform slate grey, and Chique matched strides with him like she'd found a familiar face in a foreign country. Maybe there was hope, because Nate was sure Wampum would fire, and perhaps that would rouse the filly out of her wallowing.

They turned for home, and Wampum jumped into action, the mess of kickback breaking over him like a wave. Nate asked Chique to go with him—but Chique just let him go.

Liv didn't look surprised to see him, or concerned he'd let himself in. He'd brought pizza—with two dark days ahead, he could manage the indulgence, and knowing Liv, she hadn't eaten and wouldn't have any food, since her mother had returned to Ontario. He set the box on the kitchen table, and called towards the living room.

"Get in here, trainer, and tell me what's going on in that head of yours."

He opened cupboards until he found a couple of wine glasses, and poured from the bottle of red he'd brought.

She appeared in the doorway in an oversized sweatshirt and shorts, her hair pulled loosely back. The way she leaned on the doorframe, that slight curve of her lips accompanying her raised eyebrows...none of it intended to be alluring, but totally...*no*. He shook it off, and set out plates.

Awkwardly, without crutches, she came over, which probably wasn't surgeon-approved—not that hopping on the pony a week ago had been either. He pushed a glass across the table. She pushed it back.

"I'm not drinking wine with you."

"I think we can put that drunken pity party behind us, can't we? We're good. We're friends. We've established that. Declarations have been made." He pushed the glass towards her again. "One glass. To friends."

She sighed, lifting it, then held his eyes as she accepted the toast.

Right. Friends.

"How was your afternoon? You obviously got Em to the airport in plenty of time—she's already home and whining about the cold."

"It was uninspiring." He joined her at the table. "So have we recovered enough from yesterday's embarrassment to talk about it?"

"I don't think she liked the slop," Liv said out of the corner of her mouth as she bit into a piece of pizza. When her look shifted to him, they both cracked up.

"So we can agree to throw that one out?" he said.

"And pray it doesn't ever rain again when she runs?" She took a careful sip of the wine. "I'm thinking Keeneland next. How does that sound?"

"Keeneland in April...sounds amazing."

"Assuming she comes out of this okay. Dean's sending Wampum, too."

"He ran huge yesterday. I'm proud of him." Wampum's big move on the turn, leaving Chique literally in his wake, had got the colt up for third.

"Dean was thrilled, but I'm sure you know that. Any regrets about picking the wrong horse?"

"Chique will never be the wrong horse. She'll always be my girl."

Her face softened into what he wanted to think was affection, but just as quickly bounced back to business. "I think we'll opt for fillies in the Ashland this time. If Wampum goes in the Blue Grass, maybe you'll get the mount back."

"So...any chance you're thinking Churchill for the next stop? Kentucky Oaks?" A guy could dream, right?

"Let's see how she handles the Ashland. If she runs back to yesterday's performance, we'll be packing our bags and going home."

"So little faith."

"I thought picking a Grade One instead of just waiting for

Woodbine was showing faith. Are you in?"

"You keep asking me that, like you're afraid I'm going to disappear. Have I ever let you down?"

Her eyes dropped to her glass. *Oh.* Not a good sign.

"No," she finally responded.

"But you had to think about it."

"It's not like that."

He wanted to ask what she meant, but was afraid he was reading too much into it. *Because you want to. Reel it back, Miller.* "You'll get your trainer's license there?" Back to safer ground.

"It might be simpler to just let her run in Roger's name, and get Dean to saddle her. Wait till we get back to Woodbine."

"Just do it."

"Boldly go?"

He wished she'd stop looking at him like that. Did she really have no clue? "That's more like it."

She left the crust of her slice on the plate, and took another measured sip of the barely-touched wine, slipping into silence. If he'd let her down, he needed to know, didn't he? *Leave it alone.* But he couldn't.

"What did you mean, just then? *'It's not like that.'*"

A crease formed between her brows, her lips pressing into a line. She glanced somewhere over his shoulder before her eyes fell back to his, and her words unfolded slowly, like she was having a hard time working them free. "You haven't let me down, Miller. Ever. You go above and beyond, with everything. And I worry it might be too much. I worry now it might...become a problem."

Faye.

"Right." He pushed back his chair. "I'd better go. I'm leaving the rest of the pizza with you. And the wine. You need the calories; I don't."

He ducked away from her perplexed expression, out of the kitchen, out the front door, out where he could breathe.

The phone buzzed a text notification in his back pocket, and he extracted it, willing it to be Faye just in time to help him settle his pulse, bring him perspective, but he went cold at the name he saw instead.

He'd never taken Cindy out of his contacts, though at least he'd had enough self-respect never to drunk-text her on the holidays—even if he'd come close a couple of times. And since Faye, he'd almost, but not quite, forgotten she was even in there.

I thought you might want to meet your new niece and nephew.

But oh, she was there, cutting off his airwaves, draining the blood from his veins.

He unlocked the screen, finding a photo of her holding a carefully placed bundle in the crook of each arm. Their tiny faces were pink and squinty-eyed, not terribly attractive...and perfect. And she was perfect. Radiant. It left a fresh bruise on his scarred heart.

Too many worlds colliding, here and now. Liv calling him out on Faye, who had helped him see the possibility of a future different from the one he'd thought he wanted with Cindy. Cindy, who had maybe been right to break it off. And maybe Liv had been right when she did, however bluntly, point that out. But Liv had never given him a single, tangible reason to think there was any chance of them ever being more than they were right now. Cohorts. Uneasy friends.

He fired off a text to Faye.

You're coming to Keeneland, right?

Going back to the photo, his thumb hovered over the keypad. In the name of resolving at least one thing in his head, he typed *Congratulations* and hit send.

CHAPTER THIRTY-SEVEN

April

Chique emerged from the shadow, the brilliant morning sun at the head of the stretch spotlighting her against the dark wash of green behind her. Liv propped her binoculars in her right hand while her left held the reins on Paz, who had taken to Keeneland the same way the rest of them had—like he'd been meant to be here all his life. She hadn't expected Rog to offer up his pony for this side trip, but she was grateful for the veteran's steady influence on her own nerves as much as Chique's.

The filly's ears flickered forward as they got closer, but Nate's focus remained unwavering as they galloped by around the clubhouse turn. Chique's final breeze had been perfect; entries were in; post positions drawn. Now they were just counting hours, and praying for a fast track.

Nate didn't try to jar her out of her preoccupation on the walk back—he seemed absorbed in his own, like he had been more often than not in the last few weeks. No more visits with wine and pizza, an appropriate withdrawal after that evening that told her all she needed to know—he was, rightly, committed to Faye. She tried to counter her scattered thoughts by drinking in a breath of the cool, crisp air, focusing on the beauty around them—the immaculate grounds, the cherry blossom-laden trees; the sense of serenity on Keeneland's backstretch that seemed so at odds with her underlying anxiety.

He glanced at her with a smile several watts below his normal grin, then dialed it up at the sight of Faye and Dean, waiting at the barn. "Hey, you made it!"

Liv swung off Paz. "What time did you guys leave?"

"We flew to Cinci last night, rented a car, and drove the rest of the way this morning." Dean came up and gave Liv a peck on the cheek, squeezing her shoulder. "Can I take your trusty steed for you so you can look after the big filly?"

"Thanks." Maybe she could relax a little now that it felt like a grown-up trainer was here. She pulled off her helmet and hugged Faye.

"Don't expect me to do anything." Faye smiled with mock sweetness.

"Wouldn't dream of it." Liv grinned back, grabbing Chique's halter.

"You're in time to see your boy go." Nate dragged the saddle off and pulled the bridle over Chique's ears, then left the tack on the rail.

Liv wound the chain around the halter's noseband, following with her eyes as Nate drew Faye in and kissed her, then wordlessly came back to hold Chique for a steamy bath.

"Grab that cooler, Faye?" Liv asked as she scraped away the rinse water.

"I can do that much." Faye handed it to Nate, and Chique's neck snaked with a snap of teeth, sending her jumping out of the way. "Jealous?"

Liv looked sideways at Nate, but his eyes stayed on the filly.

"I'll walk her," he said while Liv threw on the cooler.

"No hotwalker?" Dean asked when she returned to the barn, finding he had Wampum already tacked up.

"Didn't think we really needed one, with just two horses.

You're not in a hurry, are you?"

"Hardly." He tilted his head to the colt. "He looks phenomenal. I'm excited about tomorrow."

"I'm terrified. It's all Nate's fault. I was more than willing to let you do the saddling honours for Chique."

"Where's the fun in that? Good job, Miller."

Nate stopped to let Chique have a drink. "You making fun of my hotwalking skills?"

"Just singing your praises. The colt's in good order, and you successfully prompted our girl here to get her trainer's license."

Liv tried and failed to read Nate's expression as Chique pulled him past.

Faye and Dean walked out with them when they took Wampum to the track, and Liv tried to pretend the new, weird tension she felt wasn't there. Putting on a cheery front wasn't exactly her forte. It exhausted her, when she was stressed enough already.

"He's going great, Liv," Dean said as Wampum galloped past. "If Touch and Go comes back good, I might have two Plate horses this year. How incredible would that be?"

His face was uncomplicated by the strain that added a beat to her own heart rate hearing *Plate*, her mind automatically calculating *twelve weeks*. She kept her own raging doubts about whether or not Chique was going to make it to herself. Three months was so close, yet forever away.

Dean stepped in to hold Wampum for his bath once they were back at the barn. "I'll buy you guys breakfast once we're done."

"I've gotta check into the room, got a couple mounts this aft, so I'm out." Nate looked lost for a moment, watching Dean take over his usual position. He turned on his heel and went to clean the tack, then left with half a wave.

There was definitely weird in the air, and it wasn't just her. Liv pulled her eyes back to Wampum. "The kitchen food is pretty good here."

When she tried to take the shank after the colt's bath, Dean shooed her away. "The least I can do is walk my big horse. Catch up with Faye while you get your filly done up."

Faye was strangely silent as Liv gathered brushes and bandages for Chique.

"Everything okay?" Liv eyed her.

Faye waved her hand around in a non-answer.

"I thought things were good in Florida," Liv ventured.

Faye sighed. "It was. Florida was amazing. I'm just not sure it was real."

"That makes no sense at all."

"You don't see it, do you?"

"What, Faye? I'm trying to get this filly ready for a race, not monitor the state of your relationship."

"The writing," Faye said, looking overly dramatic, even for Faye, as she swept her arm through the air. "It's all over the wall."

A hint of white showed in the corner of Chique's eye as she rolled it at the real umbrellas and the makeshift ones, programmes perched over horseplayers' heads like little paper rooftops. Her feet lifted off the path in an ultra-slow jog, and she curled into the groom with her teeth squeaking as she mouthed the bit. She looked ready...but whether or not she was going to play today was anyone's guess.

"She's not the only speed, so if she does end up on the front end, well...do what you can to keep her happy without burning her up."

It wasn't as if they hadn't discussed the race already, but there needed to be words to fill the air, so Nate didn't care that Liv was repeating what had already been said. He had to ignore his doubts, doubts justifiably inspired by a filly who had a penchant for making things up as she went along. It was only her sixth start, they'd reminded each other. She was still learning, and they were still learning how she operated. It was an ongoing odyssey.

"*Riders up!*"

He grasped the lines at Chique's withers, bouncing as Liv

lifted him into the tack.

"Bonne chance." She glanced up. "Stay safe."

He met her eyes. "Thanks."

The drizzle wasn't enough to alter the track condition, so it remained fast. Nate nodded at the pony rider when it was acceptable to break out of the line of the post parade—like the groom, the woman on Paz was a hire for the day. Chique leapt into a gallop, leaving Paz behind without hesitation and powering the wrong way around the turn.

He tried to time it so they weren't left milling with the others behind the gate too long before they were loaded. Their reunion with Paz was short before the starter's assistant came for them, leading them into the fourth stall. He felt Chique's muscles tense.

"Easy, there," he murmured. "We have to wait for everyone else."

Chique shifted her weight beneath him, but she stood, ears swiveling as the activity carried on around her. The filly next to them started pawing and popped, prompting some pointed words from her handler and the jock. Chique tilted her head at the commotion, rocking her left shoulder to the side of the frame.

"C'mon, let's keep her straight," Nate grumbled at the assistant. Their neighbour stilled, and the starter sprang them from the barrier.

That second of distraction before the bell cost Chique the break, and Nate cursed as she jumped out a beat behind. He took a careful hold, leaving the other speed horse to assume the lead—praying the filly bought into the plan. She was quick enough to regain the ground she'd lost and let him park her out from the rail where she had a clear path, and couldn't complain about kickback.

He didn't like being three-wide around the clubhouse turn, but it was a matter of compromise—better than being buried on the inside. When they straightened into the backstretch, Chique neatly swapped leads and zeroed in on the frontrunner. He let her close the gap until she had her nose at that filly's saddle cloth, pressing the pace with her ears laced back, but wonder of wonders, she was waiting for him to tell her the next move.

Inching closer around the turn, the leader pressed into Chique, floating her wide—completely intentional on the rider's part. *Sure, let's give the new kid a hard time.* There was nothing he could do about it. Someone crept up on his right, drawing even, wedging Chique in the middle. Chique pinned her ears, but Nate was happy to let them go by...until that filly dropped in before she was clear, leaving him scrambling to check Chique—too late. She stumbled, staggering, tossing him forward as he grappled for her mane. Clambering to her feet—freaky athletic thing that she was—she threw him back into the tack, and he groped for the lines so he could help her out.

Shuffled to the inside now, the kickback came full force. *And here's where she packs it in.* But instead, Chique was mad, her adrenaline pumping as much as his. She was eyeballing the rail, which was a ridiculous option—there wasn't enough room. But who was he to tell this filly what to do? She thought she could fit. He picked her up and chirped, sending her.

It was so tight his boot scraped the fence, and he all but closed his eyes. Chique crept up, fighting even though she was tiring. He was afraid to hit her—it was crowded enough that an over-reaction would have a dangerous domino effect. So he pushed and pleaded with each stride, hollering in her ear until the mirror flashed past on his left. She let up as soon as he did, the blow from her nostrils sounding like a freight train.

The grandstand was shrouded in a fine mist as they came back, his anger smouldering. Liv approached with the groom —he couldn't remember if he'd seen the crutches since they'd arrived in Lexington.

"Is she all right?" Liv tore off the dirty blinkers, scanning Chique with concern.

"I think so. She got bounced around out there pretty good though—she'll be sore tomorrow. So will that bastard, if I have anything to say about it." He fired his whip at his valet.

"Forget it, Miller. You don't want any trouble. Especially

with Ricky Acosta."

"Is that who it was?" He dismounted, face set as he reached down to release the overgirth. "Where'd she finish?"

"Third. She ran huge, Nate."

Liv's face made him pause—here he was getting all riled up, when Chique had saved his ass, and still run her guts out. "She grew up a little out there." He planted a kiss on the clean spot the blinkers had left on the filly's cheek and went to weigh in.

Liv fell into step beside him. "That was a risky move, taking her up the rail."

"What was I supposed to do? Go down the middle of the racetrack?"

"Anything would have been better than putting yourself in that position."

"I didn't know if she was going to run at all. If I'd told her not to go, you know exactly what she would have said back. Anyway, what does it matter, as long as she's all right?"

"Let's just hope she is."

"We'll talk after the Blue Grass, okay?"

She nodded, and he started jogging back to the room. And headed straight for Ricky Acosta, shoving him against the wall, pressing into him.

"What the hell was that?"

"It's called race-riding, kid."

"My ass."

Acosta's laugh taunted him. "Get out of my way, or it will be. Maybe you'd better run along back to Canada where they play nice."

"So help me, if there's anything wrong with that filly—" He was trembling now, he wanted to hit Acosta so bad.

"C'mon, pretty boy, take a swing. Give me an excuse to mess up that face of yours. He's not as pretty as our princess, though, is he boys? She don't seem so sad anymore. You have something to do with that?"

Acosta stepped closer with a smirk and Nate shifted his weight and snapped his fist back. A vise-like grip seized his wrist before he could follow through and dragged him away. He spun and twisted out of the hold, ready to strike....and stopped dead.

"I told you to forget it," Liv hissed, grabbing his arms and pushing him back. "I'd throw you under a cold shower if it was in any way appropriate."

"Like this was?" he snapped, glaring at her. He could feel eyes on them as she glared back.

"Put this behind you and get ready to ride Wampum. Who knows, if he runs well enough, you might get to ride in the Derby. You wouldn't want to screw that up, would you?"

His gaze dropped to the floor.

"Good luck." She stepped away. "I'm going back to check on Chique. Stay out of trouble."

The looks and whistles as she retreated seemed to have no effect on her, but Nate kept his eyes averted, sure the smirk was still on Acosta's face.

He washed away the dirt and dressed in fresh breeches, pulling on Northwest's red and white silks. Boots wiped clean, his helmet ready with a red cover and new goggles, courtesy of his valet. Nate grabbed his whip and took a moment to breathe before riders were called outside.

Faye and Dean were waiting—Dean watching Wampum, Faye watching Nate. He had to keep her out of his head until after the race.

"How's the filly?" Dean asked.

"Appears to be fine." He couldn't let himself think about Chique, either, or his anger flared again. "This guy's been loving the track, so here's hoping."

"Maybe we'll get a piece of it."

And the Derby points that went with that.

The same pony rider, using Paz, accompanied them to the post. Added to the list of things Nate didn't want to think about was his post position: Ricky Acosta, on the favoured Buck Ruler, set to start next to him.

Wampum got away clean, and Nate took him back, letting the speed horses go. Everything was going according to plan, around the clubhouse turn and into the straightaway. Nate sat like a stone, aware of Acosta on Buck Ruler, right beside them. He relaxed slightly. Really, what was Acosta going to do? Certainly not ruin his own chances to mess up Nate's trip. But right now Buck Ruler had Wampum boxed in, and as they travelled around the turn, the two colts bumped. Wampum faltered, backing off, and Nate getting after him didn't help. Acosta picked up Buck Ruler as they hit the head of the stretch, and the big colt went into overdrive.

And then it was déjà vu.

Acosta cut in front of Wampum. Wampum clipped Buck Ruler's heels. Hard and fast, with no hope of a save.

Nate hit the dirt, air rushing from his lungs as the momentum rolled him under the rail. Gulping in a breath, he dragged himself to all fours on the turf, catching glimpses of horses flying around Wampum. He pulled himself to his feet, grasping the rail to get his bearings, then ducked under, grabbing Wampum as the colt lurched up. Wampum hopped around him, eyes wild, but he used all four legs equally. Nate exhaled, talking the colt down. Talking himself down.

In no time he was surrounded—track ambulance, horse ambulance, state veterinarian…random maintenance person taking over at Wampum's head so he could slide off the saddle. Then Dean was there, resting a hand on his shoulder.

Nate shrugged him off. "I'm fine. I think he's okay."

"We'll take that ride." Dean nodded at the van. "You should do the same, Nate. Come back when you can."

Wampum marched up the ramp, still not favouring anything, but adrenaline could cover up pain. It was best to take precautions. The ambulance attendants were battering Nate with questions as he climbed into the back. He brushed them away. His ankle was starting to hurt, that was all. Back in the room he collapsed in a heap on the bench, trying to regroup, then changed without showering, and skulked out.

Fog hung over the backstretch, masking the barns and bringing dusk prematurely. All he wanted to do was go back to his room, with or without Faye; put this wretched day behind him and figure out his head in the morning. He didn't trust it right now. He might have done just that, except for the shit he'd find himself in if he didn't check in.

"You okay?" Liv scanned him, half scrutinizing, half worried.

Faye rushed over, her arms folding around his shoulders, face pushed into his neck. He should have probably felt something, but he didn't.

He ducked away from her and went to Chique, then Wampum, both of them done up to their eyeballs—poultice to their knees, sweated to their hocks. Chique bumped him with her nose.

"How are they?" He didn't look at Liv, but could feel her hovering just behind him.

"Seem to be all right. We'll see how they are in the morning."

"Guess none of us are going to Churchill this year. Should we grab something to eat?" Trust Dean to be practical.

"As long as there's wine." Faye shivered, shoulders hunched in her coat, even though it wasn't that cold.

Liv glanced from Faye to Nate. "Meet you guys there?"

His stomach gnawed at him even though he wasn't hungry, and he led the way to the Mustang, Faye's silence as unnatural as the murky atmosphere. The twinge in his ankle was getting worse.

"Are you okay? Really?" She frowned, twisting in her seat once he was behind the wheel.

He grimaced, depressing the clutch and popping the car into gear. "Fine."

"How can you be fine? I'm certainly not. That was terrifying."

"I get it. It's scarier when it's someone else."

"Apparently."

The traffic leaving the parking area was heavy now that the big races were done, and his ankle screamed each time he rolled the car to a halt. They would have been better off waiting, because no one was going anywhere fast at the moment. He just wanted to get out of there.

"It was a spill, Faye. They happen. If you can't deal with it, maybe you're dating the wrong guy." *Shit.* That wasn't the right thing to say.

"Maybe you're right."

He'd handed her the knife she'd just pushed between his ribs, sending this conversation in an unintended direction. He wasn't up for this, not now.

"Are you going to tell me what's going on?"

He could throw that one right back at her—but he'd already dug himself a hole. "It's just been a shitty day, all right?"

"What about yesterday?"

"You were the one who opted out of staying with me."

"I told you, I didn't want any trainers mad at me because I kept you up."

"Well it's not like I slept very well anyway."

"Why would that be? Your conscience getting to you?"

"What the hell are you talking about?"

"What's going on with Liv?"

She blindsided him with that one, and he choked back a laugh. "She's your best friend, so I'm pretty sure you know the answer to that is a big fat nothing."

Her exhale was audible. "We really need to talk."

"Can't it wait? We could skip dinner, grab a bottle, go back to my room. I don't think either of us is particularly rational at the moment."

"I'm quite rational, thank you. This is as good a time as any, don't you think? Seeing as we're stuck here, and you're already having a shitty day."

He dislodged a hand gripping the wheel to rub his eyes, trying to ease the throb behind them.

"Tell me if I'm wrong," Faye began. "The only reason you decided to sleep with me in Florida is because you were feeling guilty about spending so much time with Liv after her accident. And, lo and behold, you were starting to have feelings for her. What no one seems to want to admit, though, is she has feelings for you."

"Liv? Feelings?" If only he were that convinced. "See what I mean? That's totally irrational."

"Is it, really? What happened New Year's Eve?"

"What? I was in bed by eight. Slept through it." Made sure of it, this time.

"Not this year. Last year."

"She told you about that?" That just reinforced Liv had laid it to rest, because he was sure she wouldn't have said anything to Faye about that night had it actually meant something to her. "For one, you and I weren't even seeing each other then. And for another, it was nothing. We finished off a bottle of wine after dinner at Roger and Hélène's. At midnight I kissed her. It was just a kiss, Faye. A stupid Happy New Year kiss." Which hadn't made either of them happy.

"It's never just a kiss." She looked out the passenger window, hiding her face from him. "I can't deal with it anymore. I can't compete with a horse, let alone whatever this thing is you two have going on. It's not going to disappear."

"Why can't you see all she and I will ever be are friends?"

"Because I don't believe it anymore. It's just a matter of time."

It made no difference that she was wrong—she'd clearly made up her mind. The pounding in his head crept to his neck, shooting into his shoulders. "So this is it, then." His voice sounded as flat as he felt.

Faye's fingers flew over the keypad on her phone. "Just take me back to the hotel, please."

He didn't argue.

Liv rapped on the door, then crossed her arms, shaking from a chill she couldn't keep at bay. The damp weather, the sequence of events...it came from one of them, or all of it.

Maybe he'd gone to get something to eat on his own. Maybe she should leave well enough alone. She turned away, then the door clicked.

Nate left it open as he retreated.

"You're hurt." The crease between her brows deepened as

she caught it, hovering on the threshold.

"It's nothing." He hobbled a step, his face screwing up.

Her shoulders dropped with a sigh, and she stepped in, the door shutting behind her. "Let me look at that. Get on the bed."

"Never thought you'd be the kind of girl to take charge in the bedroom." He took another bad step, his smirk falling away as his jaw tightened. "Guess I shouldn't be surprised. You're a control freak with everything else."

"Grow up," she snapped, heat flushing her cheeks as he perched on the edge of the mattress and carefully rolled off his sock.

His foot felt cold and bony between her hands, but the ankle was hot and starting to swell. She rotated it like she would have a horse, checking mobility, and he winced, pulling away.

"Easy!"

"Well you didn't want to let a professional check it out." She straightened, squaring her shoulders, hands on her hips. "You need to get that x-rayed."

"It's just bruised."

"Don't be an idiot. Or am I too late for that?" Could she just smack him? She'd feel so much better. She grabbed his key card from the end table. "Stay here."

"Got nowhere else to be."

She should just leave him to suffer. But she came back with her crutches, a six-pack of beer from the gas station downstairs, and a bucket of ice.

First she twisted a can free and handed it to him, then made an ice pack with a damp hotel towel. "Put this on it. And stay off it."

"You going to give me a lesson on how to use those?"

"Google it. Here."

He closed his hand on the two capsules of Advil she dropped into his palm, cracked open the beer with a tight smile and washed them down. "Not joining me?"

Just one good cuff? He totally deserved it. Instead she reached for a can, and walked around the bed to the chair on the other side, letting the first sip sting her tongue. "This stuff is disgusting."

"You bought it."

"Forgive me, I'm not a connoisseur." The second swig didn't taste as bad as the first.

He propped the pillows against the headboard and swung his legs up onto the bed. "I know why Faye's mad at me, but what's your problem?"

"Faye is my friend. She was my friend long before you. You put me in the middle of this."

"So why are you here?"

"She didn't want to talk to me." Liv tried another mouthful before abandoning the can to the small table next to her. "I'm guessing it's over."

"So it is."

And with that went her safety net. Why was she here, really?

"Listen, you don't have to stay. Thanks for checking in. Go find Dean and have some dinner." He adjusted the ice pack, focusing on it like it required his full attention.

Dean would still be in the hotel restaurant. Not that she felt like eating, or needed company, but it would be a much more logical option than this. This though...something kept her here. "You hung out with me in Florida when I'm sure you had better things to do. I think I can return the favour." That was it, right?

His eyes flitted over. The defensiveness faded from his expression. "You haven't got it all wrong, you know."

She frowned. "Well, thanks, Miller, but what?"

"Your philosophy on relationships."

"Which would be?"

"That they're best avoided. Am I wrong?"

She leaned forward, resting her arms on her knees, her gaze drawn to him. "Not entirely. I'd think you of all people would have figured that out before this."

"Just because I got burned once doesn't mean I want to be alone for the rest of my life. I couldn't know Faye wasn't the one."

"Oh come on."

He shot her a dark look. "You say that like I deserved to be dumped."

"Faye's MO is to sleep with a guy without getting invested. You made her get invested, then you slept with her. That was significant."

"I didn't make her do anything." He dropped the ice pack on the floor, and grabbed the beer. With the way he threw his head back as he tipped it to his lips, he must have downed half of it. "You know Faye called it off because of you, right?"

The hairs on the back of her neck tingled, and she reached up like she could smooth them into submission. "What?"

"I told her about New Year's Eve."

Her chest spasmed as his words conjured up the forbidden memory. *Control, Liv. Get it back.* "Great. So now she hates me, too."

"She's decided we have a thing for each other." His eyes, which had mostly been avoiding her, settled on her now, challenging.

"Do we?" She felt strangely calm, then her heart gave a deliberate thud, balanced on a precipice. One nudge would send it from safety into danger.

"I can only speak for myself."

"And?" Another thump, waiting for his answer, when she didn't think it would be a surprise.

"I've been talking myself out of it for three years." He crushed the can in his hand. "If I thought there was any chance in hell you felt the same, I'd say what are we waiting for? In the last three months we've both seen our lives flash before our eyes. Life's too short not to run with it."

It was the way he said it, like it was their destiny, curled her fingers into fists; drew her back from the edge.

"That's not how this goes, Miller. Faye dumped you because you were an asshole. You want me to step up to the line and say sign me up? No thank you." She strode around the bed, crouching to pick up the pieces of ice that had scattered from the pack, and handed it back to him. "I don't mean to kick you when you're down. I'm sorry about you and Faye. But I'm not going along with your little plan."

She didn't look back, desperate to tidy the messiness of it all in her head, and didn't breathe until the door clicked shut behind her.

CHAPTER THIRTY-EIGHT

May

The mosquitoes were brutal in the woods, and Nate ran faster, Switchfoot in his ears spurring him on. He burst out to the clearing by the stallion barn, leaving most of them behind, slowing to swat the last one off the back of his neck—but not before it left a fresh welt. Then *We're Gonna Be Alright* started playing, trumping his aggravation. There was really no proper response but to take a dance-like-no-one's-watching moment. Because who would be, out here? Any why would he care, anyway? Sing it out, believe it.

He opened his eyes with the last beat, and folded over, laughing. *Of course.*

"Don't let me interrupt you." The corners of Liv's mouth curved up as she pulled the elastic from her hair, resetting her ponytail. "Seriously, carry on."

She left him standing there, running towards the path he'd just left. He turned and sprinted after her, because he had nothing to lose but more blood.

Her eyes flashed over when he caught up, and he waited for her to tell him to get lost.

"Try to keep up, Miller," she said, picking up the pace, skipping over a root onto the narrow trail.

The sky had an eerie green cast when they broke out on the other side, trees coming to life like Ents as the wind whipped through them. Liv kicked it up another notch, and Nate wiped his mouth and matched her stride.

"Come on, girls!"

Mares and foals in the adjacent paddock took off, summoned by the farm worker's call and the rattle of chain on metal. Nate and Liv raced past the gate, the rain starting with cold, heavy, drops that soon turned to a downpour, drenching them.

Chique and Claire huddled in the corner of their paddock next to the barn, Chique's shrill whinny a clear indication the current situation was unacceptable, if not outright abusive. Nate grabbed a shank from Liv, and Claire shuffled over, but Chique stayed put—quarters spun resolutely to the wind, head at knee level, tail streaming between her hocks.

Water gushed into his runners as he sloshed through the stream that coursed through the paddock. He snapped on the lead and dragged her in. As soon as he pried off her sodden halter, Chique dropped to her knees and rolled with a grunt. She rose, snorting as she shook off the loose straw, then buried her nose in the pile of hay in the corner, too disgusted to even search for peppermints.

"It doesn't look like it's going to let up anytime soon, does it?" Liv stared at the sheets of rain, wincing at the crack of thunder that followed a particularly brilliant shard of lightning.

"You can come upstairs for a bit and wait it out if you want."

She caught a drip on her forehead with the back of her hand. "Okay."

He'd expected her to say no, to come up with the excuse of some paperwork in the office and wait out the storm there. Things hadn't exactly been awkward since Kentucky—Liv was, if nothing else, professional to a fault at work—but they'd reverted to just that. Friends, like Jo or Michel were friends, because they'd been working together for three years and didn't hate each other. Nothing more. Maybe all they would ever be.

This, like the run that had led to it, crossed a line she'd redrawn in black in his hotel room in Lexington. The sting of truth from her little tough love speech had eased, both his bruised ego and ankle recovering, but the line had remained. Until now. He led the way up the stairs, almost tripping as his legs shook—and not from fatigue.

She left her waterlogged shoes and socks in a puddle by the door and gravitated to the picture window framing a still-angry sky. Rain pattered steadily against the pane.

"I'm surprised you're still here. I would have thought you'd want to live closer to the track."

He probably should have moved, considering he wasn't even a farm employee anymore, but they'd never asked him to leave, and he'd never wanted to. "It'd be hard going back to living in the city after this. Besides, right now it means I can get on Chique before I head in."

"You couldn't possibly leave that to me." There was a hint of affection in her expression, and he bathed in it for a moment before it drifted away.

"Still planning to ship her in tomorrow?"

Liv nodded, dragging a hand over her wet hair. The Ashland had left Chique battered enough Liv had brought her to the farm when they'd come home, and a couple of weeks of turnout had turned into five. She'd been galloping for three of them, and had started pulling out his arms again, so it was time. Time to get serious, and see if the Plate, just seven weeks away, was still possible. Chique had fared better than Wampum, at least. The Northwest colt was on stall rest with a stress fracture in his shoulder and was out of the Plate for sure.

"I should get you a towel." He dragged himself away and went to the bedroom, peeling off his t-shirt, fantasizing he'd brought her with him. *Dream on, Miller.*

She was looking down at the picture frame on the piano

when he returned, and it chased off the fantasy as he cursed himself once more for never putting it away. Then again, what was he worried about? She knew most of the story already.

"I'd forgotten this was up here." She looked away from the photo quickly, and fingered the piano keys.

"Do you play?" He kept himself from staring at the way her t-shirt clung, handing her the towel on his way to the kitchen.

"I took lessons for a bit as a kid. One of my mother's failed attempts to instill something other than horses. You?"

"It's what sold me on the job." That and the fact he'd needed to get his head out of his ass. "Want something to drink?"

"Water?"

She accepted a glass, her eyes lingering on his face before wandering back to the piano, and the frame. "Is that New Year's Eve girl? She's beautiful."

There was no jealousy in her voice; she was merely making an observation, appreciating an aesthetic. He stood behind her, looking over her shoulder and inhaling, the scent of her a mixture of rain and sweat and something tropical, and he had to step back. Forget lines, he needed a force field.

"Yeah. Cindy."

It was after one of those adventure races. He had an arm around Phil on his left, Cin on his right, little brother Tim next to Phil. All of them wearing huge smiles, and a whole lot of mud. Good times. *One big lie.*

"She came home from school with Phil one day. They were supposed to be studying. We hit it off right away."

Liv set the picture back on the piano, her gaze landing on him as she turned. If he'd stayed where he'd been, she would have been close enough to...*damn it.* She moved away like she could read his thoughts—though talking about the past was a good antidote for that.

"She was supportive of everything my dad hated—my music, the horses. Drove him nuts. He had a big problem with us being together. My mother loved her, though." *Still does.* "I really just went to U of Calgary because of her. I thought if I was the guy with the degree that got the steady job that she'd want to be with me." He shrugged. "You know how that went."

"How long were you together?"

"Three years, four months." He could have told her right down to the number of minutes.

"Four years ago. So why is it still with you? What are you leaving out?"

It was eerie that she'd figure out he was withholding details. Or maybe he just wanted to believe they had a special connection, that she could read into his soul and see the holes there.

"She had twins in February."

There was a question mark etched on her face when he handed her his phone, open to a photo of those twins—fair, what did she care about babies? It did seem a strange way to explain. The creases in her brow deepened in confusion.

"This is crazy, but I want to say...they look like you." She stared at it again. "That's impossible, right? Or..."

"I didn't go back for a random fling last year, if that's what you're thinking. She married my brother."

"Holy shit, Miller."

He almost laughed—he didn't think he'd ever heard her swear before.

"I should have known I was just a passing amusement." He backed up to the piano, dropping to the bench. "Phil was going to law school. He really was the guy I was trying to be. All kinds of ironic, really. I only started flirting with her that day he brought her home to piss him off. Guess he got the last laugh."

He swung to face the keys, resting his fingers on them, another of his mother's favourite songs coming to him when he thought of how blindsided he'd been when he'd found out they were together. *Why is love always the last to know?*

Liv pulled up a chair from the kitchen, tucking her knees to her chest as she rested her bare toes on the edge of the bench.

"So what did you do for...eight months? You quit school

267

after she turned you down. You could have been here for the start of the season. Everyone's looking for good exercise riders in the spring."

"You make it sound like I should have been thinking straight. She dumped me, I quit school, my dad kicked me out. I spent the rest of the winter working on the farm and nightwatching mares for Al, the trainer I worked for, and he gave me a place to crash. Seemed a good place to hide. I stayed till the wedding, because I thought I should. Because I thought it would make my mother happy. Which was stupid. She of all people would have understood I never should have been there."

There was a strange stillness to her voice when she finally spoke. "How do you get over something like that?"

"I'm not sure I'm qualified to answer that. I haven't been very successful."

"I fell apart over much less. You seem to have handled it pretty well."

"Hardly. I got drunk and bolted in the middle of the reception, and I've never been back."

"You started fresh. Successfully."

"How long did it take me to get to that point? Sure you went through a dark patch, but you put things back together."

"Only because you kept after me. You had no one."

"I had Geai. I had Em. But I still kept running away. Until you gave me Chique."

"Because I was so totally incapable of dealing with her myself."

"Like this is some kind of competition."

She smiled, but there was sadness in her eyes. "So why tell me all this?"

"Because even though you might be completely baffled by it, you still hear it, and feel it. Sometimes I think we're opposite sides of the same coin."

Her eyes flashed and she rose, hands wringing as she walked away. "That doesn't mean we should be together."

Nate spun around on the piano bench, silently begging her

not to leave. Not now, when they'd come so far. "Isn't it worth a shot?"

She stopped, turning but avoiding his gaze. "It took me a long time to make it here. I don't want to ruin what we already have. We work well together. Why isn't that good enough?"

"There's got to be more to it than that, doesn't there? Or do you really think you're better off alone?"

"You said my philosophy had merit. Relationships are best avoided. Doomed to fail, especially in this business. What makes you think it would be any different with us?"

"Hope, I guess." Some crazy belief that some things are meant to be. "What if we don't fail?"

"Is that resilience, or stupidity?"

It was blunt, but it triggered a smile, because he'd spent a lot of time pondering the same thing.

"It's not that easy, though, is it?" she continued. "What about Faye? I couldn't do that to her. How could you? And please don't tell me life's too short. I can't live like that."

It was, though, couldn't she see? But he kept quiet, letting her work it through.

"I don't want things to be awkward. I don't want anything distracting either of us before the Plate. I have enough going on in my head right now. You don't even know what you'd be signing up for, Miller."

Maybe he didn't. Maybe that's all this was, the thrill of the unknown, the risk of it all. That's what they did—put their necks out there, throwing a leg over the crazy. But who wanted to stay on the ground?

"Just tell me we won't go backwards from here." It was a plea, but he didn't care.

"Are you looking for a promise?"

He threw his eyes at the ceiling, wanting badly to go to her and pull her into his arms, to kiss her speechless. "You sure like to overthink everything, don't you?"

"You think you have me figured out."

Her smile toyed with him, driving him a little nuts. "Not even close."

She glanced past him, and he looked over his shoulder to the window. The storm had moved on, patches of rich cobalt growing through wispy clouds.

"I should get going."

He wanted to cling to this, afraid they would never recover it, but short of holding her hostage, it wasn't going to happen.

"I'll come downstairs with you."

Everything glistened from the rain, the air earthy and cool as a light breeze offered to dry up the puddles.

"*À demain*, Miller."

It wouldn't be dinner and movies; a two-year engagement; one-point-five kids—or twins. But how could they know what it could be, if they didn't try?

They'd win the Plate, then continue this discussion. He had to believe that, the Switchfoot song playing in his mind feeding his conviction.

CHAPTER THIRTY-NINE

June

Chique quivered, transfixed by the buzz on the other side of Woodbine's main track. Nate matched her stare with the same focus.

Liv gave a gentle tug on the bit. "Okay?"

The filly's ear flicked, and Nate nodded. Liv nudged Paz forward. A few jog steps, and they popped into a gallop.

This was the day that would define the Queen's Plate, three weeks away. They'd had options: both the Canadian Oaks and the Plate Trial Stakes went this afternoon at a mile and an eighth. Instead, she'd sought and received permission from the stewards to work Chique a mile in between races—her idea of a compromise.

She could deal with the haters saying she was just ducking Touch and Go in the Trial, and Penny Postcard in the Oaks, both of them last year's divisional champions. Her own doubts, the ones that questioned her gut—a gut that insisted Chique wasn't ready for a race yet after her roller derby experience at Keeneland—were harder to dismiss.

Paz matched Chique's strides until Liv let go inside the

271

sixteenth pole. She steered him to the middle of the track to avoid the flying clods of dirt as Chique swept away, Nate crouched flush to her back as the filly sailed around the clubhouse turn.

She tried to track their progress as best she could, but it was mostly futile. Why she'd turned down Nicole's offer to take Chique to the pole, she wasn't sure, except maybe watching was harder than not, when she wasn't up herself.

Nate's smile was the first thing she noticed through the shimmer of heat radiating off the new dirt track when Chique glided into the backstretch, galloping out. He pulled her up, slowing to a jog and turning in beside Paz. Liv reached over and removed the blinkers, and Chique resumed her stare: nostrils flaring, a sheen of sweat on her neck, a heightened look in her eye as she gazed into the distance over her big white shadow roll.

"Time?" They'd announce it, but Nate would know.

"Thirty-nine and change, last quarter in twenty-four, galloped out a mile and a quarter in two-o-six. Or thereabouts."

There was no dodging the emotions that slammed her when he flashed that grin, totally prepared to admit she wasn't immune to it anymore. *Never say never.* Each time he looked at her like that, it seemed just a little less crazy.

Back at the barn, she stuck her head under the hose, cold water shocking the warm fuzzies back into hiding. It was the closest she'd get to a shower on the backstretch. There were races to be watched and competition to assess on the front side.

Emilie was waiting for her by the walking ring as the horses for the Plate Trial started coming up the path. "Cheeky looked great!"

"What did they catch her in?"

"One thirty-nine and three; out in two-o-six flat."

Or thereabouts. Emilie gave her a strange look as she laughed.

They watched the Trial from the box, Touch and Go

emerging as the leader mid-stretch, drawing away from the field under Dave Johnson.

"He won't have any trouble getting the mile and a quarter," Liv commented dryly.

No surprises in the Oaks, either—Penny Postcard equalled Touch and Go's time for the mile and an eighth. Someone would note how fast Chique had completed the same distance in her gallop-out for comparison. For what any of it was worth, because anything could happen on Plate Day.

Faye had been scarce since they'd got back from Keeneland, but Liv found her at Dean's barn after the races, sitting on a bench outside looking bored as a couple of exercise boys tried to chat her up. In her current state she was probably particularly fierce. Definitely not looking very celebratory after a win that would likely send Touch and Go off as favourite for the big race.

"Filly breezed good," one of the guys said to Liv.

She nodded with a curt, "Thanks." That seemed enough of a hint to chase them away, and she sat cautiously next to Faye. "How long does this go on for, then?"

Faye tucked one side of her hair behind an ear. "I don't know. It's all new to me." She gazed across the lawn, zeroing in on Nate as he congratulated Dean. "I don't know if I'd feel better or worse if you told me I was right."

"Right about what?"

"Right to break it off with him." Faye hesitated. "Right about you. It's pretty ironic the only guy to ever get to me is the one who's perfect for you, isn't it?" Her eyes shifted to Liv, her smile wan. "Don't use me as an excuse, sweetie. I'll get over it."

Daylight was slow in coming, a dense haze hanging over the track, the smog of the big city burning Nate's throat as he inhaled. Chique, on the other hand, seemed oblivious to the humidity that was making human tempers short and working uncomfortable. She was everything she should be coming up to tomorrow's Plate: both her body—so carefully sculpted by the meticulous conditioning—and her mind, always the wildcard.

They detoured though the walking ring so she could see the ensuing mayhem of the Queen's Plate Festival—the huge mechanical arm for the television camera, the tents, the concert stages, the temporary fencing.

"No giant Pegasus. No fire-breathing dragon." Nate stroked Chique's neck, dark with sweat from air that was practically at the point of saturation. It had to rain soon. This humidity had to break.

Paz snorted his approval, while Liv eyed Chique protectively from the pony's back, preoccupation all but seeping from her pores like the perspiration on her skin.

Back at the barn Nate held Chique for her bath, catching a glimpse of a photographer stopping to take a shot with a telephoto lens. Chique noticed too, ever the diva, striking a pose, suds shimmering in a slick film over her inky coat. There was no mistaking her awareness of the electricity in the air, the undercurrent humming through Woodbine's backstretch as obvious as the plunging barometric pressure.

He passed Chique to Liv once the filly was bathed and sponged, giving her arm a squeeze. "I'll see you at the end of the morning."

When he returned, there was a cluster in front of Chique's stall, and he kept his distance. The week had been full of press engagements, starting with the media barbeque on Monday, and Wednesday's Plate Breakfast and post position draw.

The filly embraced the role of Queen's Plate darling: head poked over the webbing, bumping Liv with her nose like she was trying to encourage her trainer to do the same. Liv remained straight-faced, answering questions, while Chique butted her haynet, twirling it over her head and scattering blades of timothy and alfalfa leaves though Liv's hair. The filly finished the performance with a big green snort that finally did Liv in, the tension temporarily washed away.

It was good to see her laugh. It made him laugh. Maybe she was right. Maybe this was enough. He might have to accept that it was and make the best of it. He waited till the crew cleared before sneaking in.

"She'll teach you not to be so serious." He pulled out a peppermint, and Chique dove for it, then tossed her forelock around, hoping for more. "They're predicting rain tonight."

Liv set her jaw, staring out into the gloom. "I can't believe it hasn't started yet. Can't you do something about this, Miller?"

"I'll get right on that." He smiled. "That's just the point. We can't do a thing. Maybe it'll pour all night, and stop in time for everything to dry up. Or seeing as it's held off this long, maybe it'll just wait and rain on the amazing Plate Party we're going to have."

"Do you ever get tired of being so reassuring?"

"It's work. But someone has to hold you together, right?'

CHAPTER FORTY

Plate Day

The resounding boom startled Liv out of a restless slumber, her spirits sinking with the torrential downpour that followed. She rolled out of bed, her thin tank top sticking to her, and stumbled to the open window.

Leaves battered the pane, rain blowing in through the screen. Sliding it shut felt like cutting off her supply of oxygen —of course the central air had decided to conk out during a heat wave on a long weekend. She dozed, lightning brightening the room at regular intervals, shattering cracks of thunder at times so close the windows trembled jolting her back awake.

It was like the universe was laughing at her, years building to this day; all of it potentially obliterated by a force of nature. Did it really come down to this? But if Chique truly were the best horse out there this afternoon, she would overcome. That's what Nate would say. They would still need a good dose of luck, when it felt like luck had abandoned them.

At four AM she gave up on sleep. The heart of the storm seemed to have passed, but the heavy rain persisted, settling in all too comfortably. She wandered to the bathroom she shared with Emilie to shower, envying her sister's ability to sleep through anything.

It was too early to head to the track, so she drove to the office barn. Claire and her new companion were happy to eat an early breakfast and she left them with grain in their tubs and a flake of hay in the corner.

The strip of track lighting in the office highlighted the pictures on the walls—the large framed images of Just Lucky winning his Plate, Sotisse's Oaks, and the oil painting of the two together, posed on the lawn outside the Triple Stripe stallion barn. Geai, standing between them, smiled at her from the canvas.

"Do you think he knew? You, me, the filly…"

She didn't startle at the voice. Who but Nate would be up at this hour, with a brain so in tune to her own?

She turned slowly, facing him. "It would be nice to think that. I just wish he were here to see it."

"Me too."

"It's still raining."

"It doesn't matter. I'll take care of her."

How did he do that? He had this knack for somehow addressing her fears—ones that worried about more than a poor performance this afternoon, because the track condition raised the issue of safety. He couldn't be sure Chique would handle the slop, but stood by her, ever confident. Nate had believed in this filly every step of the way.

"I thought you might want this today."

He held out a fist, and she stepped towards him, raising her eyebrows.

When she recognized the lightweight chain and tiny medallion he placed in her open palm her eyes blurred, blinking back tears she'd never shed. She turned the pendant over, trying to focus on the exquisite miniature painting of Ste-Anne and her Claire lookalike, no words coming.

Fingers closed around her wrist and Nate gently pulled her forward, directing her towards the door. "Come on. Time to go face it."

Liv detoured to Claire's stall, medallion clenched in her hand, and pushed it to the grill to meet the pink nose.

"Wish us luck, mare."

Claire blew softly in response.

Nate's headlights stayed in her rear view mirror the whole drive in, her wiper blades beating a monotonous rhythm. Jo, Michel, and Sue were already on the shed, carrying out a routine that was so familiar, but today surreal. Liv went through the motions, sweat pouring freely from her brow, stinging her eyes.

Chique pushed against the webbing after Liv turned her loose, her *tap, tap, tap,* demanding hay that wasn't coming. When a drowsy hotwalker from the other side of the barn came around the corner, the filly's neck snaked out. The kid ducked, which probably saved him from tripping over the fan Liv had left in place to keep the air circulating in the stifling stall.

"Sorry," she said sheepishly as the kid walked by. She was going to earn herself a fine if security came by to find Chique's screen still open and the fan in the way.

The kid waved it off with a sleepy grin. "Good luck today!"

Liv forgot for just a moment the feeling that everything was against them.

"Nothing wrong with her." Roger stopped at a healthy distance. "Let's get some horses out there so we have an idea of what the track's like. Are Nicole and Emilie here yet?"

Liv's face fell. "I forgot all about Emilie."

"It's going to be a long day." Jo patted her on the back. "There they are."

"Sure, thanks, sis," Emilie chided. "Good thing I called Nic last night as backup. Now will someone please put her on a horse?"

Liv scuttled to the tack room, but stopped short in front of the door. Someone had written on the whiteboard, in a neat, flowing, script.

Good things come.

It could only have been Nate. He must have stopped by after the races last night to check on Chique. Her face crinkled into a smile. *That guy.* He even had nice handwriting.

The gallopers were a moderate distraction, but after the last set, it was time to get Chique out for a bath. Emilie held her, Chique's head bobbing and teeth gnashing as Liv scraped off the excess water.

"Thanks, Em. I'll take her."

She glanced at the time every pass of the tack room. Nine o'clock. In just over seven hours, the Plate horses would start the walk over to the front side. Each time Chique acted out, squealing and bouncing her way around the shed, Liv winced. *Just hold it together for seven more hours.*

They were still walking—now that Chique had settled, Liv could call it that—when the commission vet arrived. Liv broke into a controlled jog, but the filly sprang into a canter-in-hand. Once she managed to get enough of an even trot both ways to satisfy the vet, she held Chique still, fixing her with a stern look as he examined her legs.

He straightened, and stroked Chique's neck, smiling. "Good luck."

Liv nodded thanks, collecting all the *good lucks* and tucking them away like she might amass enough of them to ensure success.

One more turn, and she'd put the filly in...to wait some more.

"Short on hotwalkers?"

Nate waited just beyond Chique's stall, his grin distracting Liv from her nerves for a moment.

"You think I was going to let someone else walk her? I'm not putting that kind of pressure on anyone today."

"Just me, right?"

"You signed up, remember." She turned Chique loose in the stall, snapping the screen shut and hanging the shank on the door.

"You seem almost cheerful."

"It's the calm before the storm—forgive my choice of

clichés."

"Maybe the calm between storms."

She leaned on her hands, the cold cinder block wall cooling her palms as the tension crept back. "What did you think of the track?"

"It's a lot better than I thought it would be. They closed it early, but there're nine races to run over it before they get to the Plate. And if it stops raining, it's gonna get real slow."

"I can't believe we're hoping it doesn't stop."

He stepped forward, holding an empty hand out to a disappointed Chique. "I'd better go. Try not to self-destruct, all right? I'd hate for you to miss it if we win." He left with another of his grins, Liv wondering if he was really that calm, or just did a better job at keeping his nerves under wraps.

Ten o'clock.

She fed Chique a reduced portion of grain for lunch and started checking tasks off her list. Halter and shank cleaned; brass polished. Bridle and bit immaculate. Shadow roll pristine —maybe Chique would keep it that way, running on the front end. Blinkers too. Busy work, all of it.

Next, something she'd only do for the Plate. The traditional hunter braids in the top half of the filly's mane fed her need to control whatever minutiae she could, tiny even plaits tied with yarn and bumped with a crochet hook. It was a shame to have to switch to elastics for the bottom, but they needed to be easily removed. Something for Nate to do as they walked out for the post parade, leaving him mane to grab in the gate.

Chique shook her head as water dribbled down her neck, and Liv dabbed the drops away with her sponge. "You have my sincerest apologies, miss." The filly was no more comfortable getting dressed for the occasion than she would be herself.

Now there was really nothing left to do. Emilie napped on the couch in the office. Liv gave her a nudge.

"Let's go."

"You sure?" Emilie grinned through her yawn.

The rain backed off to a steady drizzle on the drive home,

Liv distractedly punching at the stereo, advancing through the tracks searching for just the right music to match her mood. It wasn't happening. That song wasn't written yet.

A shower to wash away the stickiness, a French braid in her damp hair, a simple sleeveless navy linen dress. She smoothed the skirt with her hands, and dug the little medallion from the pocket of her jeans, fumbling with the clasp. When she placed the ivory hat on her head to check her reflection, fingering the pendant unconsciously, she saw someone, pretty enough, in an outfit befitting Woodbine's most prestigious day. Funny it was her.

"You look great," Emilie said, inching open the door. "Might be a little too distracting for Nate."

Liv rolled her eyes to keep the smile from her lips. "Better not be. Let's get back there."

Once she dropped Emilie off on the west side of the grandstand, she headed to the barn, the humidity assaulting her as soon as she left the air-conditioned car. Chique dozed in the corner of her stall. Probably a good thing, but maybe she should check the filly's temperature to be safe. Nate would laugh at her. *Breathe.*

If only there was a fast forward button to skip through the next few hours. All she really had left to do was put on the rundown bandages, and it was too early for that.

The PA system crackled. *"Bring them over for the fifth…"*

A squeal and a thud sent her flying back onto the shed. Chique pressed to her screen, vibrating, fixed on the procession assembling not far from the barn. So she was fine, unless she'd sprung a shoe or cracked a bone with that kick.

Possibly more terrifying than Gulfstream's Pegasus and the fire-breathing dragon—the Horse Guards. They gathered with the open landau, preparing to pick up the Lieutenant-Governor General, this year's Royal delegate. Liv touched Chique's neck, warm and damp beneath her hand. *Just a few more hours, filly. Please?*

"We'll give her a quick hose-off once they're gone." Jo hovered behind Liv. "At least she hasn't rubbed her braids out."

"Yet. Better check her shoes, too."

Chique huffed and dropped her head, letting the fan blow in her face.

The calls came at half hour intervals, counting them down. Each time Liv recalculated, obsessively—*the seventh was coming back, the eighth over there, they're calling for the ninth…the next call will be ours.*

One and a half hours until the Plate went off.

"I can do that, you know." Jo stood, hands on hips as Liv gathered what she'd need when it was finally time to put on the rundowns.

Liv just shook her head.

She wasn't taking any chances today with that track—bandages all round. She wound the white vetraps with fanatical precision, the perfect V in front, rundown patches just so, smoothing everything and finishing with two strips of white electrical tape around the top for added insurance.

"Get them ready for the tenth…"

Jo would take care of the rest. Liv left Chique with a kiss on the nose, and the sense of helplessness began, clinging to her more than the sticky air.

So many people on the front side, getting in her way as she skipped around puddles. At least the rain had finally let up. *Relax.* The horses hadn't even begun to arrive yet. But that made her twitchy, wondering why they weren't here already as she waited in the saddling stall.

One by one they appeared, and at last there was Chique's dark face with the big white shadow roll, eyes bugging out of her pretty little head.

"Give me your hat." Emilie elbowed her as the valet showed up with the tack.

She froze, wishing it were Roger putting it on. She'd only done it that one time in Keeneland—what if she screwed up, today, the most important of days? Her hands shook as she pulled the elastic girth up and found the last hole.

"Right to the top here." Her voice quavered.

The valet's helmet bobbed, and her nerves dissipated slightly as they secured the overgirth.

"Good luck." He scurried off as she thanked him, and she stashed that one with the others before stretching out Chique's forelegs.

Halter off, blinkers on, double-check the tack. "Okay Jo. See you outside."

"Hang on." Emilie grabbed her arm. She set the hat back on Liv's head and adjusted it, then nodded in approval. "Okay."

Outside Emilie squeezed between Nate and her father, standing by their number. Em bounced on her toes, and Liv wanted so much to do the same, to disperse some of her anxiety, but it didn't seem befitting the trainer of a Plate horse.

Her mother's arm weaved around her waist. "I know your original plan was to be the one riding today."

"At least this means you can watch." Liv smiled. "Chique picked him. Who am I to get in the way of that?"

"You're quite the team, the three of you."

"So we are." Her composure faltered for a second when she saw her mother's glistening eyes. "Thank you." She wrapped her arms around Anne's shoulders, then Nate's gaze drew her away.

She grasped his outstretched hand, unflinching.

"So formal," he said.

His grin launched her pulse into a whole different tempo, but she didn't let go. "It is the Queen's Plate."

"*Looks like we made it...*" He sang it softly, and she laughed.

That guy. Singing Barry Manilow in the paddock before the biggest moment of their lives, just to ease the tension enough that she didn't explode under the pressure.

She compressed all her emotions into a compartment, and pulled her pragmatism back out. "This far. It's not over yet. Safe trip. *Bonne chance.*"

Sending her collection of *good lucks* along with him, they walked up to Chique.

There was no room for emotion back here.

Besides, there was enough of it flowing, the gate crew in a struggle that had already been going on too long with a behemoth of a colt. They squeezed him in. He banged against the sides, the jock scrambling onto the frame. The colt settled. The jock got back on.

Chique flicked an ear back at Nate as the assistant starter inched her forward.

You want me to go in beside that?

Yeah. Sorry. Gotta trust me, Cheek. We won't be there long.

He pulled out the last elastic, his thoughts shooting briefly to Liv—she'd be riding this with him every step of the way. He was barely aware as the last horse filed in beside them.

The doors crashed open, and a jarring impact from the left slammed Chique mid-leap, sending her nose-diving sideways into the quagmire. Nate pitched forward, swallowing a string of offensive phrases, sure he was headed for the bog below, but she scrambled, somehow finding her feet.

Chique fought him, climbing in the slop but showing no sign of pain—as if he could trust that. He eased his hold enough to let her settle, and the lengthening of her stride convinced him she was okay, but now there was a lot more than a bad track to overcome. She would use up everything in her heart trying to catch up if he asked, and he wasn't sure he had that right.

She channeled her fury into the chase, zeroing in on the trailers as they raced past the grandstand for the first time. The behemoth was at the back of the pack, and the last thing Nate wanted to do was take Chique wide around the turn, but it was that or keep her behind the unpredictable colt who had assaulted them. After recovering from such a major setback, he hated to ask her to wait, so he let her go.

Picking up more horses as they reached the backstretch, one thing was clear: she wanted the lead, though she was still nowhere near it. Nate closed his hands on the lines, asking her to take a breather. Her ears swiveled, acknowledging. *Okay, maybe just a little one.*

Touch and Go sat behind the front-runners and just wide,

staying out of the messy kickback, inching stealthily up as the field rounded the next turn. Nate tucked Chique neatly in behind the favoured colt, letting her cruise in his slipstream. Chique went with Nate's decision, putting up with the mud pelting her face. Maybe they would have a say in the result of this Plate after all—there was still something there, though where it was coming from, he had no idea. Just over a quarter of a mile to go, and the real running had yet to begin.

Touch and Go shifted into gear and surged to the front, eclipsing the leaders. Nate swung Chique out to avoid the tired pacesetters and sent her after him. She lined the colt up, pounding through the slop, steadily wearing him down.

Nate didn't bother cocking his stick, Chique digging deep to access assets she possessed that he could never truly understand. She drew even with Touch and Go. With each thrust of her neck, each reeling stride, the finish loomed. He gathered her and threw everything at the wire with one last ask.

Chique pulled herself up, exhausted, and Nate dropped his eyes to her neck, reaching up to stroke her reverently. All that fearlessness and grit in such a small package. Then he finally dared to look around. The outrider was headed towards them.

Who cared if the sun didn't shine? Nate beamed as the outrider escorted them onto the turf course. Everyone in the packed grandstand was on their feet, cheering, and he waved a salute before dropping the lines. Throwing his arms wide, he grinned down at Chique as if presenting them with their new Queen's Plate champion, then leaned forward and wrapped himself around her neck.

Liv pushed through the throng of photographers, reaching up and grasping his hand, pressing it against Chique's shoulder. She didn't let go until the blanket of purple daisies with its yellow crown was draped over the filly's withers, taking the shank from Jo to lead them across the muddy track to the winner's circle—with a detour to the hose to give Chique a cool shower and a drink.

Head high, nostrils flared, eyes rimmed red from the assault of the track, Chique posed with her people gathered. Nate didn't even look at the camera, he just looked at her.

Stepping on the scales made it official: winner of the Queen's Plate, *Chiquenaude, dark bay or brown three-year-old filly by Just Lucky, out of Sotisse.* Jo and Sue led her away to a fresh ovation, and Nate passed the tack and his helmet to his valet and clapped with them. Then he raced to the base of the podium, throwing his arms around Liv and spinning her.

"Oh, sorry." Remembering he was soaked through and wearing half the racetrack, he set her down, grinning. He brushed some of the sand off her bare shoulder before he could stop himself.

"Sure you are." She laughed, and they joined the presentation.

Maybe she stayed at the test barn too long, but it wasn't until Chique's breathing normalized—her thirst lessening, her walk becoming less agitated—that Liv felt she could leave. Besides, it was peaceful here, the routine the same as after any race, from a cheap claimer to this. Barn Five would be anything but.

A breeze chased off the humidity, snatches of blue sky widening as the clouds broke apart. The lawn was alive. Liv waved away the glass of champagne Roger tried to press into her hand. There would be champagne, but it wasn't happening without Nate.

"What's all this?" Three men checked equipment and tuned guitars beneath the tent her father had rented.

Emilie sipped bubbles from a plastic glass. "What's it look like? Nate asked his buddies to come play at the party."

Faye put an arm around Liv's shoulders and pressed her lips to her cheek. "Way to go, sweetie."

"Sorry we had to beat Touch and Go. He ran a gutsy race."

"If anyone was going to beat us, I'm glad it was you."

Liv returned her attention to the musicians. "How come I didn't know about this?"

"Oh please." Emilie rolled her eyes. "You've been in your own little world."

"Who's that, Em?" Faye sized up the strangers. "The guy with the guitar there, do you know?"

"Kinda tall for you, isn't he?" Emilie quipped.

"Maybe that's where I've been going wrong."

"You're gonna have to wait for Nate to make introductions. Nice to have you back though." Emilie nudged Liv. "You should grab some food while there's still some left. I bet you haven't eaten all day."

Liv managed to fill a plate, and nibbled at it between accepting kudos and keeping an eye on the shed, waiting for Chique to return. She saw Jo first, but the filly wasn't far behind. The hotwalker took her a few turns before coming out, and Chique's head dropped before she was even off the asphalt apron, tearing at the blades. The only time she came up for air was when Nate's old Mustang pulled up.

After checking in with Chique, he pushed his way gradually through the crowd, cleaned up and turned out in his navy suit and tie. Emilie launched herself at him before he could speak, and Faye commended him with an impressive show of congeniality as he waved over someone from the band.

"This is my friend Will. Liv Lachance, her sister Emilie, and Faye Taylor."

Will shook hands with each of them in turn, and Faye held on just a little bit longer. Emilie was right.

"I think this is going to be the best Plate Party ever." Faye peered after him when he excused himself with the promise of music.

Emilie looped her arm through Faye's. "Let's get it started, then. Looks like we've got some dancing to do."

They wandered towards the tent, and Liv turned to Nate. "Come on, Miller. Time for some real champagne." When they got to the shed, she disappeared into the office, emerging with a fat bottle and two crystal flutes.

"Don't be popping corks in this filly's face while I'm trying to put bandages on," Jo warned as the hotwalker brought Chique to her stall, "or I'll just leave her for the two of you. You put rundowns on in that outfit, Liv. I'd like to see you do her up in it, too."

Nate removed his jacket and draped it over the rail. "Here." He plucked the hind cottons and two bandages from Jo's arms.

Jo added some sheet cotton, plastic, and a tub of furacin. Nate Miller, leading apprentice in North America, Plate-winning jockey, putting bandages on his Plate horse. *So much more than just a pretty face.* Liv snapped a photo with her phone, because, really, that needed to be broadcast.

"Stay for champagne?" She peeled the foil from the bottle's neck as Jo dumped her bucket of poultice water.

"I think there's plenty out there. You two go ahead."

Liv threw a clean rub rag over it and held the cork, carefully twisting the body.

"Gah, are you kidding?" Nate grabbed it and popped the cork, slipping his thumb over the top and letting the towel fall as he shook it.

He released the spray between them, then handed it back, froth coursing messily over the neck. Liv held it at arm's length, laughing, then filled the flutes and passed him one. No toast could cover it, so she said nothing, silently holding out her glass. He clinked it, locking in her eyes, even as the bubbles hit the back of her throat.

Chique stretched her neck out, poking him. He poured some into his cupped hand and she pressed her muzzle to his palm, but withdrew, upper lip contorting.

"Fine, all the more for us. This better?" With a toss of her forelock she swept up the peppermint that appeared from his pocket.

Liv didn't stop him when he topped them both up, the band starting behind him. "This was your idea, obviously."

"I told you we were going to have a great Plate Party this year." He set his glass on the rail and held out his hand. "Dance?"

She looked from the hand, to his eyes, a slow smile spreading over her face. One more swallow of champagne, and she put the glass down and folded her fingers over his. His hand went easily to her hip, his shoulder firm against her palm. And then it was just the two of them, the music irrelevant as he drew her closer, a tremor in her fingers she couldn't tell was his or her own spreading through her with their gentle sway.

"Geai wanted us to be together."

The words were barely a whisper in her ear. She froze, ducking the intense blue of his focus, blocking out the timbre of his voice and pulling away. "That's not fair."

It was the perfect out; the last excuse. His face, though. He wouldn't say it if it wasn't true. She'd done it again, spooking more often than any horse she'd been on, always afraid a man would get in the way of her dream. Meanwhile, Nate had become its whole foundation.

She willed herself to stop shaking, slipping trembling hands to his chest, feeling his heartbeat as much as her own. The hurt on his face fell away as her mouth tasted the tang of champagne on his.

"Don't worry, I told him he was crazy," he murmured with a muted version of the grin that had always made her just a little bit insane. Easy solution this time. She just kissed him again.

He wrapped her in, her knees threatening to give way. If her arms hadn't been coiled around his shoulders, if his hadn't held her up, she'd have fallen. So what. Control was overrated.

"You do crazy so well, Miller."

His lips hovered. "It got us this far."

"What now?"

Chique's throaty rumble interrupted, and Liv felt his laugh.

"Now we feed the guest of honour her dinner, apparently. Then, I don't know, my memory's a little fuzzy at the moment, but I think there's a party going on out there."

"Parties are definitely overrated."

"It's for a good cause."

Chique *tap-tap-tapped.*

Liv took in the filly, and the guy, and the crazy they both sent through her.

"That it is."

Next Up

Want more Chique, Liv and Nate? Here's a teaser for the continuation of their story, *All Good Things*, available now.

CHAPTER ONE
August

Voices, nervous laughter, peripheral movement; on the fringes of her consciousness, none of it important. All that was worthy of her focus was skin sliding over muscle, muscle extending and contracting. Liv analyzed every stride down to each footfall, and tried to gauge the ever-unknown unpredictability factor in the sleek filly before her.

Chique was light years away from the unraced two-year-old she'd been a year ago. There was a swagger to her step now, the glint in her eyes behind the blinkers self-important, if you could say that about a horse. With eight races under her belt, at five different tracks—five of them wins—the professionalism she displayed here in Woodbine's walking ring, willow branches whispering overhead, wasn't unexpected. Liv just didn't trust it.

A touch broke her concentration, her head snapping to the side like the wind whipping from the northwest had picked it up in a gust. She didn't bother to fix the dark hair flying around her face. She should have put it up. She was usually practical about such things, like the "turf shoes" on her feet— flats, when heels would have punched through the rain-soaked carpet of grass. Not that she ever wore heels.

She extracted a hand from the depths of her trench coat pocket, and Nate returned the firmness of her grasp, the amusement playing on his features a contrast to the seriousness of her own. She could tell what he was thinking. *No, Miller, it wouldn't be appropriate for the rider to kiss the trainer in the walking ring.*

"So?" He crossed his arms, stick tucked under his elbow.

"Stay off the inside," she responded, though she wasn't saying anything he didn't already know. They'd discussed strategy ad nauseam, walked the full mile-and-a-half of the rain-sodden E.P. Taylor turf course that morning, and he'd ridden over it in an earlier race. The course was soft, but safe.

"Breathe," he said. He squeezed the elbow of the arm that was now folded over her chest in a less-assured reflection of his posture.

"Sure, Miller. It's only the Canadian Triple Crown on the line. But if you're cool, that's what matters."

This was the first possible first in her fledgling training career. A woman trainer had won the Queen's Plate before her. A woman trainer had won the Prince of Wales, the second jewel of the crown. A woman trainer had won this, the Breeders' Stakes, third and final jewel. But no woman had won all three.

The paddock judge gave the riders up call. Liv glanced at Nate.

"Let's do this," he said with a nod, trying to be serious before he let go the grin that was the only thing with any hope of distracting her from the stormy sky, the very un-August-like cool, and everything that was on the line.

"*Bonne chance.* Don't screw up. Come home safe." She threw him up onto the moving filly, and felt the too-familiar helplessness seep in.

He was so sure about Chique. Like he was so sure about them. Liv envied his confidence in both—but now wasn't the time to think about it.

Read the rest of the story: *All Good Things* is available at Amazon.

Acknowledgments

I'd like to start by thanking a stellar group of beta readers. Sheri Keith—we've gone from penpals when we were teenagers, to writing/accountability buddies. Our virtual co-writing sessions got me here! Allison Litfin, who read an early rewrite many years ago, a chapter a week, when we were both dog training instructors, and has read every draft since. Juliet Harrison, fellow artist and Saratoga traveller, who also reps my artwork at her wonderful Equis Art Gallery in Red Hook, NY; unrelated to Andrea Harrison, fellow writer and Thoroughbred advocate here in Ontario. Nathalie Drolet who made sure my French was okay! Dr. Kristen Frederick, who checked the accuracy of the veterinary bits and shared tidbits about going to OVC. Mara Dabrishus, author, who was willing to read an early draft, providing feedback that inspired me to tear it apart and put it back together as something much better —and who has been incredibly supportive ever since.

Kim Santini and Sheona Hamilton-Grant, more of my amazing artist friends, who fed me musical inspiration.

Michelle Lopez, author and business accountability partner, who helped keep my scattered brain organized.

Natalie Keller Reinert, who made the book look amazing, going above and beyond, and as an author herself, is an inspiration to inspiring equestrian writers like me.

And of course the horses, most notably Quidi Vidi, Chique's real-life double; and Moxy (Are You OK), who inspired significant behavioral inspiration.

About the Author

It was an eight-year-old me, frustrated that all the horse racing novels I read were about the Derby, not the Plate, who first put pencil to three-ring paper and started what would become this story. Needless to say, we've both grown up a bit since then.

I began working at the track before I finished high school, and after graduating the following January, took a hotwalking job at Payson Park in Florida. Once back at Woodbine, I started grooming and galloping. While the backstretch is exciting, I found I was more at home on the farm—prepping and breaking yearlings, nightwatching and foaling mares. Eventually I started my own small layup/broodmare facility, and in the last few years I've transitioned into retraining and rehoming. Somewhere along the way I did go back to school and get a degree. I should probably dust it off and frame it one day.

I live on a small farm in Ontario, Canada, with my off-track Thoroughbreds and a young Border Collie, and I'm probably better known for painting horses than writing about them. If you like my covers, you can check out my artwork at www.lindashantz.com

If you enjoyed this book, I'd love to hear from you! I'm always happy to talk horses and racing. I'd also be forever grateful if you'd leave a review on Amazon and/or Goodreads. It doesn't have to be long, but reviews go a long way to supporting and encouraging authors, so we can keep doing what we do.

You can contact me through my artist website, www.lindashantz.com/contact

Printed in Great Britain
by Amazon

78781496R00173